DUMBARTON OAKS
MEDIEVAL LIBRARY

Jan M. Ziolkowski, General Editor

RICHER OF SAINT-RÉMI

HISTORIES

VOLUME I

DOML 10

Histories

RICHER OF SAINT-RÉMI

VOLUME I

BOOKS 1–2

Edited and Translated by

JUSTIN LAKE

DUMBARTON OAKS
MEDIEVAL LIBRARY

HARVARD UNIVERSITY PRESS
CAMBRIDGE, MASSACHUSETTS
LONDON, ENGLAND
2011

Copyright © 2011 by the President and Fellows of Harvard College
ALL RIGHTS RESERVED
Printed in the United States of America

Library of Congress Cataloging-in-Publication Data
Richer, of Saint-Rémy, 10th cent.
  [Historiae. English & Latin]
  Histories / Richer of Saint Rémi ; edited and translated by Justin Lake.
    p. cm. — (Dumbarton Oaks medieval library; 10)
  Latin with facing English translation.
  Includes bibliographical references and index.
  ISBN 978-0-674-06003-6 (v. I : alk. paper) — ISBN 978-0-674-06159-0
(v. II : alk. paper) 1. France — History — To 987 — Early works to 1800. 2.
France — History — Capetians, 987–1328 — Early works to 1800. I. Lake,
Justin. II. Title.
  DC70.A3R513 2011
  944'.01 — dc22   2011008840

Contents

Introduction

Between the years 991 and 998 an otherwise unknown monk named Richer, of the monastery of Saint-Rémi at Reims, wrote a four-volume history of the West Frankish kings beginning with the accession of Odo, count of Paris, to the throne in 888 and ending in a series of annalistic notices, the last of which is datable to 998.[1] In the prologue to his *Historia,* Richer declares that he was prompted by his dedicatee, Archbishop Gerbert of Reims, to write a book that would compile "the conflicts of the Gauls" *(congressus Gallorum).* He goes on to define his purpose more precisely: "to recall to memory in writing the frequent wars waged by the Gauls during the reigns of these kings, their various struggles, and the different reasons for their undertakings."

The West Frankish kings and their wars were a fertile topic for history in the late tenth century. When Richer set about writing, he could look back on a century of political upheaval in West Francia[2] driven by two distinct but interrelated developments: the struggle between the Carolingian and Robertian/Capetian houses for control of the West Frankish throne, and the emergence of a series of powerful independent principalities that threatened and sometimes directly challenged royal authority. Both developments grew out of the political instability of the late ninth century, when the Carolingian empire fractured into a handful of indepen-

dent kingdoms and the great landed magnates took advantage of the quarreling between the heirs of Charlemagne to win increasing power and authority for themselves. After enduring a series of divisions at the hands of the sons and grandsons of Louis the Pious (d. 840), the empire was briefly reunited during the inglorious reign of Charles the Fat (884–887). But when Charles died in January of 888, having been forced to abdicate several weeks earlier, there was no obvious successor, and the constituent parts of the empire were left to go their own way. In each of the successor kingdoms that emerged, non-Carolingian kings quickly assumed power.

In West Francia there remained a legitimate Carolingian heir to the throne: Charles, the eight-year-old son of King Louis the Stammerer (877–879) and the half-brother of kings Louis III (879–882) and Carloman (879–884). But when the magnates assembled at Compiègne in February of 888 to elect a new king, they passed over Charles and elevated Odo, count of Paris, to the throne instead. They did so for practical reasons: "not as traitors," Richer says, "but as men indignant against their enemies."[3] These enemies were the Vikings, who had inflicted tremendous damage on the Carolingian empire in the latter decades of the ninth century and posed a continual threat to West Francia, with its long coastline and easily navigable rivers. In contrast to Charles, who would not reach the age of majority for several more years, Odo was an established military commander with a secure power base who could confront the Viking threat immediately. As count of Paris and Orléans and lay abbot of Saint-Martin of Tours, he was one of the most powerful magnates of the realm. Moreover, he had won considerable

renown for leading the defense of Paris against a substantial Viking siege that threatened the city for over a year in 885–886.

As could be expected, Charles and the faction arrayed around him did not accept the validity of Odo's election. In 893 Archbishop Fulk of Reims crowned Charles king, leading to four years of civil war that came to an end only in 897, after Odo agreed to recognize Charles as his successor. When Odo died a year later, Charles became the uncontested king of West Francia, but Odo's election had created a destabilizing precedent, for there were now two different families that could lay claim to the throne. Thus, when the West Frankish magnates became displeased with Charles's entanglements in Lotharingia and his unseemly devotion to his Lotharingian favorite, Hagano, Odo's brother Robert became the focal point of their resistance. Robert rebelled against Charles and had himself crowned king in 922. Although his rival was killed a year later at the Battle of Soissons, Charles did not regain his throne. He was instead betrayed and imprisoned by Count Heribert of Vermandois, whereupon Robert's son-in-law, Radulf, duke of Burgundy, became king. When Radulf died in 936, Robert's son, Hugh the Great, engineered the return of Charles's exiled son Louis from England (for reasons that are not entirely clear), and the Carolingians were reestablished on the throne. The authority of Louis IV (936–954), however, was severely circumscribed by Hugh, who assumed the grandiose title "duke of the Franks" and sought to exercise a supervisory role over the king whom he had brought to power. Louis and his son Lothar (954–986) maintained control of the West Frankish throne for fifty years, but on the death of Lothar's son Louis

in 987, the magnates rejected the claims of Louis's uncle Charles, duke of Lower Lotharingia, and chose Robert's grandson Hugh (later known as Hugh Capet) as king. The result was a rebellion by Charles that nearly succeeded in toppling Hugh. The century of conflict between the Carolingian and Robertian royal houses for dominance in West Francia was only brought to a close—although this could not have been obvious to Richer or his contemporaries—by the defeat and imprisonment of Charles in 991 and the uncontested accession of Hugh's son Robert five and a half years later.

The decades-long Carolingian-Robertian conflict helped undermine the power of the West Frankish monarchy, and with royal authority ineffective or nonexistent throughout much of the realm, ambitious magnates seized every opportunity to aggrandize themselves, frequently at the expense of the king. The pages of Richer's *Historia* are filled with stories of the audacity, cunning, and rapacious violence of the great magnates of West Francia, men such as Hugh the Great, Heribert of Vermandois, Arnulf of Flanders, Odo of Blois, and Fulk Nerra of Anjou. Factional strife among the leading men—*dissidentia principum*—was a fact of life in tenth-century West Francia, both a cause and a symptom of the weak monarchy. The struggles of the West Frankish kings to make their authority felt in the face of the internal disorder generated by the magnates and the external threats posed by the Vikings, Hungarian raiders, and the German kings east of the Rhine constitute the principal subject matter of Richer's work.

The scope of his history extends beyond the West Frankish kings and their wars, however. Interwoven with the

stated theme of the "conflicts of the Gauls" *(congressus Gallorum)* is a second narrative thread of equal importance, the church of Reims. Richer's monastery of Saint-Rémi was located less than a mile from Reims and was closely tied to the archiepiscopal see. Saint-Rémi housed the relics of its eponymous patron, Saint Remigius, the "apostle of the Franks," who had converted the Frankish king Clovis to Christianity and anointed him with oil from a sacred vial, by virtue of which future archbishops of Reims claimed the right to consecrate the king of the Franks. In Richer's day Reims was a nerve center of political and ecclesiastical power in West Francia. The archbishop of Reims exercised authority over eleven episcopal sees and wielded supreme power in the county, making him one of the kingdom's most powerful magnates. The position was thus highly sought-after, and Richer's history narrates in detail two long-running disputes over control of the archbishopric, the first pitting Heribert of Vermandois's irregularly elected son Hugh against his sometime replacement Artald, and the second involving Gerbert's acquisition of the see and his efforts to hold on to it following the deposition of his predecessor, Arnulf, at the synod of Saint-Basle in 991.

Books 3 and 4 of the *Historia* focus heavily on Gerbert, Richer's patron and dedicatee, and Archbishop Adalbero (969–989), who was responsible for bringing Gerbert to Reims and who helped to inaugurate a period of intellectual and cultural revival in his see. The scion of a noble Lotharingian family who had been educated at the reformed monastery of Gorze, Adalbero came to Reims from Metz, where, like his predecessor Odelric, he had been a cathedral canon. Upon taking office he undertook a series of reform mea-

sures, renovating the cathedral of Reims and bringing the canons together under a communal rule, reorganizing the monasteries of Mouzon and Saint-Thierry, and traveling to Rome to secure a papal privilege for the monastery of Saint-Rémi.[4] He also advanced Gerbert's career when he arrived in Reims, appointing him to be head of the cathedral school[5] and (according to Gerbert himself) eventually designating him as his successor.[6]

Richer's account of Gerbert's early career and curriculum at Reims is justifiably one of the best-known parts of his history.[7] Educated at the monastery of Saint-Gerald of Aurillac in the Auvergne, Gerbert was sent to Spain by his abbot after a visit from Count Borrell of Barcelona, who subsequently entrusted him to the care of Bishop Hatto of Vich for instruction. He later traveled with Borrell and Hatto to Rome, where he so impressed Pope John XIII with his intellectual talents that he was given an audience with the German emperor Otto I. This proved to be a meeting of lasting importance, for it began a relationship between Gerbert and the Ottonian emperors that would last for three decades and see Gerbert promoted to a series of increasingly prominent Church offices with help from the backing of his German patrons. Gerbert left Rome for Reims shortly thereafter in order to study *logica* (the arts of dialectic and rhetoric) with the celebrated schoolmaster Gerannus, and in 972 Adalbero appointed him master of the cathedral school.

Perhaps as a result of his time in Spain, with its access to the riches of Arab learning, Gerbert possessed an unparalleled knowledge of the quadrivium (the arts of arithmetic, geometry, music, and astronomy), and Richer describes in

detail how he introduced innovations such as the abacus and the armillary sphere at Reims. He was also a self-professed Ciceronian and a devoted student of classical rhetoric, and his surviving letters bear witness to his diligent efforts to seek out new manuscripts of authors such as Cicero and Quintilian. Gerbert's tenure as *scholasticus* at Reims secured his reputation as one of the most learned men in the Latin West. It was partly as a result of his growing fame that he was brought to Ravenna by Otto II of Germany to engage in a disputation with the Saxon scholar Otric of Magdeburg, who had impugned his taxonomy of the parts of philosophy. The disputation was a triumph for Gerbert, who was rewarded by Otto with the prestigious Italian abbey of Bobbio. In Italy, however, Gerbert found himself beleaguered by refractory monks and hostile landowners, and in 984 he returned to Reims to take up his former position at the cathedral school.

After the death of Adalbero in 989, Hugh Capet passed over Gerbert and appointed Arnulf, the bastard son of King Lothar, to the see of Reims as part of an attempt to neutralize Carolingian opposition to his rule. Shortly after swearing an oath of fealty to Hugh, however, Arnulf threw in his lot with his rebellious uncle Charles and delivered the city of Reims to him. Charles and Arnulf were subsequently betrayed and captured by Bishop Adalbero of Laon in the spring of 991, marking the end of Carolingian resistance to Hugh. At the synod of Saint-Basle in June of 991, Arnulf was forced to abdicate his office, and shortly thereafter Gerbert was chosen archbishop in his place. A significant opposition faction refused to accept Arnulf's deposition, however, and Gerbert's position remained uncertain at Reims, where Ar-

nulf still had considerable support. At the synod of Mouzon in 995, which was presided over by a legate of Pope John XV, Gerbert agreed to suspend saying mass temporarily until the dispute could be settled. He spent the next two years in an ultimately vain attempt to defend his claim to the see of Reims against Arnulf's supporters, and in 997 he left Reims for the court of Otto III of Germany, who appointed him archbishop of Ravenna (998) and then pope (999–1003), at which time he took the name Sylvester II.

Richer includes an abridged version of Gerbert's own *Acta* of the synod of Saint-Basle in Book 4, and he intended to include a similar account of the synod of Mouzon, although this section either dropped out of the manuscript or was never completed. The narrative portion of the *Historia* comes to a stop at the conclusion of the synod of Mouzon. It is followed by a series of brief notes (apparently material for a future continuation), the last two of which report on Gerbert's appointment to the see of Ravenna and Pope Gregory V's decision to allow Arnulf to resume his former position as archbishop of Reims. Richer evidently stopped writing when it became clear that Gerbert was not returning to Reims, but he found a way to transmit the manuscript to him. Our sole surviving copy of his history is found in the cathedral library of Bamberg, where Gerbert's personal library was deposited after his death.

Given that Richer dedicated his history to Gerbert, described his "enlightenment" of Gaul in panegyrical tones, and reproduced (or intended to reproduce) major portions of Gerbert's *Acta* of the synods of Saint-Basle and Mouzon in his work, it is clear that the *Historia* was intended at least in part to burnish Gerbert's reputation and recapitulate his

arguments for the validity of his claim to the see of Reims. Whether Richer was instructed to write his *Historia* by Gerbert is less clear. He alludes to a command from Gerbert in his prologue, but the invocation of a commission from a dedicatee was one of the most common of medieval prefatory topoi, and it should not be taken as proof that Gerbert actually asked Richer to write. It is equally possible that the strongly pro-Gerbertian tone of the *Historia* stemmed from Richer's desire to win Gerbert's esteem and patronage, or perhaps some more tangible reward. The precise nature of the relationship between the two men eludes us. It is frequently assumed, on the basis of Richer's detailed knowledge of Gerbert's curriculum, that he must have been a student of Gerbert, but this cannot be proven. The two men did, however, share common intellectual interests, notably rhetoric and medicine, and Richer had access not only to Gerbert's synodal acts but also to his letters, which suggests that they were on familiar terms. Whether or not Richer was ever a student of Gerbert's at the cathedral school of Reims, he clearly viewed Gerbert as an intellectual mentor.

Our knowledge of Richer himself is limited to what can be gleaned from the pages of his history. His father, Rodulf, was a vassal *(miles)* of King Louis IV, and he continued to serve Queen Gerberga after Louis's death in 954. In Richer's telling, Rodulf was one of the king's closest advisers—a prudent counselor and clever military tactician who devised a successful scheme to retake the city of Laon from Hugh the Great in 949 and engineered the capture of the stronghold of Mons seven years later.[8] Rodulf's ties to Louis IV help to explain Richer's entrance into the prestigious monastery of Saint-Rémi, which was closely associated with the Carolin-

gian kings. There is no way of knowing when Richer entered Saint-Rémi, nor does he describe his time there, but the *Historia* reveals that he was a person of considerable learning and intellectual ambition. He was widely read in the historians of classical and late antiquity (notably Caesar, Sallust, Livy, and Hegesippus), and the *Historia* is full of direct and indirect echoes of their work.[9] He was also capable of describing the technical aspects of Gerbert's curriculum in language that indicates he had received a thorough training in the liberal arts. Like Gerbert, he was devoted to the study of classical rhetoric, and he composed dozens of speeches to put into the mouths of his characters. Indeed, the importance of persuasive speaking is one of the distinguishing features of the *Historia,* in which almost every important event is preceded by a formal oration of some sort.

Richer also reveals a keen interest in two subjects that fell outside of the scope of the standard medieval curriculum: siege craft and medicine. On three occasions he describes the construction of siege engines in precise technical detail, and he demonstrates a particular fondness for describing the mortal illnesses of his characters, with detailed lists of symptoms drawn from medical textbooks.[10] In a fascinating autobiographical excursus, he gives an account of an arduous journey that he took to Chartres to read medical manuscripts at the behest of his friend Heribert.[11] Given the level of Richer's learning and his desire to parade that learning in the pages of his history, it is safe to assume that he was part of the learned elite in his own community and probably tied into a broader network of scholarly monks and clerics in West Francia.

Richer saw himself as the continuator of a distinguished

tradition of historical writing at Reims, a tradition inaugurated by Archbishop Hincmar (845–882), who wrote both a *Life of Saint Remigius* and the third and final section of the so-called *Annals of Saint-Bertin*. In his prologue Richer presents his history as a continuation of Hincmar's annals, which came to an end at his death in 882. Hincmar found a worthy successor in Flodoard (894–966), a canon of the cathedral of Reims who wrote two of the most important works of tenth-century Latin historiography: *Annals* covering the years 919–966, and the massive and enormously erudite *History of the Church of Reims*.[12] Richer used both of Flodoard's histories as source material, but the *Annals* were his most important source by far. Indeed, much of the first half of his history (from 1.15 to 3.21) is a rewriting of the *Annals* in one way or another. Reworking the material of one's predecessors was standard practice for medieval historiographers, but Richer was keen to show that he was not merely compiling a tissue of excerpts from Flodoard. He states in the prologue that he "did not use the same words" as Flodoard, "but different ones," and that he employed "a very different style." In fact, the manuscript shows that in his first draft Richer boasted that his rhetorical style was "far superior" to Flodoard's, before he reconsidered and toned down his language. Stylistic concerns were thus of paramount importance to Richer, who sought to take the bare-bones structure of Flodoard's *Annals* and transform it into a true narrative history in the classical mold.

Despite the importance accorded to his work as one of the only narrative sources for the political and ecclesiastical history of late tenth-century West Francia, Richer has won few admirers as a historian. Robert Latouche, who produced

the last translation of the *Historia* over seventy years ago, could scarcely contain his irritation at the author's casual relationship with the truth.[13] There is no denying that Richer was a careless and frequently inaccurate historian. His account of the royal lineage of Charles the Simple, for example, is highly confused.[14] He incorrectly calculates Louis IV's age at his death and the length of Lothar's reign, despite the fact that the necessary information was readily available to him.[15] He frequently invents or exaggerates army sizes and casualty statistics, in one case quoting Flodoard as a source for a number not found in either of his predecessor's historical works.[16] Equally frustrating to those who turn to Richer as a source for the history of tenth-century West Francia is his fondness for rhetorical *inventio,* the imaginative generation of material needed to make a narrative believable to its audience. In Richer's case, *inventio* most frequently takes the form of freely invented speeches and conversations and detailed descriptions of battles, siege engines, and diseases for which he was highly unlikely to have had access to eyewitness accounts.

Richer's tendency to embellish the material he took from Flodoard's *Annals* by adding circumstantial details and inventing speeches was neither arbitrary nor unusual, however. On the contrary, it was entirely consistent with the conventions of classical historiography. When Richer tells the reader in his prologue that he intends to treat his subject matter "plausibly, clearly, and concisely," he is not merely recycling a well-worn prefatory topos. He is citing the three "virtues of narrative" recommended by the rhetorical handbooks of classical antiquity, thereby signaling to the reader his intention to treat his history as a *narratio* governed by

the rules of classical rhetoric. To make his history "plausible," he was obligated to flesh out his source material through a process of amplification and rhetorical invention. The result is a history that juxtaposes events that actually happened *(quae vere gesta sunt)* with the kinds of things that very well could have happened *(quae geri potuerunt)*.

Richer's intended audience and the ultimate purpose of the *Historia* remain matters of debate. It is clear that much of what he wrote was intended specifically for Gerbert's eyes, and the focus on the archbishopric of Reims and the monastery of Saint-Rémi suggests that it was intended to be read by the monastic and clerical community of Reims. The second half of the *Historia* can be read in part as an apologia for Gerbert and a defense of his claims to the see of Reims. But if Richer wrote with the specific intention of helping Gerbert, it is not immediately obvious why he chose to embed his pro-Gerbertian material within a four-book history of the West Frankish kings and their wars.

Because Richer's stated theme is political history, and because he wrote in the aftermath of the failed rebellion of Charles of Lotharingia, scholars have long been interested in determining how his own political allegiances may have shaped what he wrote.[17] On the basis of his father's service to Louis IV and his generally favorable portrayal of the Carolingian kings, some have identified Richer as a Carolingian partisan. Others have pointed to Adalbero's speech in favor of the election of Hugh Capet in Book 4 as evidence that Richer had reconciled himself to support the Capetian dynasty backed by both Adalbero and Gerbert.[18] In truth, the text of the *Historia* does not present unambiguous support for either dynasty. The Carolingian kings are generally pre-

sented with sympathy, but Richer is not shy about criticizing Charles the Simple's foolish devotion to Hagano or the immaturity and vanity of Louis V.[19] With the possible exception of Lothar, whose reign ends with a modestly successful military campaign in Lotharingia, the impression left of the Carolingian kings in the *Historia* is primarily one of weakness and persecution. By contrast, the Robertians—Odo, Robert I, Hugh the Great, and Hugh Capet—for the most part exude strength and competence, but their legitimacy is frequently called into question. On several occasions Richer refers to Robert as a "tyrant" and a "usurper," and Hugh the Great, who is himself frequently called a "tyrant," admits that his father acted unjustly in ruling while Charles the Simple still lived.[20] Hugh Capet is depicted as being conscious of acting wrongly in assuming the throne in place of Charles of Lotharingia, and on the final folio of the manuscript Richer refers to the "treachery" of Robert the Pious, Hugh's son and successor, for having released Arnulf from captivity.[21] In sum, it is difficult to support the argument that Richer wrote as part of an attempt to burnish the claims of either the Carolingian or the Robertian house. To the degree that the *Historia* presents a consistent political viewpoint, it is a conventional one: the desire for a strong and legitimate king who could stamp out civil strife (*dissidentia principum*) and bring peace to the realm.

The *Historia* itself is unfinished and its survival a matter of good fortune, for it does not appear to have circulated widely in the Middle Ages. Only one copy is extant: Bamberg, Staatsbibliothek MS Hist. 5, which was discovered by the Bamberg librarian Heinrich Joachim Jaeck in 1833 and presented to Georg Heinrich Pertz, coeditor of the fledg-

ling *Monumenta Germaniae Historica* and Richer's first editor.[22] Not only is Bamberg MS Hist. 5 the sole surviving copy
of Richer's history, it is also his autograph manuscript. Its
fifty-seven folios are filled with corrections, erasures, and
expunged but still-legible passages that testify to various
stages of composition and revision. At Bamberg, where the
Historia is attested in a twelfth-century library catalog, three
authors are known to have used it as a source. A fragment
from an anonymous eleventh-century *Historia Francorum*
draws on Richer's account of the "Customs of the Gauls" at
1.3.[23] The medieval historian Frutolf of Michelsberg (d. 1103)
and the German Renaissance humanist Johannes Trithemius
(1462–1516) also drew on Richer as a source. Interestingly,
both of these authors restrict themselves to the first two
books of the *Historia* (Trithemius refers to it explicitly as
a two-book history), and both disagree with Bamberg MS
Hist. 5, making it very likely that another redaction of Richer's history once existed at Bamberg.[24] The monastic
chronicler Hugh of Flavigny (ca. 1065–1114) borrowed from
Richer's account of Gerbert's career for his *Chronicon,* but
there is no evidence that he took a trip to Bamberg;[25] hence
it is possible that another edition of the *Historia* similar to
that which is contained in Bamberg MS Hist. 5 once existed
in northern France.[26] We have no way of knowing whether
Richer's own monastery preserved a copy of his work, since
most of the holdings of the library of Saint-Rémi were destroyed by fire in 1774.

A few aspects of Richer's diction deserve brief mention.
The word *virtus,* which in classical Latin encompassed quali-
ties such as bravery and perseverance that were associated
with ideal manliness, acquires a certain vagueness in Ri-

cher's hands.[27] It has thus been variously translated as "virtue," "excellence," "power," "strength," "skill," and "courage," depending on the context. Richer uses *tyrannus* not necessarily to refer to despots but to designate those who, like Heribert of Vermandois, Hugh the Great, and Charles of Lotharingia, challenge legitimate royal authority. The word *oppidum* is a general term that describes any kind of fortified settlement (a stronghold or a fortified town), whereas *castrum* appears, for the most part, to refer to a particular kind of fortification: a stone fortress surrounded by walls.[28] The word *miles* is used in three overlapping senses in the *Historia,* to mean soldier, vassal, and member of "the warrior class" *(ordo militaris).*[29] What unites all three of these definitions is that in every instance the *miles* was a professional warrior who provided military service to a lord. *Eques* ("knight") overlaps to a large extent with *miles,* so that *ordo militaris* ("warrior class") and *ordo equestris* ("knightly order") probably refer to the same group of people. This was not a particularly elite group, as is evident from Adalbero of Reims's criticism of Charles of Lotharingia for taking a wife *de militari ordine* (4.11) or an expunged passage in which Richer explains that Odo (a *vir militaris* whose father was of the *ordo equestris*) was unable to repress feuding among the *milites* because "they sometimes scorned to be subject to a person of middling status" *(eo quod milites mediocri interdum subdi contempnerent).*[30]

Richer's geographical terminology is idiosyncratic and occasionally confusing. Lacking a word to denote the territory that historians today call West Francia, he employs the classical moniker Gaul, and drawing on Caesar's *Bellum Gallicum,* he divides Gaul into three parts: Aquitaine, Celtic Gaul, and Belgica.[31] These territorial divisions did not, how-

ever, accurately reflect the political realities of tenth-century Francia, and even this anachronistic terminology is not used consistently. In his geographical prologue, for example, Richer, following Caesar, defines Aquitaine as the area between the Garonne River and the Pyrenees (1.2). Yet he immediately abandons this definition and uses Aquitaine in its traditional medieval signification to refer the area between the Loire and the Garonne. He uses *Belgica* as a synonym for Flodoard's *regnum Lotharii* to denote Lotharingia, but (again following Caesar) places its western boundary at the Marne River instead of the Meuse, the traditional western boundary of Lotharingia since the Treaty of Verdun in 843. This had the effect of putting cities like Reims (1.14) and Soissons (1.21) inside Belgica, even though neither was considered part of Lotharingia. *Gallia Celtica* is defined early on as the area between the Garonne and the Marne (1.2), but in the *Historia* itself Richer treats it as the area between the Loire and the Marne. Richer may in fact have ended up confusing himself by using Caesar's tripartite division of Gaul, since at 1.12 he includes Reims within Celtic Gaul and two chapters later puts it in Belgica.[32] His decision to use this terminology probably stems in part from his classicizing tendencies, but he may also have chosen to use *Gallia Belgica* over *regnum Lotharii* to make a comment about the legitimacy of West Frankish overlordship in Lotharingia. For there could be no question but that the king of *Gallia* should by rights exercise dominion in *Gallia Belgica*.

The translator's task has been made substantially easier by the work of Hartmut Hoffmann, who published a new edi-

tion of Richer's *Historia* for the *Monumenta Germaniae Historica* in 2000 and an accompanying study in *Deutsches Archiv für Erforschung des Mittelalters.* Serious students of Richer will need to consult the notes in Hoffmann's edition, which also contains a facsimile of the manuscript. I have benefited from being able to consult the previous translations of Jerome Guadet, Karl von der Osten-Sacken, and Robert Latouche, and I have been fortunate to receive help from many people. In particular I would like to thank Jan Ziolkowski, Danuta Shanzer, Greg Hays, Michael Winterbottom, David Bachrach, Bruce Eastwood, and Mayke de Jong. These volumes are dedicated with gratitude to my parents.

Justin Lake
January 2011

NOTES

1 For the dates of composition, see Hoffmann, "Die *Historien* Richers von Saint-Remi," esp. pp. 446 and 453–55.

2 "West Francia" was not a name used by Richer, or any contemporary author, but a term of convenience adopted by scholars to describe the territory ceded to Charles the Bald at the Treaty of Verdun in 843, lands that formed the core of the later kingdom of France. It was the lack of a generally agreed-upon designation for this territory that led Richer to adopt the anachronistic term *Gallia.* See Jean Dunbabin, *France in the Making* (New York: Oxford University Press, 1985), pp. 1–5.

3 *Hist.* 1.4.

4 *Hist.* 3.22–42.

5 *Hist.* 3.42.

6 *Hist.* 4.102.

7 *Hist.* 3.43–54.

8 *Hist.* 2.87–90, 3.7–10.

9 For a complete catalog of Richer's citations of and allusions to classical authors, see the index in Hoffmann, *Richeri historiarum libri IIII*, pp. 315–25.

10 For siege engines, see *Hist.* 2.10, 3.105, and 4.22. Richer's medical knowledge is analyzed by MacKinney, "Tenth-Century Medicine as Seen in the *Historia.*"

11 *Hist.* 4.50.

12 See Philippe Lauer, ed., *Les Annales de Flodoard.* Collection de textes pour servir à l'étude et à l'enseignement de l'histoire (Paris: Alphonse Picard, 1905), and Martina Stratmann, ed., *Flodoardus Remensis: Historia Remensis Ecclesiae, Monumenta Germaniae Historica SS* 36 (Hanover: Hahn, 1998).

13 Latouche, *Richer: Histoire de France.* See, for example, vol. I, p. xi: "Il est donc dangereux de le suivre et son témoinage est toujours suspect," and vol. I, p. 133 n. 2: "Richer n'a pas de scrupules d'historien."

14 *Hist.* 1.4.

15 *Hist.* 2.103, 3.109.

16 *Hist.* 1.46. See also 1.49, 1.51, 2.35, and 2.85 for invented or exaggerated casualty figures.

17 See Wolfgang Giese, *"Genus" und "Virtus,"* pp. 10–16, and Gian Andria Bezzola, *Das Ottonische Kaisertum in der französischen Geschichtsschreibung des 10. und beginnenden 11. Jahrhunderts* (Graz: Hermann Böhlau, 1956), pp. 105–45. The most recent summary of scholarly approaches to the political ideology of Richer's *Historia* is found in Glenn, *Politics and History in the Tenth Century,* pp. 5–6.

18 See Kortüm, *Richer von Saint-Remi,* pp. 46–49.

19 *Hist.* 1.14–16, 3.95. For Richer's portrayal of the West Frankish kings, see in particular Giese, *"Genus" und "Virtus."*

20 *Hist.* 1.21, 1.45, 2.2. Hugh is called a tyrant at 2.22, 24, 26–28, 36, 48, 81, 82, 85, and 87.

21 *Hist.* 4.39, 4.109.

22 For an account of Jaeck's presentation of the manuscript to Pertz and his traveling companion, Johannes Böhmer, see Glenn, *Politics and History,* pp. 269–73.

23 See Hoffmann, "Die *Historien* Richers von Saint-Remi," pp. 520–25.

24 See ibid., pp. 508–20.

25 G. H. Pertz, ed., *Chronicon Virdunense seu Flaviniacense, Monumenta Germaniae HistoricaSS* 8 (Hanover: Hahn, 1848), pp. 288–502, here p. 367. See Patrick Healy, *The Chronicle of Hugh of Flavigny: Reform and the Investiture Contest in the Late Eleventh Century* (Aldershot: Ashgate, 2006).

26 Hoffmann, "Die *Historien* Richers von Saint-Remi," p. 509. The libraries that Hugh was likely to have made the most use of were those of Saint-Vanne at Verdun and Saint-Bénigne at Dijon. See Healy, *Chronicle of Hugh of Flavigny,* p. 102.

27 See Hoffmann, "Die *Historien* Richers von Saint-Remi, p. 505.

28 Bernard Bachrach, "Fortifications and Military Tactics: Fulk Nerra's Strongholds Circa 1000," *Technology and Culture* 20, no. 3 (1979): 531–49.

29 J. M. Van Winter, "Uxorem de militari ordinem sibi imparem," *Miscellanea Mediaevalia in memoriam Jan Frederik Niermeyer* (Groningen: J. B. Wolters, 1967), pp. 113–24.

30 Fol. 2v, 16–17. The sheer number of *milites* available to do battle on behalf of the kings and great magnates also speaks to their middling status. In one of his campaigns against the Vikings (*Hist.* 1.7), King Odo is able to summon 10,000 knights *(equites)* to his side from Aquitaine and Septimania, but only 6,000 foot soldiers *(pedites)*.

31 *Bellum Gallicum* 1.1.

32 *Hist.* 1.12: *Ex Celtica vero Remorum predictus metropolitanus;* 1.14: *Inde quoque omnibus obtentis rediens, Belgicam repetit ac sanctum Remigium donis egregiis honorat.*

HISTORIES

Prologus

Domino ac beatissimo patri Gerberto[1] Remorum archiepis-
copo, Richerus monachus:

Gallorum congressibus in volumine regerendis imperii
tui, pater sanctissime Gerberte, auctoritas seminarium dedit. Quam, quia summam utilitatem affert, et rerum materia
sese multiplex praebet, eo animi nisu complector qua iuben-
tis mira benivolentia pertrahor. Cuius rei initium a vicino.
ducendum existimavi,[2] cum res multo ante gestas dignae[3]
memoriae Hincmarus, ante te in pontificatu VIII,[4] suis an-
nalibus copiosissime annexuit.

Tantoque superiora lector ea inveniet quanto a nostri
opusculi exordio per eius regesta sese attollet. Et hoc inquam ne Karolorum aliorumque frequens in utroque opere
repetitio operis utriusque ordinem turbet. Ubi enim rerum
ordo non advertitur, tanto nitentem error confundit quanto
a serie ordinis errantem seducit. Unde cum hic atque illic
sepe Karoli, sepe Ludovici notae offeruntur, pro tempore

Prologue

To my Lord and most blessed father Gerbert,[1] Archbishop of Reims, the monk Richer:

The authority of your command, most holy father Gerbert, provided the seedbed for the conflicts of the Gauls to be compiled in a book. Because the advantages to be realized are so great, and because the subject matter is so abundant, I have embraced this task as eagerly as I was drawn by the marvelous goodwill of the one making the request. I have judged it best to begin with recent events because Hincmar[2] of blessed memory, who was eighth in the office of archbishop before you,[3] so comprehensively wove together the deeds of the more distant past in his own annals.[4]

The further back the reader goes from the beginning of my work through Hincmar's history, the earlier the material that he will find. I say this so that the frequent repetition of the name Charles and of other names in each work will not cause any confusion about their respective order. For when the sequence of events is not attended to, error will confound the struggling reader to the degree that it leads him astray from the proper order. Therefore, because the names Charles and Louis appear often in both works, the careful reader will distinguish between kings who share the same

auctorum prudens lector reges aequivocos pernotabit. Quorum temporibus bella a Gallis saepenumero patrata variosque eorum tumultus ac diversas negotiorum rationes ad memoriam reducere scripto specialiter propositum est. Si qua vero aliorum efferantur, ob incidentes rationes quae vitari non potuerunt id evenisse putetur. Sed si ignotae antiquitatis ignorantiae arguar, ex quodam Flodoardi presbiteri Remensis libello me aliqua sumpsisse non abnuo, at non verba quidem eadem, sed alia pro aliis longe diverso[5] orationis[6] scemate disposuisse res ipsa evidentissime demonstrat. Satisque lectori fieri arbitror, si probabiliter atque dilucide breviterque omnia digesserim.[7] In dicendo enim recusans effluere, plurima succincte expediam. Ac totius exordium narrationis aggrediar, breviter facta orbis divisione Galliaque in partes distributa, eo quod eius populorum mores et actus describere propositum sit.

EXPLICIT PROLOGUS.

name by referring to the different time periods of the authors. My particular goal is to recall to memory in writing the frequent wars waged by the Gauls during the reigns of these kings, their various struggles, and the different reasons for their undertakings. If the affairs of others are mentioned, let it be assumed that this is due to incidental reasons that could not be avoided. Now if I am accused of being ignorant of the unknown past, I do not deny that I took some things from a certain book of Flodoard,[5] a priest of Reims, but the content itself shows very clearly that I did not use the same words, but different ones, and that I employed a very different rhetorical style. I think that the reader will be satisfied if I have set forth everything plausibly, clearly, and concisely. For by declining to be long-winded, I will reveal many things succinctly. I will begin the prologue to the work as a whole after I have briefly made a division of the world and divided Gaul into its parts, since it is my intention to describe the customs and deeds of its inhabitants.

HERE ENDS THE PROLOGUE.

BOOK ONE

Divisio orbis

Orbis itaque plaga quae mortalibus sese commodum praebet a cosmographis trifariam dividi perhibetur: in Asiam videlicet, Africam, et Europam. Quarum prior, a septentrione per orientis regionem usque in austrum extrinsecus oceano disterminata, interius a Ripheis montibus usque ad terrae umbilicum Thanai, Meothide, Mediterraneoque ab Europa distinguitur. Ab umbilico vero usque in austrum Nilo fluvio ab Africa est seclusa. Africam vero et Europam, exterius quidem ab austro in septentrionem oceano circumdatas, Mediterraneus[1] interiectus discriminat. Ab Asia vero interius earum alteram Nilus, alteram vero Mediterraneum, Thanaisque ac Meotis, ut dictum est, seiungunt. Quarum singulae cum proprias habeant distributiones, Europae tamen partem unam quae Gallia a candore vocatur, eo quod candidioris speciei insigne eius oriundi preferant, in suas diducere partes ratum duxi.

I

The Division of the World

According to cosmographers the area of the world suitable for human habitation is divided into three parts: namely, Asia, Africa, and Europe.[1] The first of these, Asia, stretches from north to south across the eastern region of the world. Its outer boundary is the ocean, and it is separated from Europe by the Don River, Lake Maeotis, and the Mediterranean, starting at the Riphaean mountains and going down to the navel of the earth.[2] From the navel of the earth southward, Asia is divided from Africa by the Nile River. The internal boundary between Africa and Europe is the Mediterranean, which lies between them, and on the outside they are bounded from south to north by the ocean. Interior Asia is separated from Africa by the Nile and from Europe by the Mediterranean, the Don, and Lake Maeotis, as previously mentioned. Although each one of these areas has its own internal divisions, I have only chosen to divide into its constituent parts that area of Europe that is called Gaul on account of its whiteness,[3] since the inhabitants of this land exhibit the distinguishing feature of a rather fair complexion.

2

Istius Galliae in[2] partes distributio

Gallia ergo et ipsa in tria distincta est: in Belgicam, Celticam, Aquitanicam. Quarum prior, Belgica, a Rheno, qui Germaniam ab oceano determinat, quae multarum gentium ferax a germinando nomen accepit, exporrigitur usque in fluvium Matronam. Ab utroque vero latere, hinc quidem Alpibus Apenninis, inde vero mari vallatur, cuius circumfusione insula Brittannica efficitur. Celtica autem a Matrona per longum in Garunnam distenditur,[3] cuius latera oceani Brittannici et insulae Brittannicae limites efficiunt.[4] Quicquid vero a Garunna distenditur in Pireneum[5] Aquitanica appellatur, hinc Rhodano Ararique[6] atque inde Mediterraneo conlimitans. Constat itaque totius Galliae spatium ab oriente quidem Rheno, ab occidente Pyreneo,[7] et a septentrione mari Brittannico, ab austro vero Mediterraneo cingi.

2

The Division of Gaul into Parts

Gaul itself, then, is divided into three parts: Belgica, Celtic Gaul, and Aquitaine.[4] The first of these, Belgica, extends from the Rhine to the Marne. The Rhine all the way down to the ocean marks the boundary with Germany (which takes its name from "germination"[5] because this land is productive of many peoples). Belgica is hemmed in by the Pennine Alps on one side and the sea that makes Britain an island on the other. Celtic Gaul extends over a vast area from the Marne to the Garonne. Its sides form the boundaries of the Britannic Sea and the island of Britain. The region between the Garonne and the Pyrenees is called Aquitaine; it is enclosed on one side by the Rhone and the Saône and on the other side by the Mediterranean. It is agreed, therefore, that the territory of Gaul as a whole is surrounded by the Rhine in the east, the Pyrenees in the West, the Britannic Sea in the north, and the Mediterranean in the south.

3

Mores Gallorum

Omnium ergo Galliarum populi innata audatia plurimum efferuntur, calumniarum impatientes. Si incitantur, cedibus exultant, efferatique inclementius adoriuntur. Semel persuasum ac rationibus approbatum vix refellere consuerunt. Unde et Hieronimus 'Sola,' inquit, 'Gallia monstra non habuit, sed viris prudentibus et eloquentissimis semper claruit.' Praeter haec quoque Belgae rebus disponendis insigniores, robore atque audatia non impares. Maxima quaeque magis ingenio quam viribus appetunt. Et si ingenio in appetendis cassantur, viribus audacter utuntur. Cibi etiam potusque adeo parci. Celtae vero ac Aquitani consilio simul et audatia plurimi, rebus seditiosis commodi. Celtae tamen magis providi, Aquitani vero precipites aguntur plurimumque in ciborum rapiuntur appetitum. Quod sic est eis innatum, ut preter naturam non appetant. Hinc et Sulpicius, 'Edacitas,' inquit, 'in Grecis gula est, in Gallis natura.' Hos[8] omnes populos, etsi natura feroces, ab antiquo fere per omnia prospere egisse, etiam cum[9] pagani essent, historiae tra-

3

The Customs of the Gauls

All the peoples of Gaul are carried away by their native boldness and are unwilling to suffer an insult. If provoked, they revel in slaughter, and when enraged they attack without mercy. But once they have been convinced of something and its truth has been demonstrated to them through arguments, they tend not to dispute it. For this reason Jerome says: "Only Gaul did not contain monstrosities, but was always famous for prudent and eloquent men."[6] Apart from this, the men of Belgica are particularly distinguished for their skill at organization, and they are by no means inferior in physical strength and daring. In any major undertaking they prefer to use strategy rather than force, but if their designs are thwarted when employing the former, they use the latter boldly. They are also quite moderate in eating and drinking. The Celts and Aquitainians are distinguished both by prudence and daring, although they are prone to rebellion. The men of Celtic Gaul, however, exercise greater foresight, while the Aquitainians act rashly and are particularly driven by their appetite for food. This characteristic is so native to them that their appetite cannot be regarded as unnatural. Hence the saying of Sulpicius: "Voracity in the Greeks is the product of gluttony; in the Gauls, it is the product of nature."[7] The histories tell us that from ancient times all of these peoples, although savage by nature, were

dunt. Post vero a sancto Remigio baptizati, adprime clara semper victoria[10] emicuisse feruntur. Quorum quoque primus rex christianus Clodoveus fuisse traditur. A quo per succedentia tempora imperatoribus egregiis res publica gubernata fuisse dinoscitur, usque ad Karolum, a quo historiae sumimus initium.

4

Quod ob infantiam regis et principum dissidentiam pyratae Gallias irruperint

Hic patrem habuit Karlomannum regem, avum vero paternum Ludovicum cognomento Balbum, abavum[11] autem Karolum Calvum, Germannorum atque Gallorum imperatorem egregium. Biennis adhuc patrem amisit, matre vix per quadriennium superstite.[12] Ob cuius infantiam cum regnorum principes nimia rerum cupidine sese preire contenderent, quisque ut poterat rem dilatabat. Nemo regis pro-

successful in almost everything that they did, even while they were pagans. But after they had been baptized by Saint Remigius, they are said to have shone continually in very famous victories.[8] It is said that Clovis was their first Christian king. Starting with him and through the succeeding years, the kingdom is known to have been ruled by illustrious emperors, down to the time of Charles,[9] with whom I shall begin my history.

4

How Because of the King's Youth and the Dissension among the Leading Men the Pirates Invaded Gaul

Charles's father was King Carloman, his paternal grandfather was Louis (surnamed "the Stammerer"), and his great-grandfather was Charles the Bald, the celebrated emperor of the Germans and the Gauls.[10] At the age of two he had already lost his father, and his mother lived for barely four years after that.[11] Because Charles was still a child, the leading men of the realm were each striving to get ahead of one another in their lust for wealth, and each was seeking to enrich himself as much as he could. No one was looking out for the king's interests or trying to protect the realm. Every-

879

vectum,[13] nemo regni tutelam quaerebat. Aliena adquirere summum cuique erat, nec rem suam provehere videbatur qui alieni aliquid non addebat. Unde et omnium concordia in summam discordiam relapsa est. Hinc direptiones, hinc incendia, hinc rerum pervasiones exarsere. Quae cum immanissime agitarentur, piratae qui Rhodomensem provinciam incolebant, quae est Celticae Galliae pars, ad rerum immanitatem incitantur. Haec gens ab insulis oceani septentrionalis remotioribus diu ante exierat. Et per maria errando classe devecta, summam hanc Galliarum partem attigerat. Saepe quoque eam armis impetivit, saepe etiam a terrae principibus devicta occubuit. Quod cum multoties inter sese moverent, visum fuit Gallie primatibus ut dono regum haec provincia ei conferretur, ita tamen, ut idolatria penitus relicta, christianae religioni se fideliter manciparet, necnon et regibus Galliarum terra marique fideliter militaret. Huius provinciae metropolis Rhodomum esse dinoscitur, sex tantum urbibus, Baiocis videlicet, Abrincanto, Ebrocis, Sagio, Constantiae, Lisoio vim suae dominationis intendens. Hanc itaque ex antiquo a piratis possessam esse manifestum est. Sed paterna tunc sevitia ducti, in principes dissidentes moliri conantur. Unde et latrociniis ac discursionibus Brittanniam minorem, quae est Galliae contigua atque militans, infestare aggrediuntur. Reique occasionem nacti, fidem penitus abrumpunt ulteriusque procedunt in Galliam. Ac circumquaque palantes, longe lateque diffun-

one's chief goal was to acquire the property of others, and no one was thought to have increased his fortunes unless he had added someone else's possessions to his own. As a result, universal harmony lapsed into complete and utter discord, and outbreaks of pillaging, burning, and seizures of property followed. While these acts of savagery were being perpetrated, the pirates who inhabited the territory around Rouen (which is a part of Celtic Gaul) were themselves roused to savage deeds. This nation had long ago left the distant islands of the northern sea, and after traversing the seas with their fleet in a haphazard fashion, had reached this corner of Gaul.[12] They attacked it many times, and many times they were vanquished and laid low by the leading men of the land. After both sides had engaged one another in battle on many occasions, the magnates of Gaul agreed that this province should be turned over to the pirates by virtue of a royal grant, but only on the condition that they completely abandon idolatry, faithfully dedicate themselves to the Christian religion, and serve the kings of Gaul loyally as their vassals on land and on sea.[13] (Rouen is the metropolitan see of this province, and its authority extends over just six cities: Bayeux, Avranches, Évreux, Sées, Coutances, and Lisieux.) It is clear, then, that the pirates have held this territory from the distant past. But at that moment, driven by their ancestral savagery, they attempted to take advantage of the dissension among the leading men. They advanced into Brittany, which borders on and is held as a fief of Gaul, and harried it with pillaging and raids. Then, seizing the opportunity that was before them, they completely broke the agreement that they had made and marched into Gaul. Scattering in all directions, they spread far and wide, carrying off

duntur, feminarum, puerorum, pecudum, ceterarumque rerum non modicam predam abducentes. Recipiuntur vero cum his omnibus secus Sequanam loco qui Giuoldi fossa nuncupatur. Ac idem sepius aggresi, Galliae Celticae partem quae Sequanae Ligerique fluviis interiacet, quae et Neustria nuncupatur, totam pene insectati sunt. Hisque animo inerat interiores Galliarum partes irrumpere earumque gentes aut a finibus pellere aut gravissimis substituere tributis. Id etiam ante fieri quam in consensum principes revocarentur accelerabant, huiusmodi dissidentia pecunias Galliarum sese asportaturos certissime rati. Quorum impetus Catillo principe ferebatur. Principes, tanta barbarorum ignominia confecti, de pace habenda per legatos inter sese admodum quaerunt. Nec diu morati, iure obsidum in unum consulturi conveniunt. In quo conventu, sapientium usi consilio, fidem pacti, in concordiam maximam rediere, contumelias a barbaris iniectas ultum ire parati. Et quia Karolus vix adhuc triennis erat, de rege creando deliberant, non ut desertores, sed ut in adversarios indignantes.

a considerable haul of women, children, livestock, and other property, after which they withdrew with all of this plunder to a place called Jeufosse on the Seine. Through constant raiding they harried almost all of that part of Gaul that lies between the Seine and the Loire, which is called Neustria. Their intention was to invade the inner regions of Gaul and either drive the inhabitants from their lands or subject them to very heavy tribute. Indeed, they were hastening to do this before the leading men could be reconciled with one another, for they reckoned that given the level of discord among them, the wealth of Gaul would surely be theirs for the taking. Their invasion was led by their chief, Catillus. Overcome by the enormity of the disgrace caused by the barbarians, the leading men sought earnestly through the exchange of envoys to make peace. Nor did they delay any longer before they came together to deliberate under the surety of hostages. During this meeting they heeded the advice of wise men, and after pledging their faith to one another, they returned to a state of complete harmony, ready to avenge the insults inflicted on them by the barbarians. And because Charles was barely three years old at the time, they entered into deliberations to elect a king,[14] not as traitors, but as men indignant against their enemies.

5

Regis genus atque fortuna

Anno itaque incarnationis dominicae DCCCLXXX-VIII, <. . .> Martis, V feria, communi decreto Odonem, virum militarem et strenuum, in basilica sancti[14] . . . regem creant. Hic patrem habuit ex equestri ordine Rotbertum, avum vero paternum Witichinum, advenam Germanum. Creatusque rex, strenue atque utiliter omnia gessit, preter quod in militari tumultu raram componendi lites potestatem habuit.[15] Nam pyratas signis collatis intra Neustriam septies fudit ac in fugam novies compulit.[16] Atque hoc fere per quinquennium.[17] Quibus repulsis, fames valida subsecuta est, cum triennio terra inculta remanserit. Iam enim mensura frumenti quae sedeties ducta modium efficit decem dragmis venibat.[18] Gallinatius quoque quatuor dragmis, ovis vero tribus unciis, atque vacca iabo tollebatur. Vini nulla coemptio erat, cum vinetis ubique succissis, vix eius aliquid habebatur. Rex interea per loca[19] quae piratis irruentibus aditum prebebant munitiones exstruxit ac in eis militum copias ponit, ipse[20] in Aquitaniae partes secedens, non ante se

5

The Lineage and Fortunes of the King

On Thursday the 29th of February in the year 888 of the 888 Lord's incarnation, in the church of Saint <. . .>, by communal decree they made Odo, a vigorous warrior, their king.[15] His father, Robert,[16] was of the knightly order, and his paternal grandfather, Witichin, had emigrated from Germany.[17] After he was elected king, Odo carried out all of his tasks energetically and successfully, except that when armed violence broke out, he had limited power to settle the disputes.[18] Within Neustria he defeated the pirates in pitched 888–892 battles seven times and compelled them to flee nine times. This went on for about five years. After the pirates had been driven out, there was a severe famine because the land had remained uncultivated for three years. At that time one-sixteenth of a bushel of grain sold for ten drachmas and a chicken for four, while a sheep sold for three ounces and a cow could be purchased for eleven.[19] Wine could not be bought because the vines had been cut down everywhere, and there was scarcely any to be had. Meanwhile the king built fortifications throughout the areas that were serving as entry points for the invading pirates, and he stationed garrisons of soldiers there. He himself withdrew into Aqui-

rediturum proponens quam supradicta modii frumentarii mensura duabus dragmis veniret, gallinatius vero denario, atque ovis duabus itidem dragmis, vacca vero tribus unciis venumdaretur.

6

Pyratae Brittanniam impetunt ac devastant

Interea rege apud urbem Anitium rem publicam procurante, pyratae a finibus Neustriae[21] pulsi eum ad interiora Aquitaniae concessisse[22] dinoscunt. Confluunt itaque ac classem parant, atque Brittanniam repentini irrumpunt. Brittanni repentino barbarorum impetu territi, saevientibus cedunt.[23] Cuique vitam tantum salvare satis fuit. Rerum suarum ereptionem nemo quaerebat. De vita solummodo agitabant. Unde et suis fere omnibus derelictis, pyratae passim rapiunt.[24] Quaeque commoda asportant ac cum multa rerum preda nullo renitente redeunt. Tam felici ergo successu elati,[25] per exteriores Brittanniae fines secus Andegavum Aquitaniam irrumpunt, multaque depopulatione terram devastant. Abducunt viros ac mulieres puerosque. Quorum

taine, declaring that he would not return until the afore-mentioned bushel of grain sold for two drachmas, a chicken for a denarius,[20] a sheep for two drachmas, and a cow for three ounces.

6

The Pirates Attack and Devastate Brittany

Meanwhile, while the king was attending to affairs of state in the city of Le Puy, the pirates who had been driven out of Neustria learned that he had withdrawn into the interior of Aquitaine. And so they gathered together, outfitted a fleet, and made a sudden incursion into Brittany. Terrified by the unexpected onset of the barbarians, the Bretons fled before the savage invaders. Each person thought only of saving his own life. No one tried to rescue his possessions; their only concern was survival. As a result, almost all of their property was left abandoned, and the pirates plundered far and wide. They carried off everything of value and returned with a great haul of plunder, without facing any opposition. Emboldened by such good fortune, they burst through the outer borders of Brittany into Aquitaine, near Angers, and devastated the area with widespread pillaging. They led away men, women, and children, and slaugh-

892/893

provectiores in utroque sexu obtruncant. Pueros servituti mancipant, feminas vero quae formosae videbantur prostituunt.

7

Odo rex contra pyratas exercitum parat

Sed nonnulli vario eventu elapsi, profugio salvati sunt. A quibus dum exagitarentur, mox Odoni regi relata fuere. Qui rerum magnitudine motus, quotquot ex Aquitania potuit edicto regio congregari precepit milites peditesque. Ex Provintia quoque, quae Rhodano et Alpibus marique ac Gothorum finibus circumquaque ambitur, Arelatenses ac Aurasicanos habuit, sed et ex Gothia Tholosanos atque Nemausinos. Quibus collectis, exercitus regius in $\overline{X}^{bus}$ equitum, peditum vero $\overline{VI}^{bus}$ erat. Procedit itaque secus Briddam, sancti Iuliani martiris castrum, iter agens. Sanctumque regiis donis veneratus, Arvernicum pagum ingreditur. Huc iam hostes advenerant ac castrum quod Mons Panchei dicitur vehementi hostilitate premebant. Rex principibus Francorum atque Aquitanorum stipatus, licet ancipiti deliberatione, tamen

tered the more aged members of both sexes. They delivered the children into slavery and gave the most attractive women over to prostitution.

7

Odo Musters an Army Against the Pirates

Yet a number of people managed to escape in one way or another and find safety in flight. As they were being driven away, they brought news of what had happened to King Odo. Dismayed by the gravity of the situation, he issued a royal edict commanding as many knights and foot soldiers as possible to assemble from Aquitaine. In addition, from Provence (which is surrounded on all sides by the Rhône, the Alps, the sea, and the territory of the Goths) he had at his disposal men from Arles and Orange, and from Gothia he had men from Toulouse and Nîmes. Once they had assembled, the royal army consisted of ten thousand knights and six thousand foot soldiers. They set forth and made their way to Brioude, the castle of Saint Julian the martyr. After honoring the saint with royal gifts, they entered the county of the Auvergne. The enemy had already arrived there and was mounting a violent assault upon the fortress of Montpensier. The king was attended by the leading men of the Franks and the Aquitainians, and although they were

belli dispositionem apud eos pertractabat, illos ad pugnam hortans ac eorum magnanimitatem ex natura plurimum attollens. Aliis quoque gentibus eos esse potiores tam viribus quam audatia et armis memorabat. Eorum quoque maiores pene totum orbem debellasse, ipsumque caput orbis Romam immaniter attrivisse.[26] Unde et oportere paternam animositatem in filiis renovandam asserebat,[27] ut patrum magnanimitas filiorum virtute commendaretur.

8

Impetus Odonis regis in pyratas, bellique qualitas

Quibus dictis cum persuasisset, utpote vir audax ac violentus, cum $\overline{\text{XVI}}$ signis illatis barbaros aggreditur.[28] Sed peditum copias premittit[29] atque ex eis primum impetum infert. Ipse cum equitatu succedens, peditum fortunam op-

wavering in their counsel, he went over the plan of attack with them in detail, urging them into battle and repeatedly extolling their native courage. He declared that they were superior to other peoples not only in strength but also in daring and skill at arms. Moreover, he reminded them that their ancestors had subjugated almost the whole of the earth and had inflicted severe damage on the city of Rome, the very capital of the world. Hence they should revive this hereditary valor among themselves so that the courage of their forefathers would be commended by the bravery of their descendants.

8

Odo's Assault on the Pirates and the Outcome of the Battle[21]

After persuading them with these words, in keeping with his daring and aggressive nature, Odo marched forward to attack the barbarians with sixteen thousand troops. He sent the foot soldiers ahead to make the first assault, however, while he followed up with the knights, waiting to see how

periebatur. Nec minus et barbari acies ordinaverant ac indivisi adversarios excipere cogitabant. At regii pedites hostibus directi, primo certamine sagittas iaculantur; densatique, lanceis obversis, in illos feruntur. Excepti vero a barbaris, plurimi dilabuntur, non tamen preter adversariorum ruinam. Nam et eorum alii precipitati, alii vero quamplures sauciati sunt. Post pedites vero et regius equitatus succedit ac acies hostium, copiis peditum divisas, multo nisu irrumpit. Sternitque, ut fertur, $\overline{\text{XIII}}$, paucis fuga salvatis.[30] Et cum iam potiretur victoria spoliisque diripiendis instaret, barbarorum $\overline{\text{IIII}}$, quae insidiose in abditis latuerant, ex obliquo viarum irruere. Qui cum gradivo incessu propinquarent, armorum luce ab observatoribus cogniti sunt. Factoque signo, exercitus in unum redit. Rex multo plures advenire arbitratus, suos hortatur stipatores ut priores animos resumant, immo et non amittant; decus pro patria mori, egregiumque pro christianorum defensione corpora morti dare multis sermonibus asserens. Exercitus itaque densatus, licet anterioris belli vulneribus aeger, tamen obvenire non distulit.

the infantry fared. The barbarians had also drawn up their battle lines, intending to meet their adversaries without breaking their formation. The royal foot soldiers who had been sent against the enemy fired arrows at the outset of the battle; then they crowded together in a group, turned their spears toward their foes, and attacked. Many of them fell when they were met by the barbarians, but not without severe cost to their enemies; for some of them were struck down and many more were wounded. The king's knights came up behind the foot troops and charged with tremendous force into the enemy lines, which had already been broken up by the infantry. Thirteen thousand of the enemy are said to have been slain, and only a few managed to flee and save themselves. Just at the moment when the victory was theirs and they were setting about seizing the spoils of their enemies, four thousand of the barbarians, who had been lying in wait to ambush them, rushed out from side paths. As they steadily drew nearer, however, the gleam of their arms betrayed them to the lookouts. The signal was given, and the army formed up again. The king reckoned that many more of the enemy were on their way, and he urged the men around him to summon up their former courage and not to lose heart. He spoke to them at length, declaring that it was glorious for them to die for their country and that it was a noble thing for them to sacrifice themselves in the defense of Christians. And so the army formed up in rank once more, and although they were still suffering from the wounds they had received in the earlier engagement, nonetheless they did not shrink from going to meet the enemy.

9

Ingo ex mediocribus regis signifer[31] bellum ingreditur

Et cum agitaretur quis regium signum efferret, eo quod in tanta nobilium manu nullus sine vulnere videbatur, idque omnes evitarent, e medio omnium Ingo prosilit, ac militatum sese offerens, inperterritus dixit: 'Ego ex mediocribus regis agaso, si maiorum honori non derogatur, signum regium per hostium acies efferam. Nec fortunam belli ambiguam expavesco, cum semel me moriturum cognosco.' Ad haec Odo rex, 'Nostro,' inquit, 'dono ac principum voluntate signifer esto.' Ille signum excipiens, agmine densato circumseptus incedebat. Factusque cunei militaris acumen, hostes vibrabundus ingreditur. Precipitantur barbari, viresque amittunt. At regius exercitus rediens, iterum irrumpit sternitque. Tercioque adortus fere omnes opprimit. Ex quorum tumultu cum aer densatus multo pulvere pinguesceret, Catillus cum paucis per caliginem fuga sese surripuit atque in dumetis sese abdidit. Qui cum lateret, a victoribus passim

9

Ingo, a Man of Middling Status, Enters the Fray as the King's Standard-Bearer

At this point there was some debate as to who was going to carry the king's standard into battle, since out of so many noblemen not one could be found who had not been wounded, and they were all avoiding the task. Thereupon Ingo leaped forth from their midst and volunteered to serve in this capacity, saying, without a trace of fear, "I, a man of middling rank and a stable officer of the king, will carry the royal standard through the enemy lines, if it does not detract from the honor of my superiors. Nor do I fear the uncertain fortunes of war, since I know that I shall die only once." In response King Odo declared, "By virtue of my dispensation and the will of my leading men, you shall be my standard-bearer." Taking up the standard, Ingo advanced in the midst of a close-packed formation. Positioning himself at the tip of a wedge of soldiers, he advanced toward the enemy while brandishing the standard. The barbarians were thrown headlong, their morale broken. The king's army, wheeling back toward them, attacked and cast them down a second time. After a third assault they had slaughtered almost all of them. As the air became thick and clouded with dust from the fighting, Catillus and a few of his men stole away and fled in the haze, concealing themselves in some bushes. But while he was hiding, he was discovered and

palantibus repertus atque captus est, suisque qui secum latuerant gladio[32] transfixis, post spolia direpta Odoni regi[33]
oblatus est.

10

Tiranni baptismus
et interfectio

Utiliter ergo patrata victoria, rex tirannum captum secum Lemovicas ducit, ibique ei vitae ac mortis optionem
dedit, si baptizaretur vitam, sin minus mortem promittens.
Tirannus mox absque contradictione baptizari petit, sed du-
bium an fidei quicquam habuerit. Quia ergo Pentecostes
instabat sollempnitas, ac episcoporum conventus regi aderat, ab episcopis ei triduanum indicitur ieiunium. Die vero
constituta cum in basilica sancti Marcialis martiris post
episcoporum peracta officia in sacrum fontem ab ipso rege
excipiendus descenderet, iamque trina immersione in nomine patris et filii et spiritus sancti baptizatus esset, Ingo

taken prisoner by some victorious soldiers who were ranging widely over the field of battle. They put his companions who had hidden with him to the sword, and after seizing spoils from them, they brought Catillus before King Odo.

10

The Baptism of the Tyrant, and His Murder

After securing this profitable victory, the king brought the captured tyrant with him to Limoges. There he gave him a choice between life and death, promising him life if he were baptized and death otherwise. The tyrant requested baptism immediately and without any argument, but it is doubtful whether he had any faith. Now because the feast of Pentecost was approaching and there was a group of bishops with the king, they proclaimed a three-day fast for Catillus. On the appointed day, after the bishops had performed the divine offices in the basilica of Saint-Martial, when Catillus was going down to the sacred font to be received by the king himself, having already been baptized with a threefold immersion in the name of the Father, Son, and Holy Spirit, Ingo, the former standard-bearer, drew his sword and fatally

ante signifer, gladio educto, loetaliter eum transverberat ac fontem sacratum vulneris effusione immaniter cruentat. Rex tantum facinus indignans, principibus frementibus homicidam rapi ac trucidari iubet. Ille gladio proiecto fugiens, sancti Marcialis aram complexus est, indulgentiam ab rege ac primatibus postulans atque loquendi locum multis clamoribus petens. Et iussu regio de commisso facinore responsurus sistitur. Orsusque sic ait:[34]

II

Oratio Ingonis pro se apud regem et principes suasorie habita

'Deum voluntatis meae conscium testor, nihil mihi fuisse carius vestra salute. Vester amor ad hoc me impulit. Ob vestram salutem in has me miserias precipitavi. Pro omnium vita tantum periculum subire non expavi. Grande quidem est gestum negotium, sed maior est negotii utilitas. Re-

ran him through, monstrously staining the sacred font with the outpouring of blood from the wound. The king was furious at the perpetration of such a terrible crime and he ordered the incensed magnates to seize the murderer and put him to death. Throwing away his sword, Ingo fled and grasped the altar of Saint Martial, beseeching the king and his leading men for pardon and asking them with repeated cries for an opportunity to speak. At the orders of the king he was allowed to stand before them to answer for the crime that he had committed, whereupon he addressed them as follows:

II

Ingo's Persuasive Speech on His Own Behalf Before the King and His Leading Men

"I appeal to God, who is privy to my intentions, that nothing was dearer to me than your safety. It was love for you that drove me to this. It was for your safety that I cast myself down into these misfortunes. It was for the sake of all of your lives that I did not fear to run so great a risk. Certainly it is a serious crime that has been committed, but the advantages to be derived from it are greater still. I do not deny that I have offended against the sovereignty of the

giam maiestatem me laesisse quidem non abnuo, sed multa commoda in facinore comparata assero. Consideretur auctoris animus, animadvertatur etiam futura facinoris utilitas. Tirannum captum metus causa baptismum petiisse adverti, eumque postquam dimitteretur pluribus iniuriis vicem redditurum, suorumque stragem[35] gravissime ulturum. In quem, quia futurae cladis causa visus est, ferrum converti. Haec est mei facinoris causa. Haec me ad scelus impulit. Hoc ob regis suorumque salutem peregi. Et utinam morte mea patriae libertas rerumque tranquillitas consequantur. Sed si occidor, ob regis primatumque salutem occisus videbor. Cogitet iam quisque an pro huiusmodi mercede ei militandum sit, et an pro fide servata tali habendus sit retributione. Ecce capitis et pectoris laterisque recentia vulnera. Patent precedentium temporum cicatrices, dispersique per reliqua corporis membra livores. Quorum assiduis doloribus confectus, nihil post tot mala nisi mortem, malorum finem, exspecto.' Qua conquestione[36] alios ad benivolentiam traxit, alios vero ad lacrimas impulit. Unde et milites pro eo agentes regem demulcent et ad pietatis clementiam suadent, nihil regi prodesse asserentes si suorum quispiam intereat; immo in tiranni occisione gaudendum, vel quia vitae datus sit si fidelis decessit, vel quia eius insidiae penitus defecerint si in dolo baptismum susceperit. Quibus rex animum temperans, tumulato barbaro, Ingonem in gratia resumit. Et insuper castrum

king, but I maintain that many benefits have been achieved through this crime. You must consider the intent of the agent and you must also take into account the future advantages that may result from the crime. I realized that it was out of fear that the captured tyrant asked to be baptized, and that when he was released he would requite the many wrongs done to him and exact the severest vengeance for the slaughter of his men. I turned my sword against him because I saw that he would be the cause of future calamity. This was the reason for my crime. This is what drove me to such a wicked act. I did this for the salvation of the king and his men. And may my death bring about freedom for our fatherland, and peace![22] But if I am put to death, it will be clear that I died in order to save the king and the leading men. Let every man now ask himself if he is bound to serve the king in return for this sort of reward, and whether loyal service merits such a punishment. Behold the fresh wounds to my head, my chest, and my side! The scars of the past are plain to see. Bruises are spread over the remaining limbs of my body. Debilitated by unceasing pains from these injuries, I look forward to nothing after so much suffering except death, which is the end of suffering." With this lament he won the goodwill of some and drove others to tears. As a result, some of the king's knights, acting on Ingo's behalf, tried to assuage their lord's anger, urging him to be merciful and show pity. They declared that the death of one of his own men would be of no use to him. Instead he should rejoice in the tyrant's death, because if he had died a believer, then he had been given over to life, whereas if he had undergone baptism in bad faith, then his schemes had come to nothing. In response the king tempered his anger,

quod Blesum dicitur ei liberaliter accommodat, eo quod is qui castri custodiam agebat, in bello pyratico occisus esset. Eius quoque uxorem derelictam dono regio in matrimonio Ingo sibi accopulat. Regis exinde ac principum gratia admodum usus, prospere ac feliciter omnia gerebat. Verum id in brevi. Nam vulnerum sanies male a cirurgis amputata, cum sub recutita superficie tumorem intrinsecus operaretur, nimio humoris reumatismo plus biennio vexatus in lectum decidit. Unde et intercluso reumate, penitus intumuit. Sicque toto erisipilato corpore, vitam amisit, Gerlonem filium parvum superstitem relinquens. Qui ab rege tutori commissus, patrimonium cum matre possedit.

12

Promotio Karoli in regnum[37]

Interea rex a Lemovica urbe dimotus, Echolisinam petit ac ibi quaeque gerenda disponit. Nec multopost petens Petragoram, nobilium causas quae litibus agitabantur ibi ae-

and after the barbarian had been buried, he took Ingo back into his favor. In addition to this, he generously granted him the stronghold of Blois, since the previous castellan had been killed in the battle against the pirates. Ingo also married this man's widow with the king's dispensation. Thereafter he enjoyed the favor of the king and the leading men, and he met with success and good fortune in all that he did. But this did not last very long. For the surgeons who had cut away the infected matter from his wounds had done so ineptly, and although the outer layer had been removed, it swelled up underneath. After he had been tormented by great discharges of humors for more than two years, he took to his bed. Since the discharge was confined within, he swelled up deep inside. As a result his whole body was stricken with erysipelas and he died. He left behind as his heir a young son named Gerlo, who was entrusted to a guardian by the king and entered into his inheritance jointly with his mother.

12

The Elevation of Charles to the Throne

Meanwhile the king left Limoges for Angoulême, and there he dealt with whatever needed his attention. Not long after this he went to Périgueux, where he ruled fairly and

quissime ordinat, plurimum[38] de communibus omnium causis apud optimates pertractans. Quibus cum foret admodum intentus ibique per aliquot tempora sese moraturum proponeret, Fulco Remorum archiepiscopus de Karoli promotione in regnum apud Belgas tractabat. Videbatur etenim tunc quod presens oportunitas huic rei aliquam commoditatem pararet. Idque plurimum persuadebat Neustriorum absentia.[39] Et enim[40] cum rege in partibus Aquitaniae tunc[41] detinebantur. Suadebant quoque multiplices adolescentis quaerimoniae. Iam enim quindennis, de regni amissione apud amicos et domesticos gravissime conquerebatur regnumque paternum repetere multo conatu moliebatur. Ei ergo omnes Belgicae principes et aliquot Celticae summopere favebant. Horum quoque consensus sub Remensi metropolitano sacramenti iure firmatur. Ac tempore statuto conveniunt, ex Belgica quidem Coloniensis, Trevericus, atque Maguntinus metropolitani, cum suis diocesaneis episcopis aut eorum[42] probabilibus legatis. Ex Celtica vero Remorum predictus metropolitanus cum aliquot suis diocesaneis, Laudunensi videlicet, Catalaunico atque Morinensi. Anno autem incarnationis dominicae DCCCXCIII, V kal. Februarii, die dominica, collecti Remis in basilica sancti Remigii Karolum quindennem regem creant ac in urbe purpuratum

impartially on the legal disputes among the nobles and attended to matters of public interest with the leading men.
Since the king was occupied with what he was doing and had
decided to remain there for some time, Archbishop Fulk
of Reims entered into discussions with the men of Belgica
about putting Charles on the throne. For it appeared to
them then that the present occasion offered certain advantages to the execution of their plan. A particular inducement
was the absence of the Neustrians. For at that time they
were being kept in Aquitaine with the king. They were also
persuaded by the persistent laments of the young Charles.
Now fifteen years old, he was complaining bitterly to his
friends and the men of his household about the loss of his
kingdom and devoting all of his efforts to recovering his father's throne. As a result, all of the leading men of Belgica
and some of those from Celtic Gaul gave him their full support. Their agreement was also confirmed by an oath administered by the archbishop of Reims. At a designated time   893
the archbishops of Cologne, Trier, and Mainz,[23] accompanied by their suffragan bishops or the bishops' trusted envoys, arrived from Belgica, while the archbishop of Reims
and some of his suffragans, namely the bishops of Laon,
Châlons-sur-Marne, and Thérouanne, came from Celtic
Gaul. On Sunday, January 28, 893, they assembled in the basilica of Saint-Rémi at Reims and consecrated the fifteen-
year-old Charles king, after which they dressed him in pur-
ple and had him issue decrees in the city in the manner of

more regio edicta dare constituunt. Et ex Celtica quidem paucissimi eius partes sequebantur. Ex Belgica vero ei omnes addicti sunt. Ab illis enim devotissime exceptus, per omnes eorum urbes et oppida humanissime deductus est.

13

Odonis reditus ab Aquitania, eiusque obitus

Quod factum Odo rex comperiens,[43] ab Aquitania redit, urbemque Turonicam petens, sanctum Martinum donis regalibus honorat. Sicque Parisii receptus, sanctos martires Dionisium, Rusticum, et Eleutherium magnifice donat. Tandem fluvio Matrona remenso, Belgicam ingreditur. Ac oppido receptus quod dicitur Fara, pre nimia anxietate insomnietatem pati coepit. Quae cum nimium succresceret, mentis alienationem operabatur. Superantibusque humoribus, anno regni sui X, ut quidam ferunt mania, ut alii frenesi, finem vitae accepit. Tumulatur vero cum multo suorum lamento in basilica[44] sancti Dionisii[45] martiris.

a king. Very few men from Celtic Gaul took his side, but all those from Belgica supported him. They welcomed him with the utmost devotion and escorted him very graciously through all of their cities and strongholds.

13

The Return of Odo from Aquitaine and His Death

When King Odo learned of this, he returned from Aquitaine and went to Tours, where he honored Saint Martin with royal gifts. When he came to Paris, he likewise endowed the holy martyrs Denis, Rusticus, and Eleutherius in splendid fashion. Finally he crossed the River Marne and entered Belgica. After he had arrived at the stronghold of La Fère, he began to suffer from insomnia brought on by tremendous anxiety, and as his condition worsened, it led to dementia. Suffering from an excess of humors, he died 898 in the tenth year of his reign, some say from madness, and others from delirium. He was subsequently buried in the basilica of Saint-Denis, amid great lamentations from his followers.[24]

14

Mores Karoli

Karolus itaque rex creatus, ad multam benivolentiam intendebat. Corpore prestanti, ingenio bono simplicique.[46] Exercitiis militaribus non adeo assuefactus, at litteris liberalibus admodum eruditus; in dando profusus, minime avarus.[47] Duplici morbo notabilis, libidinis intemperans, ac circa exsequenda iuditia paulo neglegentior fuit. Galliarum principes ei animo ac sacramento annexi sunt. Necnon et Rotbertus, Odonis regis defuncti frater, vir industrius atque audatia plurimus, sese militaturum regi accommodat.[48] Quem etiam rex Celticae ducem preficit ac in ea omnium gerendorum ordinatorem concedit, eius fere per quadriennium[49] consilio utens eique admodum consuescens. A quo per Neustriam deductus,[50] urbibus atque oppidis ab eo receptus est. Urbemque Turonicam petens, plurima auri atque argenti talenta sancto Martino liberaliter impertit. A cuius servitoribus pro sese fieri deprecationes postulans, perpetim cotidianas obtinuit. Inde quoque omnibus obtentis rediens, Belgicam repetit ac sanctum Remigium donis egregiis honorat. Et sic Rotberto Gallia Celtica collata, in Saxo-

14

The Character of Charles

As king, Charles strove for great goodwill. In appearance he was outstanding, in character virtuous and without guile. While not particularly accustomed to military training, he was well educated in the liberal arts. Generous in giving, he was not at all covetous. He was conspicuous for two different failings: a lack of self-control over his lusts and a certain degree of negligence in carrying out judgments. The leading men of Gaul were bound to him both of their own volition and by oaths. In addition, Robert, the brother of the deceased king Odo, a man of energy and considerable boldness, adapted himself to serve the king.[25] The king in turn made him duke over Celtic Gaul and granted him the authority to govern the region. For almost four years he followed Robert's advice and developed a close familiarity with him. Robert escorted him through Neustria and welcomed him in his cities and strongholds. When Charles arrived at Tours, he generously bestowed many pounds of gold and silver on Saint Martin, and he asked that the monks offer up prayers on his behalf, a request they undertook to fulfill every day in perpetuity. When he had obtained everything that he wanted, he departed and went back to Belgica, where he honored Saint Remigius with splendid gifts. After he had conferred Celtic Gaul on Robert, he departed for Saxony.

niam[51] secedit. Cuius urbes sedesque regias lustrans, cum oppidis nullo renitente obtinuit. Ubi etiam Heinricum, regio genere inclitum, ac inde oriundum, ducem omnibus praeficit.[52] Sarmatas absque prelio subditos habuit. Anglos quoque ac reliquos transmarinorum populos mira benivolentia sibi[53] adegit. Vix tamen per decennium. Et forte felicissimus per omnia fuisset, si in uno nimium non errasset.

15

Nimia Karoli dilectio erga Haganonem

Nam cum multa benignitate principes coleret, precipua tamen beatitudine Haganonem habebat, quem ex mediocribus potentem effecerat, adeo ut magnatibus quibusque longe absistentibus, ipse regio lateri solus haereret; pilleum etiam a capite regis sepissime sumptum palam sibi imponeret. Quod etiam multam regi intulit labem.[54] Etenim primates id ferentes indignum, regem adeunt ac apud eum satis conqueruntur hominem obscuris parentibus natum regiae dignitati multum derogare, cum acsi indigentia nobilium

He made a circuit through the cities, royal estates, and strongholds of this region, taking control over them without any resistance. There he also appointed Henry,[26] a Saxon distinguished by his royal ancestry, as duke over all of the inhabitants. He kept the Slavs in peaceful submission, and he bound the English and the rest of the peoples across the sea to himself with remarkable goodwill. This lasted for scarcely ten years, however. And it is possible that he would have remained supremely fortunate throughout, had he not erred so grievously in one matter.

15

Charles's Excessive Love for Hagano[27]

For while the king treated the leading men with great kindness, he showed particular favor to Hagano, a man whom he had raised up from middling status to a position of power, so much so that, while all the magnates kept their distance, Hagano alone clung to the king's side. On a number of occasions he even took off the king's hat in public and put it on his own head. This proved disastrous to the king. For the chief men thought it was degrading, and they went to Charles and complained bitterly that this man of obscure birth was detracting greatly from the royal dignity, sitting as he did beside the king like a counselor, as though there were

ipse tamquam consulturus regi assistat. Et nisi a tanta consuetudine cesset, sese a regis consilio penitus discessuros. Rex dissuasionibus his minime credulus, a dilecto non cessit.

16

Indignatio Rotberti in Haganonem

Interea Belgicae[55] urbibus[56] atque oppidis firmissime optentis, in Celticam[57] redit ac urbe Suessonica recipit sese. Huc ex omni Gallia principes confluunt. Huc etiam minores multo favore conveniunt. Inter quos cum Rotbertus in maiore gratia apud regem sese haberi putaret, utpote quem ducem in Celtica omnibus prefecerat, cum rex in palatio sedisset, eius iussu dux dexter, Hagano quoque ei levus pariter resedit. Rotbertus vero dux tacite indignum ferebat personam mediocrem[58] sibi aequari magnatibusque preponi. At iram mitigans, animum dissimulabat, vix regi pauca locutus. Celerius ergo surgit ac cum suis consilium confert. Quo collato, regi per legatos suggerit sese perferre non posse

a shortage of noblemen. They said that if he (sc. Hagano) did not cease from this excessive familiarity with him, they would depart his council altogether. But the king paid no heed to these admonitions, nor did he abandon his favorite.

16

Robert's Resentment Against Hagano

When Charles had firmly secured the cities and strongholds of Belgica, he returned to Celtic Gaul and installed himself in the city of Soissons. The leading men from all over Gaul assembled there. Even the men of lesser status came with great goodwill. Now Robert assumed that among all these men the king held him in the highest esteem, since he had appointed him duke over all of Celtic Gaul. Yet when the king took his seat in the palace, he ordered the duke to sit at his right side, and Hagano to sit at his left. Duke Robert quietly resented that a person of no stature should be considered equal to himself and preferred over the magnates. Yet he controlled his anger and hid how he felt, scarcely saying anything to the king. After a while he got up and took counsel with his own men. After conferring with them, he sent messengers to inform the king that he could

sibi Haganonem aequari primatibusque anteferri; indignum etiam videri huiusmodi hominem regi haerere, et Gallorum nobilissimos longe absistere. Quem nisi in mediocritatem redigat, sese eum crudeli suspendio suffocaturum. Rex dilecti ignominiam non passus, facilius se omnium colloquio quam huius familiaritate posse carere respondit. Quod nimium Rotbertus indignatus, cum optimatibus plerisque iniussus Neustriam petit ac Turonis sese recipit, multam ibi de regis levitate indignationem[59] habens, plurima etiam ut in se transfundatur rerum summa apud suos caute pertractans. Quamvis etenim regi faveret, non mediocriter tamen ei regnum invidebat, cum sibi post fratrem hereditandum magis videret. Nonnulla quoque moliebatur in Fulconem Remorum metropolitanum, qui regem a cunabulis educaverat atque in regnum promoverat. Videbatur etenim quia si is solum deperiret, facilius refundi in sese regnum potuisset. Id etiam apud Balduinum Morinorum principem admodum agitabat. Hic enim ab eo[60] persuasus, eius partes iam rege deserto sequebatur.

not stand for Hagano to be treated as an equal to himself and as a superior to the other leading men of the realm. Indeed, he thought it disgraceful that a man of this sort should cling to the side of the king while the noblest men of the Gauls were kept at a distance. If the king did not reduce him back to his middling status, he would have him strung up and hanged without mercy. The king could not abide these insults to his favorite and replied that he would rather do without the advice of all of his counselors than his friendship with Hagano. This infuriated Robert, who departed unbidden for Neustria with the majority of the magnates and took up residence at Tours.[28] There he vented his frustration at the king's frivolity and plotted discreetly with his men to see how he could transfer supreme authority to himself. For although he was well-disposed toward the king, he greatly envied him his throne, which he thought should have passed to himself after the death of his brother. He also began to plot against Fulk, the archbishop of Reims, who had raised the king from the time he was in the cradle and elevated him to the throne. For it seemed to him that if only Fulk were dead, he would have had an easier time taking the crown for himself.[29] He discussed this matter at length with Count Baldwin of Flanders.[30] For having been persuaded by Robert, he had now abandoned the king and gone over to his side.

17

Interfectio Fulconis archiepiscopi

Quo rex comperto in Balduinum fertur ac multa obsidionis vi castrum Atrabatum ab eo aufert atque cum tota sancti Vedasti abbatia Fulconi predicto metropolitano concedit. At post aliquot tempora metropolitanus ob itineris longinquitatem causarumque[61] incommoditatem Altmarum comitem accersiens, abbatiam sancti Medardi, quam ipse comes tenebat, ab eo accipit et pro ea abbatiam sancti Vedasti cum castro Atrabato rationibus utrimque habitis ei impertit. Unde et ad nimiam pertrahitur Balduinus crudelitatem, multaque affectus anxietate, ad ultionem penitus sese convertit. Amicitiam ergo circa metropolitanum simulat; per legatos quoque multam benivolentiam mandat,[62] fidemque spondet. Illud tamen multa suorum curiositate observat, utrum privatus an cum copiis regis palatium petere consuescat, privatum multo nisu impetere cupiens. Haec dum sic haberentur, pro regiis causis contigit episcopos Belgicae

17

The Murder of Archbishop Fulk

When the king learned of this, he moved against Baldwin, and after a major siege operation he took the castle of Arras from him and granted it, along with the whole abbey of Saint-Vaast, to the aforementioned Archbishop Fulk. Some time later, however, because of the length of the journey and the inconvenience of the legal disputes involved, Fulk summoned Count Altmar, who held the abbacy of Saint-Médard, and after negotiations on both sides Fulk received Saint-Médard in exchange for the abbey of Saint-Vaast and the castle of Arras. As a result, Baldwin was driven to the depths of savagery, and in his great agitation at what had happened he devoted himself wholly to revenge. To that end, he pretended to be friendly toward the archbishop and sent envoys to express his goodwill and pledge his loyalty. At the same time, he had his men take careful notice of whether Fulk was in the habit of going to the royal palace by himself or with an escort—his intention being to mount a violent assault upon him while he was alone. In the meantime it so happened that the bishops of Belgica had assem-

apud regem congregari. Unde et metropolitanus accersitus, cum iter accelerare pararet, incautus cum paucis festinabat. Cui mox affuit quidam Winemarus cum cohorte a Balduino missus. Metropolitanus cum esset cum paucis, a cohorte cum suis interceptus est. Nulli fugae locus patuit. Omnes circumvallantur atque impetuntur. Admodum[63] utrimque dimicant, utrimque fusi procumbunt. Winemarus metropolitanum adortus, lancea inermem transfigit atque inter suos septem vulneribus sauciatum precipitat. Cui cum adhuc ictus intenderet, quidam suorum multo episcopi amore ducti super eum procumbunt, qui cum eo mox transfixi atque occisi sunt. Quatuor tantum fuga labuntur, qui rei negotium Remis demonstrant. Tunc vero magna militum manus ab urbe mox cum armis educta, adversarios persequi conatur. Sed eis elapsis, dominum occisum cum suis colligunt atque multo doloris lamento Remos deportant, cum sacerdotibus sacerdotem plurimo dignitatis obsequio condentes.

bled to hear pleas before the king. Now the archbishop had also been summoned there, and because he was trying to make the journey quickly, he was hastening there unsuspectingly with only a few men. He was soon set upon by a man named Winemar, at the head of a band of soldiers sent by Baldwin. Because the archbishop only had a few men with him, he and his followers were cut off with no chance of escape. They were all surrounded and attacked. Both sides fought fiercely, and on both sides men were struck down and killed. Winemar attacked the archbishop and ran the unarmed man through with his spear, dealing him seven wounds and striking him to the ground in the midst of his followers. While he was aiming yet another blow at him, some of the archbishop's men were prompted by their great love for their master to spread themselves over his body, whereupon they were quickly run through and killed along with him. Only four men escaped and brought the news of what had happened to Reims. Shortly thereafter, a large band of fighting men[31] left the city under arms to try to hunt down the enemy. But because the perpetrators had escaped, all they could do was gather up the bodies of their slain lord and his men and carry them with grievous lamentations to Reims. There the archbishop was laid to rest beside his fellow bishops in a magnificent funeral worthy of his stature.[32]

18

Winemari interitus

Interea collectis apud regem episcopis, talia mox referuntur. Quod etiam omnibus nimium animi incussit dolorem. Rex ipse in lacrimas dissolutus, de casu pontificis[64] adeo[65] conquestus est. Episcopi quoque in fratris morte et coepiscopi multa commiseratione condoluere.[66] Initoque consilio, Winemarum cum suis complicibus horribili anathemate damnant. Qui in brevi deficiens, insanabili ydropis morbo a deo percussus est. Ventre itaque turgidus, exterius quidem lento igne, interius vero immani incendio urebatur. Ingens tumor pedum non deerat. Verenda vermibus scaturiebant. Crura tumentia ac lurida;[67] anelitus fetidus. Viscera etiam paulatim per colum diffluebant. Super haec omnia sitim intolerabilem sustinebat. Appetitum vero comedendi aliquando habebat, sed cibi illati fastidium inferebant. Insomnietatem iugem patiebatur. Omnibusque factus intolerabilis, omnibus habitus est odio.[68] Itaque amici atque domestici ab eo dimoti sunt, multo eius corporis fetore confecti, in tantum ut nullus medicorum saltem medendi causa ad eum

18

The Death of Winemar

Meanwhile, news of what had happened was brought to the bishops who had assembled before the king, leaving them all grief-stricken. The king himself dissolved into tears and bitterly lamented the archbishop's fate, while the bishops sorrowfully mourned the death of their brother and fellow bishop. After meeting in council, they condemned Winemar and his accomplices with a dreadful anathema. Shortly thereafter Winemar grew ill, having been stricken by God with an incurable case of dropsy. His stomach became distended, while on the outside of his body he burned with a dull fire, and on the inside with a terrible fever. His feet were not spared from great swelling. His private parts swarmed with worms. His legs became swollen and sallow, and his breath grew foul.[33] Little by little, his guts began to flow out through his colon. In addition to all of this, he suffered from an unquenchable thirst. While he sometimes had an appetite, the food that was brought to him induced nausea. He suffered from constant insomnia. No one could tolerate his presence, and he became hateful to everyone. Thus, his friends and family were driven away from him, overcome by the tremendous stench of his body, which was so bad that no doctor could come near him even

accedere posset. Quibus omnibus dissolutus, omni christianitatis communione privatus, a vermibus ex parte iam consumptus, flagiciosus ac sacrilegus ab hac vita pulsus est.

19

Promotio Herivei in episcopatum

Sepulto vero domno Fulcone metropolitano, Heriveus, vir spectabilis et palatinus, episcoporum consensu et Remensium conibentia in pontificatu regis donatione succedit. Quorum uterque quanta utilitate quantaque religione in aecclesia Remensi floruit si quis ad plenum dinoscere cupit, legat librum Flodoardi presbiteri, quem ab urbe condita de eiusdem urbis episcopis uberrime descripsit. Adepto quoque Heriveus pontificatu, multa fide regem sequebatur, desertoribus adeo infestus. Erlebaldum Castricensium comi-

to treat him. Debilitated by all of these things, deprived of all Christian communion, and already partially consumed by worms, he was driven from this life a sinner and perpetrator of sacrilege.[34]

19

The Elevation of Hervey to the Bishopric

After the burial of Archbishop Fulk, Hervey,[35] a distinguished courtier, succeeded to the bishopric with the consent of the bishops, the agreement of the townsmen of Reims, and the dispensation of the king.[36] If anyone would like a full account of the efficacy and devotion with which both of these men distinguished themselves in the service of the church of Reims, he should read the book of the priest Flodoard in which he has given a copious account of the bishops of this city from the time of its founding.[37] Upon succeeding to the bishopric, Hervey proved a loyal follower of the king and an enemy to those who had deserted him. Erlebald, the count of Châtresais, who had seized property   920

tem, qui res sui episcopii pervaserat et oppidum quod vocant Macerias obtinebat, more aecclesiastico prius quidem ut resipiscat ammonet, post vero anathemate damnat. Qui cum sibi nec damnatus satisfaceret, in eum cum multis militum copiis fertur, oppidumque multa obsidione per quatuor ebdomadas vehementer adurget. Erlebaldus continuam non ferens impugnationem, clam ab oppido cum aliquot suorum dilabitur. Qui vero remanserant victi, portis mox patefactis, metropolitano cedunt.[69] Eisque eiectis, suos ibi deposuit ac de toto pago Erlebaldum profugum disturbavit.

20

Ad Rhenum mutua impetitio,[70] · ac comitis Erlebaldi occisio

Rex in pagum Warmacensem locuturus Heinrico Transrhenensi concesserat. Huc quoque Erlebaldus comes advenit, apud regem deploraturus a Remensium metropolitano sese immaniter habitum. Heinricus apud regem de rerum dispositionibus fidelissime[71] satagebat. Cui rei cum admo-

that belonged to the see of Reims and was occupying the stronghold called Mézières, was first warned by Hervey to come to his senses in accordance with ecclesiastical custom, and afterward condemned with a sentence of anathema. When Erlebald failed to make satisfaction to him even after this, Hervey moved against him with a large force of fighting men and pressed Mézières hard with an extensive siege for four weeks. Unable to endure the continuous assault, Erlebald slipped out of the stronghold in secret with a few of his followers. Those who had remained behind admitted defeat, opened the gates, and surrendered to the archbishop. Hervey then expelled them and installed his own men in their place, and he hounded the fugitive Erlebald out of the whole county.[38]

20

The Melee on the Rhine and the Murder of Count Erlebald

The king had gone to the county of Worms to speak with Henry from Beyond-the-Rhine.[39] Count Erlebald also came there to complain to the king about the cruel treatment he had received at the hands of the archbishop of Reims. Henry was applying himself with the utmost fidelity to the business at hand before the king. While he was intently engaged

dum intenderet, Germanorum Gallorumque iuvenes lingua-
rum idiomate offensi, ut eorum mos est cum multa animositate maledictis sese lacessire coeperunt. Consertique gladios
exerunt, ac se adorsi, loetaliter sauciant. In quo tumultu,
cum ad litem sedandam Erlebaldus comes accederet, a fu-
rentibus occisus est. Rex proditionem ratus, ocius surgit
suisque stipatur. Heinricus vero dolum arbitrans,[72] classem
repetit atque a regiis stipatoribus Rhenum transire cogitur.[73]
Estimabant[74] enim[75] hi qui regi assistebant eum in dolo venisse. A quo etiam[76] tempore Karolo infestus ferebatur.

21

Desertorum dolosa apud Karolum[77] persuasio de Haganonis abiectione

Hinc itaque Heinrico, inde Rotberto duce Karolus urge-
batur. Factusque eorum medius, utrimque premebatur. Post
haec ad interiora Belgicae rediens, urbe Suessonica sese re-

in this activity, some of the young men from among the Germans and the Gauls grew annoyed at the native speech of their counterparts and began a heated exchange of insults, as is customary with them. Then they came toward one another, drew their swords, and attacked, dealing out lethal blows. Count Erlebald stepped forth into the midst of the brawl to try to put an end to the dispute, but he was struck down and killed by the frenzied combatants.[40] The king suspected treachery and arose at once, surrounded by his men. Henry, for his part, thinking that this was a trick, went back to his ships and was forced to cross back over the Rhine by the king's retinue. For the men who were attending the king suspected that Henry had come there with deceitful intent. From this time forward it was reported that Henry was hostile to Charles.[41]

21

The Duplicitous Speech of the Traitors to Charles Concerning the Removal of Hagano

Henceforward Charles was threatened by Henry on one side and Duke Robert on the other. Caught between these two men, he was being squeezed from both sides. He subsequently returned to inner Belgica and took up residence

cipit, multam ex huiusmodi infortunio apud suos agitans quaerelam. Huc etiam ex Belgica quo Celticae conlimitat atque ex Celtica principes nonnulli confluunt. Sed et Rotbertus dux propinquior factus, Stampis sese recipit ac ad palatium legatos dirigit, regalia negotia inde experturus. At qui confluxere Rotberti partes tuebantur, cuius suasu capti de Haganonis abiectione apud regem pertractant, non ut id fieri velint, sed ut regnandi occasio Rotberto paretur. Abiectionem itaque Haganonis leviter suadent. Ducem etiam a se discessurum si non abiciat mediocri assertione demonstrant, quatinus levi obiurgatione rex ammonitus, coeptis insistere non formidet. Unde et post contra eum iustissimam indignationis causam se habituros arbitrabantur. Quod etiam totum ad vota eorum provenit. Nam rex nulla[78] suasione affectus, numquam[79] a dilecto sese discessurum respondit idque multis sententiarum sermonibus asserebat. Quod cum Rotbertus dux[80] in eius animo fixum perciperet,[81] Heinrico Transrhenensi per legatos de regis abiectione[82] suadet. Compererat enim eum a regiis stipatoribus in fugam coactum, unde et de se fidem continuo fecit.[83] Cuius consensu tirannus mox laetus, in sese regnum transfundere[84] diligentissime laborabat. Largitur igitur[85] plurima et[86] pollicetur infinita. Tandem[87] inductos de transfugio iam principes

in the city of Soissons, where he complained to his men at great length about his ill fortune. Several of the leading men from the region of Belgica that borders on Celtic Gaul came before him, as well as some from Celtic Gaul itself. Duke Robert had also moved into the vicinity, however, and having installed himself at Étampes, he sent envoys to the palace to find out what the king was up to. Now the men who went before the king were partisans of Robert, and he had convinced them to speak to the king about removing Hagano—not with the intention of actually bringing this about, but in order to give Robert a pretext to seize the throne. And so they gently persuaded him to cast Hagano out, pointing out with a halfhearted plea that the duke would desert him if he did not remove Hagano, so that the king, having been admonished with a mild reproach, would not fear to continue on in his current course of action. In this way they thought that they would subsequently have eminently justifiable grounds for their resentment against him. And indeed, everything turned out in accordance with their wishes. For the king was unmoved by any of their arguments, and he responded that he would never leave his favorite, reiterating his position at length. When Duke Robert saw that Charles was steadfast in his resolve, he sent envoys to Henry from Beyond-the-Rhine to try to convince him of the need to depose the king. For he had discovered that Henry had been forced to flee by the king's retinue, and for this reason he made an immediate profession of loyalty to him. Cheered by Henry's support, the tyrant began to work carefully and deliberately to usurp the throne for himself. To that end, he made generous gifts and limitless promises. At last he gathered the leading men together and spoke

aperte alloquitur, regem inquiens Suessionis sese privatum habere, Belgas preter paucissimos ad sua discessisse. Unde et rei commoditatem adesse memorabat, facillime et ex aequo regem posse capi asserens, si ipsi omnes palatium adeant acsi consulturi, in ipso quoque palatii cubiculo inter consulendum regem capiant teneantque. His favent omnes pene ex Celtica et de patrando facinore apud tirannum coniurant. Palatium ergo adeunt regemque utpote consulturi stipant. Intromissum vero cubiculo, ut paucis allocuti sunt, capiunt ac tenent.[88]

22

Heriveus metropolitanus Karolum a desertoribus captum liberat Remosque ducit

Iamque abducere nitebantur, cum metropolitanus Heriveus cum copiis repentinus urbem Suessonicam ingreditur. Regis enim sollicitus, desertorum fraudem presenserat. Et

to them openly about deserting the king, declaring that the king was alone at Soissons and that all but a handful of the men of Belgica had returned home. Hence, he told them, the time was right for this undertaking. They could capture the king easily enough and without any obstacles if they all went to the palace as though they were going to take counsel with him. Then, as they were deliberating in his personal chambers, they would seize him and hold him prisoner. Almost all the men of Celtic Gaul agreed to this, and they all swore to carry out this criminal act before the tyrant. They went to the palace, therefore, and crowded around the king as if they were there to take counsel with him, but after leading him into his chambers and speaking to him briefly, they seized him and held him captive.

22

Archbishop Hervey Frees Charles from the Traitors and Takes Him to Reims

They were still trying to take him away when Archbishop Hervey arrived suddenly at Soissons with his forces. For he was worried about the king and had gotten wind of the traitors' plot. At first it was just himself and a few men, but later his followers were admitted with the help of

ipse quidem prius cum paucis,[89] post vero sui,[90] favente Riculfo eiusdem urbis episcopo, consequenter admittuntur. Armatis itaque circumdatus, concilium desertorum stupentibus cunctis penetrat. Factusque terribilis: 'Ubi, inquam, est dominus meus rex?' Ex tam multis pauci admodum respondendi vires habuere,[91] sese penitus deceptos rati. Qui tamen cum viribus resumtis dicerent, 'Intro cum paucis consultat,' metropolitanus ostio obserato vim infert, serisque pessumdatis, cum paucis[92] sedentem repperit. Captum enim custodibus adhibitis ergastulo deputaverant. Quo metropolitanus manu apprehenso, 'Veni,' inquit, 'rex, tuisque potius utere.' Et sic a metropolitano e desertorum medio eductus est. Tunc etiam equum ascendens, cum $\overline{\text{ID}}$ armatorum ab urbe exivit atque Remos devenit. Post cuius discessum desertores pudore confusi illusos sese indignabantur. Confusique[93] ad Rotbertum redeunt atque rem non satis prospere gestam desertori transfugae reportant. Karolus vero rex cum metropolitano aliisque paucis qui a se quidem defecerant, sapientium tamen consilio ad se reversi erant, Belgicae interiora[94] repetit ac Tungros[95] concedit. Ibique episcopo tunc defuncto, Hilduinum, eligente clero ac populo favente, per archiepiscopum Herimannum presulem ordinat,[96] virum liberalem ac strenuum, sed factiosum. Nam mox episcopus ordinatus, iis Belgicae principibus qui Rotberto duci

Riculf, the bishop of the city.[42] Surrounded by armed men, Hervey entered into the council of traitors as they all looked on in astonishment. He took on a frightening aspect: "Where, I ask, is my lord the king?" Out of so many men, only a very few could summon up the nerve to respond, reckoning that they had been completely foiled. However, when they had recovered their composure they replied, "He is inside with a few men, taking counsel with them." The archbishop applied force to the locked door, broke open the bolts, and found the king sitting inside with a few men (for they had consigned their captive to a prison cell and put guards over him). The archbishop took him by the hand and said, "Come, my king, and avail yourself of your own men." And with that Charles was led from the midst of the traitors by the archbishop. Then, mounting his horse, he left the city accompanied by 1,500 armed men, and went to Reims.[43] After his departure, the traitors were confounded with shame and furious that they had been outwitted. They returned to Robert in a state of disarray and told the turncoat that they had failed to execute their plan successfully. King Charles, meanwhile, along with the archbishop and a few other men who had deserted him but subsequently come back to him after heeding the advice of wise men, returned to inner Belgica and went to Liège. The bishop of that city had just died, and when the clergy chose Hilduin to replace him and the people approved, the king had Archbishop Hermann ordain him as bishop.[44] Hilduin was a generous and energetic man, but he was prone to faction. For as soon as he was ordained bishop, he attached himself to and aided the magnates of Belgica who were supporting Duke

in regis abiectione favebant[97] mox haesit et favit, plurimum cum eis contra regem machinans. At rex bono suorum usus consilio, per Heriveum metropolitanum ducem Heinricum, qui in Saxonia omnibus preerat, accersit. Hic enim ab Rotberto persuasus, cum aliis ab rege discesserat.[98]

23

Conquestio Herivei Remensis[99] metropolitani apud Heinricum[100] pro Karolo rege

Penes quem metropolitanus vice regis sic orsus ait: 'Hactenus, vir nobilissime, tua prudentia, tua liberalitate[101] pax principum, concordia omnium utiliter floruere. At postquam malivolorum[102] invidia animum remisisti, circumcirca discordiae vis a latibulis emersit.[103] Quae res domino nostro regi apud te oratum ire suasit. Antehac enim non mediocriter ob tua merita ei dilectissimus fuisti. Tua egregia fides ei

Robert's efforts to depose King Charles, plotting with them extensively against the king. For his part the king, following the good advice of his men, sent Archbishop Hervey to summon Duke Henry, who ruled over all the men of Saxony. For he and several others had been persuaded by Robert to abandon the king.[45]

23

The Complaint of Hervey, Archbishop of Reims, to Henry on Behalf of King Charles

The archbishop addressed him on behalf of the king as follows: "Until recently, your eminence, peace among the magnates and universal harmony flourished to the common advantage due to your wisdom and generosity. But after you yielded to the envy of spiteful men, the power of discord emerged on every side from its hiding places. This state of affairs has convinced my lord the king to plead his case before you. For in former days he loved you dearly because of your many services to him. The outstanding loyalty that he

recognita in magnis periculis multam sibi fidutiam parat. Cum totius statu dignitatis rex potiretur, paululum a te oberrasse sese non ignorat. Sed id multa fide corrigere gestit. Nec est hoc inusitatum et singulare.[104] Omnium est interdum desipere, bonorum vero rationibus redire. Sufferendum est itaque atque summa benignitate indulgendum. Tu quoque, Germanorum[105] optime, nimium a recto secessisse videris. Neque id mirum. Nam dux Rotbertus omnia sitiens regique regnum immaniter invidens, incautum te[106] suasionibus illexit. Quid enim suasorie digesta non efficit oratio? Nimium, inquam, ab utrisque oberratum est. Sed iam tandem prior vobis redeat virtus. Summa utriusque ope uterque nitatur, ut tu habeas regem tibi adprime commodum, et rex habeat te virum sese dignissimum. Nam te idem prestare gestit iis omnibus qui Germaniam[107] inhabitare noscuntur. Ob hoc igitur animum ad meliora revoca. Dominum abiectum recipe, ut et tu ab eo extollendus excipiaris.'

recognized in you won you his trust amid great dangers. The king is not unaware that after he obtained his position of preeminence he became estranged from you to some degree, but he is eager to correct this in good faith. Nor is this an uncommon or unique occurrence. All men act foolishly on occasion; but good men return to their senses. For this reason you must show forbearance and pardon him with the utmost kindness. For you too, who are supreme among the Germans, seem to have strayed considerably from the path of rectitude. Nor is this surprising. For Duke Robert, coveting everything and envying Charles his kingdom to an excessive degree, enticed you with persuasive words and caught you off guard. For what is there that a persuasively delivered speech cannot accomplish? Both sides, I tell you, have made serious mistakes. But now, at long last, it is time for both of you to resume the honorable conduct of the past. Each of you must strive with all of the resources at your disposal to see to it that you have a king who is devoted to your interests and the king has in you a follower who is in every way worthy of himself. For it is his desire that you should be preeminent among all the known inhabitants of Germany. For this reason, then, turn your thoughts back to better things. Receive your lord, whom you cast away, so that you too may be received by him and raised up."

24

Responsio Heinrici[108] ad metropolitanum Heriveum de Karolo

Ad haec Heinricus,[109] 'Multa,' inquit, 'me ab his[110] dehortantur, nisi tua, pater egregie, virtus ad idem quodammodo pertrahat. Scio enim quam difficile et arduum sit ei consilium dare, cum sua inconstantia, tum suorum invidia. Non est incognitum mihi quantum pro eo domi militiaeque pridem certaverim. Illud etiam notissimum constat, quantum circa me fide debita abusus sit. Id fortassis, pater, persuades, quod cum factum erit, fecisse penitebit. Sed quia de futuro nemo satis callidus, nemo satis prudens fit, licet saepius prava quam bona consilia proveniant, ferar quocumque iubes. Modestiamque meam post tuam dignitatem demittam, virtutem tuam experturus.[111] Equidem decretum mihi fuerat ingenio, consilio, armis ab eo recedere.' Persuasus itaque per metropolitanum, Heinricus[112] regi deducitur, multoque ambitionis honore ante admittitur, ac ambo in amicitiam federantur.

24

Henry's Response to Archbishop Hervey Concerning Charles

To this Henry responded, "There are many things to dissuade me from this course of action, distinguished father, were it not that your virtue somehow draws me back to it.[46] I know what a difficult and thankless task it is to give him advice[47] both because of his own fickleness and because of the spitefulness of his followers. I have not forgotten how in former days I exerted myself on his behalf, both at home and abroad. It is also well known how much he abused the trust he owed me. Perhaps you will persuade him of it, Father, and then he will repent of what he has done. But because no one is sufficiently clever or wise when it comes to the future, and in spite of the fact that bad counsel prevails more often than good,[48] I will follow wherever you lead. I will subordinate my modesty to your authority[49] and make trial of your virtue. For my part I had resolved[50] to leave him without my wisdom, my counsel, or my arms." Thus convinced by the archbishop, Henry was brought before the king and admitted into his presence with a great display of honor, and the two men were bound together in friendship.

25

Quibus gestis, Hilduinus Tungrensium episcopus cum iis qui ab rege defecerant conspirasse in regem insimulatur, regique infensus ab eo insectabatur.[113] Cuius odii vis eo usque pervenit, ut Richerum Prumiensis monasterii abbatem promoveret et Hilduinum abdicaret. At Richerus ab rege donatus, cum ab metropolitano Herimanno urgeretur, eo quod contra fas ab rege episcopatum suscepisset super eum qui tenebat quique nulla culparum confessione victus, nullo iuditio damnatus esset, regis iussu Romam festinat ac ibi Iohanni papae et regis sententiam et sui negotii causam demonstrat. Papa in Hilduinum desertorem indignans, ab officio eum suspendit ac anathemate damnat. Richerum vero episcopum ordinat ac suae auctoritatis benedictione donat. Haec dum sic agerentur, Hilduinus prosequitur, incassum apud papam plurimam querimoniam fundens ac apud eum pro absolutione admodum laborans. Quo conquerente, Richerus redit ac sedem vacuam iussus ab rege ingreditur.

25

Subsequently Bishop Hilduin of Liège was accused of having conspired against the king with the other traitors and he was persecuted by Charles as an enemy. The king's hostility toward him reached the point that he promoted Richer,[51] abbot of the monastery of Prüm, and deposed Hilduin. After Richer had been invested with the office of bishop by the king, however, he came under attack from Archbishop Hermann on the grounds that he had unlawfully taken up the bishopric from the king over the head of the current occupant, who had neither confessed to any wrongdoing nor been convicted by any court. So Richer hastened to Rome at the king's behest and there he explained the king's decision and justified his own conduct to Pope John.[52] Roused to indignation against the traitor Hilduin, the pope suspended him from office and condemned him with an anathema. He ordained Richer as bishop in his place and invested him with the blessing of his authority. Meanwhile, Hilduin continued to press his case, complaining to the pope at length and making every effort to win absolution from him, but to no avail. While he continued to protest, Richer returned and took up the vacant see on the orders of the king.[53]

921

922

26

His ita sese habentibus, rex ad interiores Belgicae partes iter retorquet. Ibique ob multas rerum quae emerserant causas regio decreto et metropolitani iussu sinodus apud Trosleium habenda indicitur. Cui sinodo domnus Heriveus presedit, rege quoque ibidem presidente. Ubi quam plurimis quae utillima visa sunt determinatis, regis interventu et episcoporum qui sinodo interfuere consensu, domnus Heriveus metropolitanus Erlebaldum predictum Castricensium comitem a vinculo excommunicationis absolvit. Ibi etiam Rodulfo Laudunensium episcopo defuncto, Adelelmum eiusdem urbis thesaurarium multo episcoporum consensu ab rege donatum sollempniter ordinat.

27

His prospere et utiliter gestis, rex superiora Belgicae repetit, aliqua suorum ibi ordinaturus.[114] Cum equitatu itaque in Richuinum comitem fertur, eo quod et ipse desertor Rotberti partes tuebatur. Eius ergo oppidis obsidionem adhibet,

26

Under these circumstances the king went back to the inner regions of Belgica. There it was announced that by royal decree and the order of the archbishop a synod would be held at Trosly[54] to deal with the many legal issues that had arisen. Archbishop Hervey presided over the synod, together with the king. After a great many issues deemed to be of particular importance had been decided, Archbishop Hervey released Erlebald, the aforementioned count of Châtresais, from the bonds of anathema through the intervention of the king and the agreement of the bishops who were present.[55] In addition, because Bishop Rodulf of Laon had died, Hervey solemnly ordained Adelelm, the treasurer of the cathedral of Laon, as his successor with the general consent of the synod, after he had been invested with this office by the king.[56]

27

When these measures had been taken successfully and to good effect, the king went back to Upper Belgica to put some of the affairs of his subjects in order. He took a force of knights and moved against Count Ricuin,[57] because he too had abandoned the king to support Robert's faction.

vehementi expugnatione infestans. At ille equitatum intolerabilem advertens, iure obsidum victus ad regem redit. Rex
victum excipiens, animum ab ira mitigat ac eum in gratiam
resumit.[115]

28

Dum haec gerebantur, Rotbertus Celticae Galliae dux
piratas acriter impetebat. Irruperant enim duce Rollone filio Catilli intra Neustriam repentini. Iamque Ligerim classe
transmiserant ac finibus illius indemnes potiebantur. Ibant
passim palantes atque cum vehementibus manubiis ad classem sese referebant. Dux vero ex tota Neustria copias collegerat. Plures quoque ex Aquitania accersiverat. Aderant
etiam ab rege missae IIII[116] cohortes ex Belgica, quibus et
Richuinus predictus preerat. Aquitanorum vero legiones
Dalmatius curabat. Neustrios vero ipse dux Rotbertus disponebat. Sicque totus ducis exercitus in $\overline{XL}$ equitum consistebat. Dalmatium ergo cum Aquitanis in prima fronte constituit, dein Belgas[117] at Neustrios subsidiis locat. Ipse etiam
dux legiones circumiens, precipuos quosque nomine vocans,
hortatur ut suae virtutis ac nobilitatis plurimum memine-
rint, pro patria, pro vita, pro libertate certandum asserens.

Charles laid siege to his strongholds and subjected them to a violent assault. When Ricuin realized that he could not withstand the king's knights, he surrendered and returned to the king under the surety of hostages. Charles accepted his surrender, tempered his anger, and took him back into his favor.[58]

28

In the meantime, Duke Robert of Celtic Gaul was mounting a fierce attack on the pirates. For they had had made a sudden incursion into Neustria under the leadership of Rollo, the son of Catillus. Having already crossed the Loire with their fleet and taken control of the surrounding region with impunity, they were ranging all over the countryside and bringing a tremendous haul of plunder back to their ships. The duke, for his part, had mustered forces from all over Neustria and summoned many men from Aquitaine as well. The king had also sent four cohorts from Belgica. These were commanded by the aforementioned Ricuin, while Dalmatius[59] was in charge of the legions from Aquitaine. Duke Robert himself commanded the men of Neustria. The duke's army, then, numbered forty thousand knights in all. He placed Dalmatius and the Aquitainians in the first rank and kept the men of Belgica and Neustria in reserve. The duke himself went around the legions and called out each of the most distinguished men by name, urging them to be mindful of their courage and nobility and telling them that this battle was to be waged for their fa-

De morte non sollicitandum, cum ea omnibus incerta sit. Si vero fugiant, eis nihil ab hostibus esse relinquendum. His et aliis quam plurimis militum animos accendebat.[118] Quibus dictis,[119] dux[120] in locum ubi prelium erat gerendum[121] instructos ordines deducit.[122]

29

Nec minus et hostium exercitus contra hos rem militarem multa audatia ordinabant. Quorum exercitus in $\overline{L}$ armatorum consistens, ordinatim obvenientibus procedit. Rotbertus dux vim belli maximam imminere advertens, cum mille robustis ex Neustria Dalmatio in prima fronte sese assotiat. Procedit itaque cum Dalmatio et Aquitanis.[123] At piratarum legiones longo sese ordine protenderant, ipsumque ordinem ad hostes excipiendos curvaverant[124] scemate lunae quae in augmento[125] est, ut dum multo fervore hostes ruerent, exercitus circulatione exciperentur. Sic etiam ab iis qui in cornu utroque persisterent a tergo appetiti, more pecudum sternerentur.

therland, their lives, and their freedom.[60] They should have no fear of death, since its hour is uncertain to all, whereas if they fled then nothing would be left for them by their enemies. With these and many other exhortations he fired the resolve of his troops. When he had finished speaking, the duke led them drawn up in rank to the place where the battle was to be fought.[61]

29

The enemy forces likewise arrayed their troops against them with great boldness. Their army, which numbered fifty thousand armed men, marched forward in rank to meet them. Realizing that the shock of battle was imminent, Duke Robert took one thousand stalwart men from Neustria and joined Dalmatius in the front rank, marching into battle alongside him and the Aquitainians. The legions of the pirates were stretched out in a long line, and they had bent their ranks into the shape of a crescent moon to meet the enemy. Their intention was that when the enemy charged forward in a mad rush, they would be completely enveloped, whereupon the men positioned on the flanks would attack them from behind and cut them down like cattle.[62]

30

His ergo in utraque parte paratis, uterque exercitus[126] signis collatis[127] congreditur. Rotbertus et Dalmatius cum Aquitanis legiones piratarum penetrant, statimque ab iis qui in cornibus erant a tergo impetuntur. Mox quoque et Belgae[128] inprovisi prosequuntur atque piratas qui a tergo suos premebant immani cede sternunt. Neustrii quoque atrocissime instant. In qua commixtione, cum Aquitani piratis circumdati multo conamine eos quos impellebant in fugam cogerent, ii qui in cornibus perstiterant a Belgis et Neustriis hinc premebantur, inde vero ab Aquitanis conversis letaliter urgebantur. Superati itaque arma deponunt ac multis clamoribus pro vita supplicant. Rotbertus itaque tantae caedi parcere petit ac instat ut eruantur. Vix quoque ab caede quievit exercitus, multo prosperioris fortunae incitatus successu. Sedato vero tumultu, qui inter eos potiores videbantur a duce capti sunt; reliqui vero sub iure obsidum ad classem redire permittuntur.

30

Once both sides had made their preparations, the two armies charged forward and joined battle. Robert and Dalmatius, at the head of the Aquitainians, broke through the pirate legions and were immediately attacked from behind by the troops on the wings. They were immediately followed by the men of Belgica, who came up without warning and struck down the pirates who were attacking their allies from behind with tremendous slaughter. The Neustrians, too, set upon them with savage ferocity. During the melee the Aquitainians, who were surrounded by the pirates, put their attackers to flight with a terrific effort, whereupon those of the enemy who remained on the wings were attacked on one side by the Neustrians and the men of Belgica, and pressed with deadly force on the other side by the Aquitainians, who had now turned to face them. Owning themselves beaten, the enemy laid down their weapons and pleaded vociferously for their lives. Seeking to avoid a wholesale massacre, Robert urged that they be spared. The army could scarcely put a stop to the slaughter, so excited were they by the successful result of their good fortune. Once order had been restored, however, the most prominent of the pirates were taken prisoner by the duke, while the rest were permitted to return to their ships under the surety of hostages.

31

Patrata ergo victoria, exercituque soluto, Rotbertus[129] captos Parisii deponit.[130] Hos percunctans an christiani essent, nullum eorum quicquam religionis huiusmodi attigisse comperit. Misso itaque ad eos instruendos reverendo presbitero et monacho Martino, ad fidem Christi conversi sunt. Qui vero ad classem redierant, alii eorum christiani, alii pagani mixtim inventi sunt. Et hi quoque per predictum virum instructi, receptis a duce opsidibus[131] quos dederant, ad salutaria sacramenta deducti sunt.

32

Et cum de baptisterio ageretur, Wittoni Rhodomensium metropolitano eis predicandum a duce committitur. Witto vero non se solo contentus, Heriveo Remensi epistolam dirigit, per quam ab eo querit quo ordine, qua ratione gens ante perfida aecclesiae sotianda sit. Heriveus vero metropolitanus multa diligentia haec disponere cupiens, conventum episcoporum fieri iubet, ut multorum rationibus res idonee distribueretur.

31

Having thus achieved the victory, Robert disbanded his army and deposited his prisoners at Paris. When he asked them whether or not they were Christians, he discovered that none of them had the slightest knowledge of the faith. And so he sent the reverend priest and monk Martin to instruct them, and they were converted to faith in Christ. Of those who had gone back to the ships, it was discovered that some were pagan and others were Christians. They, too, received instruction from the aforementioned Martin, and after they had received back from the duke the hostages whom they had handed over, they were brought to the sacraments that bring salvation.

32

When the issue of their baptism arose, the duke entrusted Archbishop Witto of Rouen with the task of ministering to them. Witto, however, not wishing to act alone, sent a letter to Hervey of Reims inquiring about the appropriate procedure and method for incorporating a formerly heathen people into the church. Desiring to be scrupulous in attending to these matters, Archbishop Hervey convened a council of bishops so that the question might be properly submitted to a collective decision.

33

Et die constituta sinodus habita est. In qua primum de pace et religione sanctae dei aecclesiae statuque regni Francorum salubriter ac competenter tractatum est, post vero de piratarum mitigatione atque conversione uberrime agitatum. Decretum quoque de eodem ab ipsa divinitate rationem quaerendam, ieiunandum etiam ab omnibus triduo. Domno vero papae id esse suggerendum, ut invocata per ieiunium divinitate, et domno papa humiliter consulto, efficatius res ordinaretur. Revolutis itaque patrum decretis, reverendus metropolitanus Heriveus XXIIII capitula in volumine ordinavit, rationabiliter ac utiliter digesta et qualiter rudes in fide habendi sunt continentia. Quae omnia venerabili Rodomensi Witoni delegavit. Ille vero excipiens,[132] utiliter sumptum negotium consummavit.

34

Hac etiam tempestate Ragenerus, vir clarus et nobilis,[133] cognomento Collo longus, cuius etiam obitus multam rei publicae in Belgica intulit labem, communi corporis valitudine tactus et oppressus, finem vitae apud Marsnam pala-

33

On the appointed day the synod was held.[63] They first treated of the peace and faith of the holy Church of God and the condition of the kingdom of the Franks in a productive and salutary manner, and this was followed by fruitful deliberations concerning the pacification and conversion of the pirates. On this subject it was decreed that they would seek a decision from God himself and that everyone would observe a three-day fast. The matter should also be submitted to the pope, so that by calling upon God through fasting, and by humbly consulting the pope, the issue might be brought to an effective resolution. After reading through the decrees of the fathers, the reverend archbishop Hervey compiled in writing a collection of twenty-four articles, organized in a logical and practical fashion, which outlined how to deal with those new to the faith. He turned all of this over to the venerable Witto of Rouen, and after Witto received it, he successfully carried out the task that he had undertaken.[64]

34

At this time Reginar Longneck,[65] a renowned and noble man whose death proved disastrous for public order in Belgica, was afflicted with illness throughout his body and died at the palace of Meerssen. It is said that King Charles was

915

tium accepit. Cuius exequiis Karolus rex interfuisse dicitur, ac oculos lacrimis suffusus dixisse, 'O,' inquiens, 'ex alto humilem, ex amplo artissimum,' altero personam, altero monumentum significans. Peractisque exsequiis, Gisleberto eius filio, iam facto iuveni,[134] paternum honorem coram principibus qui confluxerant liberalissime accommodat.

35

Hic cum esset clarissimo genere inclitus et Heinrici Saxoniae ducis filiae Gerbergae coniugio[135] nimium felix, in nimiam pre insolentia temeritatem preceps ferebatur; in disciplina militari ex audatia nimius, adeo ut quodcumque inevincibile appetere non metueret; corpore mediocri et denso, duroque membrorum robore; cervice inflexibili, oculis infestis atque inquietis[136] sicque mobilibus ut eorum color nemini ad plenum innotuerit, pedibus omnino inpatientibus, mente levi.[137] Oratio eius ambigua ratione consistens, interrogatio fallens, responsio anceps; orationis partes raro dilucidae sibi cohaerebant; suis adeo profusus, aliena enormiter sitiens; maioribus ac sibi aequalibus coram favens, occulte vero invidens; rerum confusione ac mutua dissidentium insectatione plurimum gaudens.

present at his funeral, and that with his eyes full of tears he exclaimed, "Alas! Once high, he is now brought low, once mighty, he is now most narrowly confined," signifying the man himself with the first statement and his tomb with the other. After the funeral, in the presence of the magnates who had assembled there, he generously bestowed Reginar's holdings upon his son Gislebert, who had now reached the age of manhood.[66]

35

Gislebert was distinguished by the nobility of his ancestry,[67] and he had concluded a very favorable marriage with Gerberga,[68] the daughter of Duke Henry of Saxony, but his arrogance drove him headlong to extremes of recklessness. So daring was he in the conduct of warfare that he would not shrink from undertaking what seemed to be impossible. He was of medium size and solidly built, with strong, hardy limbs, a stiff neck, hostile, darting eyes that were so quick-moving that their color was never fully apparent to anyone, restless feet, and a frivolous nature. He dealt in ambiguities when he spoke; he was deceitful in asking questions and equivocal in answering them; and his utterances rarely fit together coherently.[69] He was quite generous to his own followers, but he had an insatiable appetite for what belonged to others.[70] In public he was obliging to men who were superior or equal to him, but he secretly envied them, and he rejoiced greatly in disorder and factional strife.

36

Talis itaque in regem nimia animositate ferebatur. Meditabatur quoque regis abiectionem admodum, ac plurimum id pertractabat apud eos qui in Belgica potiores videbantur,[138] non quidem Rotberto, sed sibi regnum affectans, sua quoque principibus pene omnia distribuens. Et maiores quidem prediis et aedibus egregiis inclite donabat, mediocres autem auri et argenti talentis efficaciter illiciebat. Fit itaque multorum ex Belgica cum eo consensus. Sed hoc satis improvide ac inconsulte. Nam licet ob magna beneficia comparatos sibi attraxisset, non tamen ex iureiurando ad patrandum facinus sibi annexuit. Leviter ergo attracti, leviter post dissociati fuere.

37

Nam cum Karolus, hoc audito, a Celtica cum exercitu rediret Belgisque bellum inferre pararet, Belgae mox non in aperto cum Gisleberto resistere nisi sunt, sed oppidis ac municipiis[139] sese recludunt. Rex vero singulis qui ab se de-

36

Gislebert, being as he was, was animated by a tremen- 919–922
dous hostility toward the king. He also plotted intently to
remove him from the throne and frequently discussed the
matter with the more powerful magnates of Belgica. Because he wanted the kingdom for himself, and not for Robert, he distributed most of his own possessions among the
leading men. He lavished splendid estates and houses on the
more powerful and successfully enticed those of middling
status with pounds of gold and silver. Many of the men of
Belgica joined him as a result. Yet he failed to show sufficient foresight or planning in what he did. For while he had
won these men over and attracted them to his side with
lavish gifts, he had not bound them to himself by making
them swear an oath to carry out this crime. As a result, those
who were quick to join him were subsequently quick to
abandon him.

37

For when Charles, having learned of this, returned from
Celtic Gaul with his army and prepared to make war on the
men of Belgica, they did not immediately join Gislebert in
resisting the king openly, but instead shut themselves up in
their strongholds and fortresses. The king, for his part, sent

fecerant legatos dirigit, per quos significabat sese regali atque sollemni donatione largiturum quicquid eis ab Gisleberto prediorum et aedium collatum est, sese quoque contra
Gislebertum pro eis certaturum, si is eis ex collatis beneficiis quicquam repetere velit. Quo capti, mox iure sacramenti
ad regem redeunt, habitisque rationibus quicquid benefi-
ciorum ab Gisleberto eis collatum fuit, regali largitate[140] firmissime unicuique donatur. Unde et a Gisleberto receden-
tes, regi constantissime resocientur ac cum eo in Gislebertum
feruntur.

38

Gislebertus vero in oppido Harburc, quod hinc Mosa et
inde Gullo fluviis vallatur, a fronte vero immani hiatu multoque horrore veprium defensum est, cum paucis claudebatur.
Huc rex cum exercitu properat locatque obsidionem, hinc
et inde navalem, a fronte vero equestrem. In cuius expugnatione cum persisteret, Gislebertus navali fuga dilabitur. Oppidani vero capti, in regis deveniunt iussionem. Gislebertus
autem cum duobus clientulis, paterna hereditate privatus,
Rhenum exulaturus pertransit, ibique per annos aliquot

envoys to each one of the men who had deserted him, declaring that he would grant to them by solemn royal charter whatever estates and houses Gislebert had conferred upon them. Moreover, he would fight on their behalf against Gislebert if he tried to take back any of the benefices that he had granted away. Persuaded by this, they immediately swore oaths and reconciled themselves with the king, and after a determination was made of which benefices had been given to them by Gislebert, each of them was given secure possession of these benefices by royal charter. And so they abandoned Gislebert and once more allied themselves faithfully to the king, whom they now joined in his campaign against him.

38

Gislebert was shut up with a few men inside the stronghold of Harburc, which was surrounded on two sides by the Rivers Meuse and Geul and defended on the front by a huge precipice and a mass of thorny bramble bushes. The king hastened there with his army and laid siege to the stronghold, positioning his ships on the two sides and his knights in front. While the king was pressing the assault, Gislebert managed to escape by ship. The garrison, however, were captured and passed under the king's command. For his part Gislebert, having been deprived of his paternal inheritance, crossed over the Rhine with two of his henchmen to go into exile. There for several years he remained in exile at the

apud Heinricum socerum deceptus exulat. Evoluto autem aliquot annorum tempore, Heinricus apud regem suasorie egit[141] ut Gislebertus revocaretur ac in regis gratiam resumeretur, ea vero rerum conditione, ut regis sententia ex collatis beneficiis intemerata, Gislebertus ea tantum regali clementia reciperet quorum possessores per tot sui exilii tempora iam obierant.

39

Ab exilio itaque revocatus, regis gratiam per Heinricum meretur, ea tamen, ut dictum est, conditione, ut a beneficiis quae insolenter diduxerat, quandiu possessores viverent, careat, ea vero quorum possessores per annos aliquot obierant regis miseratione repetat. Recipit itaque quae a defunctis quidem derelicta vacabant, maximam suarum rerum partem:[142] Treiectum, Iuppilam, Harstalium, Marsnam, Littam, Capraemontem. Quibus habitis, Karolus rex in Celticam redit, Nortmannis qui extremos Galliarum fines locis maritimis infestabant copias inferre parans. Heinrico vero trans Rhenum contra Sarmatas profecto, Gislebertus per suos immaniter vexabat et atterebat eos qui ab rege sua data ob-

court of his father-in-law, Henry, having been thwarted in his ambitions.[71] But after a few years had passed, Henry persuaded the king to recall Gislebert and restore him to favor, on the condition that the king's decision regarding the benefices that he had granted would remain unchallenged, and that Gislebert would receive, by the king's mercy, only those benefices whose proprietors had died during the course of his long exile.

39

Gislebert was thus recalled from exile and taken back into the king's favor through Henry's intervention, albeit with the previously mentioned provision that he would do without the benefices that he had so arrogantly alienated as long as their proprietors were still living. Those benefices whose proprietors had died during the intervening years he could ask to have back at the king's mercy, however. In this way he recovered the benefices that were left vacant after their proprietors had died, which included the greater part of his possessions: Maastricht, Jupille, Herstal, Meerssen, Leten,[72] and Chèvremont. Subsequently King Charles returned to Celtic Gaul and prepared to lead his forces against the Northmen who were harrying the outer regions of Gaul from their seaside bases. But when Henry set out across the Rhine against the Slavs, Gislebert sent his men to brutally torment and persecute those who had received his possessions from the king.[73] By killing some in secret attacks and

tinebant. Alios clandestina invasione enecans, alios incessanter ut sua relinquant adurgens, tandem evincit suisque
omnibus potitur, truculentius exinde in regem machinans.
Socerum itaque adit eique ab rege dissuadet, Celticam so-
lam regi posse sufficere asserens, Belgicam vero atque Germaniam rege alio plurimum indigere. Unde et ut ipse in regnum coronari non abnueret multis suasionibus permovebat.
Heinricus vero cum nefanda eum suadere adverteret, dictis
suadentis admodum restitit et ut quiesceret ab illicitis multis amplificationibus agitabat.

40

Et Gislebertus quidem, cum apud socerum non profice-
ret nec regnum sibi parare posset, in Celticam secedit ac
transit in Neustriam. Sicque cum Rotberto duce de eodem
negotio consilium confert, suadens ei de regni susceptione
ac Karoli abiectione. Exultat tirannus et[143] tiranno absque
mora favet. Deliberant itaque ambo et post pro perpetran-
dis fidem sacramento confirmant. [Et post haec Gislebertus
in Belgicam redit, municipia militibus copiis sufficientibus

forcing others to abandon their possessions through constant harassment, he eventually prevailed and regained all of his property, whereupon he began to plot more aggressively against the king. Thus, he approached his father-in-law and advised him to turn against the king, claiming that Celtic Gaul by itself was enough for Charles, whereas Belgica and Germany stood in desperate need of a separate king. And for this reason he tried to sway him with repreated exhortations not to refuse the crown for himself. But when Henry realized what kind of wickedness was being urged upon him, he turned a deaf ear to Gislebert's efforts to persuade him and admonished him repeatedly to refrain from unlawful activities.

40

Because Gislebert was not getting anywhere with his father-in-law and he was unable to procure the throne for himself,[74] he withdrew into Celtic Gaul and crossed into Neustria. There he met with Duke Robert to discuss the same issue, trying to persuade him to depose Charles and take up the throne for himself. The tyrant rejoiced and gave his support to the other tyrant without delay. And so they entered into deliberations together and afterward they swore an oath to confirm their intentions. [After this Gislebert returned to Belgica, putting garrisons of sufficient strength into his strongholds, readying everything against the king, and shoring up the walls wherever the masonry

implens, in regem omnia ordinans, sicubi rudera aditum faciebant, firmioribus claustris reaedificans. Ratus vero milites a sese deficere posse si iureiurando sibi eos non annecteret, fidem ab omnibus ex iureiurando, sed et obsides quos vult accipit, eosque in oppido Harburc quod pene inexpugnabile videbatur, deputatos recludit, in regem omnia palam ordinans. Nec minus[144] id optinuit, ut quaecumque ipse in regem machinaretur, ea socero iniuriae non essent, maxime ob id quod Sarmatarum infestatione ipse admodum pressus, alienis negotiis utiliter interesse non possit. His ergo rex in Celtica permotus, Belgicam impetit. At Gislebertus, utpote qui fidem abruperat, ad regem non solum venire contempsit, verum pecuniis ut antea atque rerum pollicitationibus ab rege quoscumque poterat subtrahebat. Et rex quidem cum patienter haec ad tempus toleranda non ignoraret, Tungris cum iis qui secum ex Celtica advenerant absque tumultu residebat, levius fieri asserens quicquid per pacienciam toleratur,[145] medium quoque sese esse hostium recognoscens, cum a Rotberto hinc in Celtica, ab Gisleberto vero inde in Belgica urgeretur. Et Rotbertus quidem de regis abiectione suique promotione adeo laborabat. Idque apud principes sic optinuit, ut contra regem cum eo fere omnes crudelissime coniurarent.][146]

had collapsed and offered a potential point of entry for the enemy. Reckoning, however, that his troops might desert him if he did not bind them to himself with an oath, he had them all swear an oath of loyalty to him, but he also took whatever hostages he wanted from them and shut them up in the seemingly impregnable stronghold of Harburc. He made no attempt to disguise all of the preparations he was making against the king. On behalf of his father-in-law he also saw to it that whatever he was plotting against the king would not cause Henry any harm, since the latter was being hard-pressed by Slavic raids and could not effectively intervene in any other peoples' affairs. All of this provoked the king to leave Celtic Gaul and set out for Belgica. But Gislebert, as befitted an oath-breaker, not only disdained to come meet the king, but also tried to lure whomever he could away from him with bribes and promises of property, as he had done before. Now the king was aware that he would have to bear all of this patiently for the time being, so he remained at Liège with those who had accompanied him from Celtic Gaul and took no action, declaring that whatever was endured with patience became easier. He realized that he was surrounded by his enemies, threatened on one side by Robert in Celtic Gaul and on the other by Gislebert in Belgica. For his part, Robert was devoting all of his efforts to deposing the king and having himself elevated to the throne. And he successfully prevailed upon almost all of the leading men to join with him in his ruthless conspiracy against the king.[75]]

41

Tempore vero constituto, cum rex Tungros redisset ibique privatus resideret, urbem Suessonicam Rotbertus ingreditur. Apud quem ex tota[147] Celtica primates collecti, qua ratione regem abiciant constantissime consultant. Nec defuit Gislebertus ab Belgica, qui mox absque deliberatione Rotbertum regem creandum perstrepebat. Communi ergo omnium qui aderant decreto Rotbertus eligitur, ac multo ambitionis elatu Remos deductus, in basilica sancti Remigii rex creatur. A cuius coronatione peracto triduo, Heriveus Remorum metropolitanus diutina egritudine vexatus interiit. Qui si eodem tempore valuisset, tanto facinori oportunitas non patuisset. Cui etiam mox succedit donatus ab Rotberto Seulfus, qui tunc urbis eiusdem officio fungebatur archidiaconatus, vir strenuus multaque rerum scientia inclitus.

41

At the appointed time, after the king had returned to 922
Liège and taken up residence there without his retinue,
Robert entered the city of Soissons. The magnates from all
over Celtic Gaul gathered before him and with great determination they deliberated about how they should go about
deposing the king. Nor did Gislebert fail to appear from
Belgica, and immediately and without any debate he began
to clamor that Robert should be made king. Therefore, by
virtue of a general decree of all those who were present,
Robert was chosen king and taken with a great deal of high-
flown pomp to Reims, where he was crowned king in the
basilica of Saint-Rémi.[76] Three days after Robert's coronation, Archbishop Hervey of Reims died, after suffering from
a long illness.[77] If he had been in good health at the time,
there would have been no opportunity for such a shameful
deed. He was succeeded shortly thereafter by Seulf,[78] then
serving as the archdeacon of Reims, who was invested with
this office by King Robert. He was an energetic man who
was renowned for his great learning.[79]

42

Interea Karolus a Gallis preter paucissimos Belgarum desertum sese comperiens, apud precipuos eorum qui a se non defecerant plurimam de suo infortunio agitabat querelam, miseriorem sese inquiens si hac urgeatur calamitate quam si oculos claudat suprema morte, cum illa dolores augescant, ista demantur.[148] Carius quoque sibi ferro occidi quam regno a pervasore[149] privari. Post regni enim privationem solummodo superesse in exilium deportationem. In quo etiam ab iis quos summo semper habuit amore, apud quos diutius conversatus sit, quibus quoque nihil umquam mali molitus fuerit, debere sese suffragia accipere memorabat.

43

Ad haec sui[150] 'Pernitiosum est,' inquiunt, 'o rex, iuratis a domino deficere, sceleratissimum vero contra dominum stare. Si de desertore ac transfugis agitur, horumque nominum si advertatur interpretatio, quicquid moliti sunt prae-

42

Meanwhile, when Charles learned that he had been deserted by all of the Gauls save for a few men from Belgica, he complained bitterly of his misfortunes to the most prominent of his remaining followers, declaring that he would suffer more if this disaster were to befall him than he would if he closed his eyes at the final moment of death, since the former would increase his sorrows, while the latter would only take them away. He would prefer to die by the sword rather than be deprived of his kingdom by a usurper. For after the loss of his kingdom all that remained for him was to be sent away into exile. In his current circumstances, he declared, he should also expect to receive help from those to whom he had always shown the greatest affection, those who had been his constant companions, and those, moreover, against whom he had never attempted any wrong.

43

In response his men declared: "It is a ruinous thing, your highness, for sworn men to abandon their master, but it is the very height of wickedness to take up arms against one's lord. If we are speaking of rebels and traitors, and if we keep in mind the meaning of these words, it follows that whatever these men have done is contrary to both law and jus-

ter ius est et aequum.[151] Unde et sine dubio si pugnae necessitas eos adurgeat, divinitatis ultionem non evadent. Id vero certissime noveris, nullo modo regnum a te repetendum, nisi bello ipsum aggrediaris tirannum. Regnum ereptum non irrumpes,[152] nisi ferro viam violenter aperias. Et quia iam nunc res pugnam suadet, sacramento fides adhibenda est, ut nobis iuratis, res in ambiguo non sit. Dein saltem L eligendi sunt qui certissime tirannum appetant vimque ei inferant, ut cum belli violentia alios in alios exagitaverit, isti tiranno tantum laborent inventumque transfigant. Quid enim proderit omnes interfici et malorum causam reservari?' Et decreto communi in Rotbertum coniurant.

44

Mox quoque et regio iussu accersiuntur ex Belgica quicumque ab rege non defecisse videbantur. Quorum collectorum numerus, ut fertur, vix in X[153] milibus putabatur. Et tamen in quantum perspici valuit, nullus militiae[154] ineptus admissus est. Omnes corpore valentes et non inertes pugnae, omnesque in tirannum unanimes.[155] His rex circumseptus,

tice. Consequently, there can be no doubt that if necessity compels them to go into battle, they will not escape divine punishment. You should understand very clearly, however, that you cannot recover your kingdom without making war upon the tyrant himself. Nor will you be able to break into the kingdom that has been snatched away from you unless you take up the sword and open a path with force.[80] Now because the present circumstances call for battle, let an oath of fealty be administered to us so that after we have sworn, there will be no doubt in anyone's mind. Then let at least fifty men be chosen and assigned the specific task of finding and attacking the tyrant, so that when the fury of battle drives foe against foe, their only goal will be to exert themselves against the tyrant and run him through once they have found him. For what good will it do you if all of the enemy are slain but the source of these evils remains alive?" Thus, they all agreed to swear an oath against Robert.

44

Shortly thereafter, all those who were not deemed to have 923 deserted the king were summoned from Belgica by royal decree. The number of those assembled was estimated to be scarcely ten thousand men, according to report. And yet as far as could be determined no one untrained in warfare was accepted. They were all physically strong and skilled in battle, and all were united against the tyrant. Surrounded by

per Condrucium Hasbaniumque procedit in hostem. Erep-
tumque regnum irrumpens, sedem regiam Atiniacum pridem suam ingreditur. Ibique aliquantisper reparato exercitu, in adversarium fertur.[156]

45

Factus vero tiranno propior, exercitum ad congressum
ordinat, $\overline{\text{VI}}$[157] robustorum premittens. Quibus etiam virum
clarum[158] nomine Fulbertum ducem constituit. Se ipsum
vero IIII[159] milibus circumseptum, labentibus primis subventurum deputat. Postquam autem per singulas legiones
discurrens, precipuos quosque[160] multum diuque ad vim
belli[161] hortatus est, instructos ordines plurimis suasionibus
incitans, ad locum ubi congrediendum erat deducit. Axonam vero fluvium transmeans, ad urbem Suessonicam tendit. Ibi etenim tirannus copias collegerat, cuius quoque
exercitus in $\overline{\text{XX}}$ consistebat. Cum ergo Karolus rex bello[162]

these men, the king marched through Condroz and Hes-
baye against the enemy. He forced his way into the kingdom
that had been usurped from him and entered the royal palace at Attigny, which had formerly been his. Then, after giving his army a chance to rest for a while, he moved against
his foe.[81]

45

When he had moved into the vicinity of the tyrant, he
arrayed his army for the battle, sending ahead six thousand stalwart men over whom he placed an illustrious commander named Fulbert. He assigned to himself and the four
thousand men who surrounded him the task of coming forward to relieve those who were first to give way. Then, going
around to each one of the legions, he urged the most prominent men forcefully and at length to fight hard in the battle,
and rousing the troops who had been drawn up into ranks
with repeated exhortations, he led them to the place where
the battle was to be fought. Then he crossed the River Aisne
and advanced toward the city of Soissons. For it was there
that the tyrant had gathered his forces, which numbered
twenty thousand men. Although King Charles wanted to

intenderet,[163] episcoporum instinctu[164] aliorumque religio-
sorum virorum qui sibi assistebant actum est ut ipse rex
bellum non ingrederetur, ne forte in rerum confusione rega-
lis stirps eo lapso consumeretur. Id etiam duces et milites
coegerunt. Ab omnibus ergo coactus, IIII[165] milibus quibus
ipse circumseptus incedebat virum clarum[166] Hagraldum
preficit. Hortatur vero plurimum ut dei[167] tantum auxilium
implorent, nihil eis metuendum, nihil de victoria diffiden-
dum memorans. Regni quoque pervasorem[168] vix uno mo-
mento duraturum asserebat, 'Cum,' inquiens, 'deus huiusmodi abhominetur, et apud eum nullus superbiae locus sit,
quomodo stabit quem ipse non munit? Quomodo resurget
quem ipse precipitat?' Et post haec cum episcopis virisque
religiosis qui aderant montem loco oppositum conscendit,
ubi etiam est basilica beatae Genovefae virginis dedicata,
eventum belli inde experturus. Interea iunctim procedit
exercitus et magnanimus gradive[169] in hostem accelerat.
Procedit quoque tirannus, animo non impar, at legionibus
potior.

take part in the battle, at the urging of the bishops and the other holy men who accompanied him it was decided that he himself would not enter the battle, lest by chance he should perish amid the fray and the royal line should be extinguished through his death. The commanders and fighting men were insistent upon this as well. Therefore, under compulsion from all sides, Charles put an illustrious man named Harald in charge of the four thousand men who were supposed to accompany him into battle. He urged them repeatedly to pray to God alone for help, telling them that they should fear nothing and have no doubt about their victory. And he also declared that the man who had usurped his throne would last but a moment. "Because," he said, "God abhors men of this sort, and pride has no place before him, how shall anyone whom he does not protect remain standing? How shall one whom he has cast down rise again?" Then, in the company of the bishops and the other holy men who were with him, he climbed the hill that stood across from them, where a church had been dedicated to the blessed virgin Geneviève, there to await the outcome of the battle. Meanwhile, his army marched forward together and advanced steadily and courageously toward the enemy. The tyrant, too, came forward, equal in valor and stronger in legions.

46[170]

Quibus utrimque visis comminus, cum maximo clamore utrique exercitus signis infestis concurrunt. Congressique innumeri hinc inde corruunt. Et Rotbertus quidem rex, cum in certamine ignotus esset et hinc inde feriendo toto campo fureret, a coniuratis conspectus, an ipse esset interrogatur. At ille intrepidus mox barbam obvelatam detegit seseque esse monstrat, multa vi in Fulbertum comitem ferrum vibrans. Ille vero, loetali ictu accepto, ab eo in dextram obliquatur. Et sic per loricae manicam lancea eum in latere gravissimo ictu sauciat, necnon et per epar atque pulmonem et sinistri lateris ypocundriam ferrum usque in clipeum transigit,[171] et circumseptus ab aliis, septem lanceis confossus precipitatur[172] diriguitque. Fulbertus mox multo[173] exhaustus sanguine et inter certantes[174] mortuus cecidit. Interempto vero Rotberto, tanta vi caedis uterque deseviit exercitus ut in parte eius $\overline{\text{XI}}$ CCC et XLIX,[175] in parte vero Karoli $\overline{\text{VII}}$ C XVIII a Flodoardo presbitero ferro interiisse

46

When the men on each side could see one another at close range, the two armies rushed together and joined battle[82] with a tremendous roar.[83] During the fighting countless men fell on both sides. King Robert was raging over the whole battlefield, unrecognized amid the fray, striking men down wherever he went, when the men who had sworn the oath caught sight of him and asked him if he were Robert. Showing no fear, he immediately uncovered his beard, which had been concealed, and revealed who he was, whereupon he struck a tremendous blow with his sword at Count Fulbert. Fulbert, having been dealt a mortal wound, was knocked to Robert's right. This enabled him to strike him with his spear through the armhole of his hauberk, wounding him grievously in the side and driving the point of his spear through his liver, his lung, and the left side of his abdomen, all the way to his shield. Robert was then surrounded by others, and after receiving seven spear wounds, he collapsed to the ground and lay there, unmoving. Shortly thereafter Fulbert grew faint from blood loss and also fell dead in the midst of the fighting. In the aftermath of Robert's death both armies inflicted such savage violence upon one another that according to the account of the priest Flodoard, 11,349 of Robert's men and 7,118 of Charles's perished by the sword.[84] At this moment the

descriptum sit. Et iam quidem Karoli victoria videbatur, eo quod tiranno occiso, qui illius[176] fuerant in fugam ferebantur, cum ecce, Hugo, Rotberti filius, vix adhuc pubescens, in prelium ab Heriberto deducitur[177] succurritque labentibus. Et licet cum copiis advenerit, tamen utpote qui patre[178] amisso omnes suspectos habebat nulloque duce fretus erat, a belli violentia quievit. Illud tantum memorabile[179] fecisse refertur, quod nullo resistente locum belli occupavit et aliquantisper in eo stetit, ac si manubias hostium direpturus. Unde et sibi victores videbantur. Karolus vero ob necem tiranni[180] victoria potiri sese putabat. Quapropter et anceps victoria fuit, cum Celtae[181] desertores regem[182] extinctum amiserint, Karolus vero nihil spoliorum attigerit. Neutrum illorum spolia diripuisse contigit. Cuius rei oportunitas cum Karolo non defuisset, nulla tamen ductus cupiditate, rem pernitiosam[183] vitavit. Nam[184] transfugis plurimum diffidens, utpote qui maximam exercitus partem amiserat, mox iter sine spoliis in Belgicam retorsit, post[185] truculentius redire disponens. Hac tempestate terrae motus in pago Camaracensi factus est, ex quo domus nonnullae subversae sunt. Unde et rerum calamitas adverti potuit, cum regni princeps preter ius captus et in carcerem usque in diem vitae suae supremum detrusus sit. Nam cum rem militarem disponeret et exercitum copiosiorem Galliis inferre pararet, Gallisque inde timor multus incuteretur, mitiore animo ferebantur.

victory seemed to belong to Charles because with the tyrant dead, his former followers had been put to flight. But just then Hugh,[85] the son of Robert, who had barely reached the age of manhood, was brought onto the battlefield by Heribert[86] and came to the aid of the losing party. Although Hugh arrived with reinforcements, he refrained from taking part in the fray of battle since, with his father dead, he regarded everyone with suspicion and had no one whose direction he could rely upon. The only memorable thing he is reported to have done is this: after occupying the battlefield without any resistance, he remained there for a while as though he were going to strip spoils from his enemies. As a result, his men deemed themselves victorious. Charles, on the other hand, thought that the victory was his because the tyrant had been killed. Thus, it was not clear who had prevailed, since the rebels from Celtic Gaul had lost their king, but Charles had not seized any spoils.[87] It turned out that neither side had done so, in fact.[88] The opportunity had presented itself to Charles, but he was not motivated by greed and he steered clear of this dangerous activity.[89] For he was quite anxious about the traitors now that he had lost most of his army, and he departed for Belgica immediately, without seizing any spoils, intending to return later in force.[90] At 922 that time there was an earthquake in the county of Cambrai, as a result of which some houses were knocked down. This was a forewarning of the calamitous circumstances to come, when the king was unlawfully taken captive and thrown into prison, there to remain until the end of his days.[91] When the Gauls learned that Charles was making arrangements for a new campaign into Gaul and raising a larger army to lead against them, they were stricken with 923

Quod Karolus rex subintelligens, per legatos revocare eos nitebatur, multisque rationibus eis id suadere querebat. Nortmannis quoque usque ad effectum suasit, adeo ut regi fidem spondere eique ut iuberet militare vellent. Qui cum regi militaturi occurrere pararent, a Gallis intercurrentibus inhibiti sunt. Unde et eorum suppetiis rex privatus est.

47

Rodulfi regis promotio, ac Karoli captio

Galli, a pertinatia nullatenus quiescentes, Rodulfum Richardi Burgundionis filium accitum, apud urbem Suessonicam, eo licet satis reclamante, regem sibi prefecerunt, virum strenuum ac litteris liberalibus non mediocriter instructum. Quod Heribertus, tantorum malorum incentor, sese velle dissimulans, Karolum regem per legatos accersit, tantis flagiciis se reniti voluisse mandans, sed a coniuratorum multi-

terror and adopted a more pliant attitude. When Charles got wind of this, he sent envoys to try to win them back to his side, using many different arguments in an effort to convince them. He was successful in persuading the Northmen, so much so that they pledged fealty to him and agreed to fight under his command. But as they were preparing to come meet the king with their army, the Gauls blocked their path and prevented them from advancing, depriving the king of their help.[92]

47

The Elevation of Radulf to the Throne and the Capture of Charles

The Gauls, refusing to cease from their obstinacy, summoned Radulf, the son of Richard of Burgundy,[93] and crowned him king at Soissons, in spite of his protestations.[94] He was an energetic man, and well educated in the liberal arts. Heribert, who had instigated these wicked acts, attempted to conceal his complicity and sent envoys to invite King Charles to come to him, claiming that he had tried to oppose these outrages, but that he had been forcefully suppressed by the crowd of conspirators. At that time there had been no opportunity for him to offer counsel, but now he had discovered the best way to make it up to him. Hence,

tudine[186] vehementissime suppressum. Tunc nullum consilii locum patuisse, nunc vero remedii partem optimam sese repperisse. Unde et maturius accedat quo ei ipse obvenire valeat, cum paucis tamen, ne si cum multis adveniant, dissidentium animositate in bellum cogantur. Et pro itineris securitate si sibi placeat, ab ipsis legatis iurisiurandi fidem accipiat. Rex horum credulus, ab legatis iusiurandum pro fide accepit ac sine suorum deliberatione proditori obvenire non distulit. Proditor dolos dissimulans, cum paucis aeque ibi venit.[187] Datisque osculis excepti, familiaribus colloquiis cousi sunt. Et inter loquendum cohortem armatorum ab abditis evocat regique incauto inducit. Qui multitudini reniti non valens, a cohorte captus est, aliquibus cum eo captis, quibusdam etiam interemptis, reliquis quoque fugatis. Ductusque Peronam, carcerali custodiae deputatur. Germani rege amisso in diversa feruntur. Quorum alii de reditu domini elaborant, alii vero a spe deiecti Rodulfo regi favent, nec tamen in eius fidem penitus concedunt. Quorum priores exspectatione diutina domini libertatem opperientes, Heribertum proditorem de fidei violatione sepe convenerunt ac inde plurimum apud male conscios conquesti sunt. Quibus persuadere non valentes, de periurii reatu nihil ruboris incusserunt, cum ira dei eis immineret.

Charles should come as soon as possible to a place where they could meet, but with just a few men, because if they both came with large retinues, then the enmity between the opposing parties might lead to open fighting. And if Charles so desired, he could also ask the envoys to swear an oath guaranteeing his safe passage. Taken in by Heribert's words, the king had the envoys swear an oath confirming their good faith, and, without giving his advisers a chance to consider the matter, he went at once to meet his betrayer. In an effort to conceal his treachery, the traitor also arrived with a small escort. The two men greeted each other with an exchange of kisses and spoke on familiar terms. While they were talking, Heribert summoned a cohort of armed men from their hiding place and directed them toward the unsuspecting king. Unable to resist their superior numbers, Charles was taken captive by them. Some of his men were captured along with him, some were even killed, and the rest were put to flight. The king was taken to Péronne[95] and consigned to a prison cell.[96] With the loss of their king, the Germans[97] were torn in different directions. Some worked to bring about the return of their lord, while others gave in and supported King Radulf, without, however, giving him their complete loyalty. The first group, who were waiting with constant expectation for their lord to be freed, frequently charged the traitor Heribert with breaking his word and complained repeatedly about this to his accomplices. They failed to change their minds or to induce any sense of shame in them for their sin of perjury, even though the anger of God loomed over these men.

48

Exactio pecuniae publicae
piratis dandae

Haec dum agerentur, pyratae[188] Gallias irruperunt, pecudum armentorumque abductione multarumque opum exhaustu cum plurimorum captivitate terram depopulantes. Quorum impetum rex dolens, suorum usus consilio, exactionem pecuniae collatitiae fieri exactoribus indixit, quae hostibus in pacis pacto conferretur. Et collata, ad votum commune paciscuntur atque in sua concedunt. Rex vero, licet merens, ad alia se contulit. Exercitum[189] itaque in Aquitaniam adversus eius principem Wilelmum parat, eo quod subdi sibi contempneret. Et tempore oportuno cum exercitu super Ligerim affuit. At Wilelmus militum copiam non patiens, obruenti per legatos occurrit.[190] Illisque fluvio interfluente, in legatorum suasionibus dies tota consumpta est. Tandem die altera fidem utrimque pacti, a se discesserunt.

48

The Exaction of Tribute to Be Paid to the Pirates

In the meantime, the pirates invaded Gaul and devastated the land, leading off flocks and herds, removing much of the portable wealth, and taking numerous prisoners. Their attacks dismayed the king, who, on the advice of his counselors, ordered his officials to levy a general tax that would be turned over to the enemy to secure a truce. Once the tribute had been paid, the pirates agreed to terms and withdrew to their own territory. In spite of his grief, the king set himself to other tasks. He mustered an army to lead into Aquitaine against William,[98] the leading man of the region, because he refused to submit to his authority. At a suitable time Radulf came to the Loire with his army. William, however, could not resist the size of the king's army, and he sent envoys to meet with the man who was bearing down upon him. While the two parties waited on opposite sides of the river, their envoys spent the whole day in negotiations. On the second day both sides finally reached an agreement and parted from one another.[99]

924

49

Congressus Rodulfi regis
cum piratis, eorumque fusio

Rex inde regressus, febre acuta apud urbem Senonicam corripitur. Qui cum die cretica convaluisset, vi recidiva rursus opprimitur. Ac de salute desperans, Remos ad sanctum Remigium sese deferri fecit. Cui dona plurima largitus, elapso mense utiliter convaluit urbemque Suessonicam alia curaturus expetiit. Ubi cum apud principes rei publicae[191] consuleret, legati adsistunt qui pyratas[192] fide violata interiores Burgundiae[193] partes irrupisse asserunt, congressosque cum Manasse ac Varnero comitibus, Iozselmo atque Ansegiso episcopis, adeo defecisse ut eorum DCCCCLX apud montem Calaum sternerentur, nonnulli capti tenerentur; reliqua vero minorum manus lapsa profugio sit; Warnerus vero, equo occiso quo vectus ferebatur, X vulneribus perfossus interierit. His rex motus, diem alteram in partibus deliberationis totam consumpsit. Et die tertia edicto regio tirones ex citeriori Gallia intra dies XV collegit. Collectosque cum aliquot magnatibus super fluvium Sequanam adversa-

49

The Battle Between King Radulf
and the Pirates; Their Defeat

In the course of his journey back from Aquitaine, the king was stricken with an acute fever in the city of Sens, and although he recovered during the day of crisis, he suffered a relapse. Despairing of his life, he had himself brought to the monastery of Saint-Rémi at Reims. After bestowing many gifts upon the monastery, he made a successful recovery within a month, and after this he went to Soissons in order to take care of some other business.[100] While he was attending to affairs of state there with his leading men, messengers arrived bringing word that the pirates had violated their agreement and invaded inner Burgundy. At Chalmont they had done battle with counts Manasses and Warnerius and bishops Gauzlin and Ansegis, suffering a serious defeat in which 960 of their men were killed.[101] Some were also taken captive, while a remaining group of lesser importance slipped away and escaped. As for Warnerius, the horse upon which he was riding was killed, and he died after being pierced through with ten wounds. These events distressed the king, and he spent the whole of the next day in deliberations. On the third day he issued a royal decree ordering recruits to be assembled from Burgundy[102] within the next fifteen days. When they had assembled, he led them and several of the magnates against the enemy forces on the

925

riis inducit. At pyratae[194] renisuri obvenientes, a Gallis in sua castra redire coacti sunt. Galli fugientes insecuti, castris ignem inmittunt, congressique vehementi conamine, victos sternunt. At alii fuga pedestri, alii profugio navali elapsi sunt, alii cum castris succensi, alii ferro ad $\overline{III}$ interfecti sunt. Quos vero fuga exagitavit, post collecti, quodam suo oppido secus mare sito collecti sunt. Cui etiam Augae nomen erat.

50

Rollonis pyratae interitus, suorumque ruina

Quorum princeps Rollo sufficientibus copiis oppidum implens, bello sese manifeste paravit. Rex inde digressus, exercitum provocanti infert, congredi non differens. Oppidum aggressus est. Et obsidione disposita, vallum quo cingebatur irrumpit. Atque sic tirones peribolum conscendentes, adversarios pervadunt. Oppidoque potiti,[195] mares omnes trucidant. Feminis intactis parcunt. Oppidum diruunt atque comburunt. Cuius incendiis aere densato ac de-

Seine. The pirates came out to oppose them, but they were forced by the Gauls to retreat to their camp. The Gauls pursued them as they fled and set fire to their camp, whereupon they engaged them in battle and inflicted a devastating defeat upon them in a fierce struggle. Some of the pirates fled on foot and others by ship; some were burned up along with their camp, while about three thousand others fell to the sword. Those who had been dispersed while fleeing later reassembled, however, and gathered at Eu, one of their coastal strongholds.[103]

50

The Death of the Pirate Rollo and the Downfall of His Men

Their leader, Rollo, installed a garrison of sufficient strength in this stronghold and made open preparations for war. In response to his provocations, the king departed and led his army against him, showing no hesitation for battle.[104] He marched to the stronghold, and by laying siege to it, broke through the rampart that encircled it, whereupon the new recruits climbed over the inner wall and overran the enemy. Once they had taken control of the stronghold,[105] they slaughtered all the men, but spared the women, leaving them unmolested. They demolished and set fire to the

nigrato, in tetra caligine nonnulli evadentes, finitimam quandam occupant insulam. Quos sine dilatione exercitus aggressus appetit ac navali pugna victos opprimit. Piratae vitae spem amittentes, alii sese fluctibus immergunt ac enecantur, alii enatantes ab observatoribus iugulati sunt, alii nimia formidine tacti telis propriis sese appetunt. Et sic omnibus ademptis predaque direpta non modica, rex Belvacum rediit ibique resedit.

51

Item piratarum interitus

Inde audito Atrabatensium regionem a piratis aliis vexari, assumpto exercitu ab his qui loca maritima incolebant, repentinus in eos fertur. Piratae comminus congredi non ferentes, ab exercitu cedere coacti sunt. Ac coartati, saltu quodam vitam tueri nitebantur. At exercitus circumquaque eos obsidens, adeo urgebat. Illi vero, noctu eruptione facta, in

stronghold, and as the air grew thick and black from the flames, some of the enemy escaped amid the foul darkness and took possession of a neighboring island. The king's army pursued them without delay, assaulting the island and visiting a crushing defeat upon them in a naval battle. The pirates now abandoned any hope for their lives. Some plunged into the waves, where they drowned. Others tried to swim away but were caught and killed by lookouts. Still others were overcome with fear and turned their own weapons on themselves. And so, after they had all been killed and a great haul of plunder had been seized, the king returned to Beauvais and took up residence there.[106]

51

Further Destruction of the Pirates

When the king heard that the region around Arras was being plagued by a different group of pirates, he assembled an army from the inhabitants of the coastal districts and quickly moved to attack them. Unable to withstand a pitched battle, the pirates were forced to retreat before his army. Finding themselves cut off, they strove to preserve their lives in a wooded area, but the king's army surrounded them on all sides and pressed the attack relentlessly. At night the pirates broke out and moved on the king's camp. But

926

castra regis feruntur. Et circumvallante exercitu penitus inclusi, miserabili fortunae succubuere. Octo namque eorum milia ibi caesa referuntur. Quo tumultu rex[196] inter humeros sauciatus, Hildegaudus vero clarissimi generis comes interemptus est aliique nonnulli, nec tamen aliquo nomine clari. Rex victoria potitus, Laudunum rediit.

52

Lunae defectio

Tunc etiam luna XIIII terrae obiectu obscurata, visibus intuentium defecit. Acies quoque igneae Remis in celo visae sunt. Quibus presagientibus signis, febrium ac tussicularum morbus evestigio irrepsit. Unde nonnulli loetaliter affecti occubuere. Cum his quoque et litium tumultuatio inter regem ac Heribertum, qui Karolum sub custodia detinebat, non modica subsecuta atque exagitata est,[197] eo quod Heribertus[198] ab rege nimia expetebat, rex vero utpote insatiabili nihil accommodabat.

when the royal army surrounded them, they were completely hemmed in and succumbed to a wretched fate. Indeed, it is said that eight thousand of them were killed in that place.[107] During the battle the king was wounded between the shoulders, and Count Hildegaud,[108] who was of a very distinguished lineage, was killed, along with several others, although none of these men were of any repute. Victorious, the king returned to Laon.[109]

52

An Eclipse of the Moon

At that time the moon was obscured in its fourteenth day by the interposition of the earth, and it disappeared from the sight of observers.[110] Fiery armies were also seen in 927 the sky at Reims. These portents presaged a sudden outbreak of fever and coughing from which many people grew mortally ill and died. On the heels of these events, a contentious dispute broke out between the king and Heribert, who was keeping Charles in captivity, because Heribert was making unreasonable demands of the king,[111] while for his part the king refused to yield to Heribert, on the grounds that nothing would ever satisfy him.[112]

53

Falsa Karoli liberatio[199]

Regi ergo minas Heribertus[200] intendens, Karolum regem a carcere eductum in pagum[201] Veromandensem deduxit, non ut regno fidelis eum restitueret, at ut ex eius eductione aliquam suspectis[202] formidinem incuteret. Nortmannis itaque accersitis atque apud oppidum Augam collectis eum deducit ibique filius Rollonis pyratae, de cuius interfectione iam relatum est, regis manibus sese militaturum committit, fidemque spondet, ac sacramento firmat.

54

Sententia in Rodulfum pe <. . .>
ab <. . . . . .> ct <. . .>[203]

Exinde Heribertus,[204] Rodulfo regi invidens, admodum insidiabatur. Unde et cum Karolo Remos deveniens, pro eo Romam legatos dirigit ac Iohanni papae epistolam mittit,

53

The Fraudulent Liberation of Charles

Heribert, therefore, by way of threatening the king, took Charles out of captivity and brought him to the county of Vermandois, not in order to restore him to the throne as a loyal follower, but to inspire fear in those whom he mistrusted through his release. And so, having summoned the Northmen to assemble at the stronghold of Eu, he brought Charles before them, and there the son of the pirate Rollo[113] (whose death has already been mentioned[114]) committed himself into the hands of the king to become his vassal, pledged fealty to him, and confirmed his allegiance with an oath.[115]

54

Judgment Against
Radulf . . .[116]

Thereafter Heribert looked upon King Radulf with hos-   928
tility and began to plot against him in earnest. Accordingly, he took Charles with him to Reims, and he sent envoys to Rome on his behalf with a letter for Pope John in which he

per quam significabat contra Karolum nec sese coniurasse, nec coniurationis conscium fuisse, coniuratis tantum invitum cessisse. Unde et se velle plurimum ut Karolus regno restituatur, qui innocens sine causa abiectus sit. Nec solum se in hac esse sententia, at optimorum quosque,[205] preter hos qui donis multiplicibus corrupti sunt.[206] Quapropter et ipse auctoritate apostolica regno restitui regem abiectum iubeat. Quicumque eius precepto refragari nisus fuerit, anathemate perpetuae maledictionis condempnet, ac pro hac re episcopis atque principibus Galliarum et Germaniae epistolam dirigat, continentem et bonorum[207] benedictionem et contradictorum maledictionem. Legati ergo Romam properant,[208] sed consumpto itineris labore, nihil mandatorum peragunt. Namque a prefecto captus papa, eo quod a se plurimum dissideret, ab eo carcerali custodia detinebatur. Unde et sine legationis effectu digressi, in Gallias remearunt. Heribertus[209] vero, ad alia sese conferens, apud Hugonem Rotberti filium de fide inter sese habenda adeo satagebat. Quem et suasionibus efficaciter allicuit ac fide pacti sibi annexuit. Hugonis itaque efficatia persuasus, ad Rodulfum redit eique reconciliatus aliquandiu hesit. Cuius in multa gratia susceptus, ut se fidelitatis exsecutorem monstraret, Karolum mox Peronae in carcerem retrusit.

claimed that he had not conspired against Charles, nor had he been a party to the conspiracy, and that he had yielded only unwillingly to the conspirators. Hence he strongly desired to see Charles, who was guilty of nothing and had been deposed without cause, restored to the throne. It was not only he who held this opinion, but all of the best men, excepting those who had been corrupted by numerous bribes. For this reason, the pope, by virtue of his apostolic authority, should order the deposed king to be restored to the throne and condemn whoever tried to oppose his command with an anathema of perpetual malediction. And as part of this effort he should also send a letter to the bishops and the leading men of Gaul and Germany containing a blessing for good men and a curse for those who opposed his will. Therefore, Heribert's envoys hastened to Rome, but after going to all the trouble of making the trip, they were unable to accomplish any of the tasks that had been set for them. For the pope had been taken captive by the prefect of the city, with whom he was engaged in a bitter quarrel, and he was being kept under guard in a prison cell.[117] And so the envoys left without completing their mission and returned to Gaul. Heribert, meanwhile, turning to other matters, devoted himself to securing an agreement between himself and Hugh, the son of Robert. Successfully enticing him with persuasive words, Heribert bound Hugh to himself with a pledge of faith. Heribert, persuaded by the force of Hugh's words, went back to King Radulf, and after their reconciliation he remained loyal to him for some time. Once he had been welcomed back into the king's good graces, Heribert immediately put Charles back into prison at Péronne to show that he was a man of his word.[118]

55

Heribertus a rege Remense
episcopium accepit

Unde et ab rege donari petens, episcopium Remense sub optentu filii sui adhuc pueri ab eo accepit. Nam et tunc hac vita dignae[210] memoriae Seulfus metropolitanus decesserat. At quia aetas tenerior puerum sacris officiis prohibebat, Odelrico cuidam, ab Aquensi episcopio pyratarum insectatione pulso, pro eo ministrare concessum est. Cui etiam abbatiam sancti Timothei martiris ad usus proprios attribuit et insuper canonicorum victum simul impertivit. Rodulfus interea rex, quanta foret aequitas suae vitae demonstrare cupiens, ad Karolum ubi servabatur accessit. Apud quem multa de eius miseriis conquestus, sermone multiplici si offenderat suppliciter veniam postulabat. Et quoniam suscepti regiminis apicem penitus amittere non valebat, quod ratio conferebat ei restituit, sedes videlicet regias, hoc est Attiniacum et Pontionem. Sicque Suessionum remeavit.

55

Heribert Receives the Bishopric of Reims from the King

Seeking a reward from the king as a result, he received from him the bishopric of Reims in the name of his son,[119] who was still a child.[120] For Archbishop Seulf of worthy memory had just died.[121] Because his tender age prevented the boy from carrying out the sacred offices, a certain Odelric,[122] who had been driven from his bishopric of Aix-en-Provence by pirate attacks, was allowed to serve in his place. Heribert also gave the abbey of Saint-Timothy to Odelric to be used for his upkeep, and he granted him a clerical prebend as well.[123] Meanwhile, King Radulf, desiring to demonstrate the rectitude with which he lived his life, went to see Charles in captivity. After bitterly lamenting the miseries that Charles had been forced to endure, he spoke to him at length, humbly asking for his pardon if he had wronged him. And because he could not completely renounce the position of supreme authority that he had assumed, he restored to Charles that which he thought reasonable, namely the royal estates at Attigny and Ponthion. And with that he returned to Soissons.[124]

925

928

56

Karoli obitus

Karolus post haec tedio et angore deficiens, in machronosiam decidit. Humoribusque noxiis vexatus, post multum languorem vita privatus est. Rodulfus vero rex, pyratas Galliam Aquitanicam irrupisse per legatos comperiens eamque hostiliter debacchantes infestasse, vim inferre cogitabat.

57

Regis ac pyratarum conflictio, eorumque fusio

Edicto ergo regio omnibus qui de militari ordine valebant accitis ex Gallia Celtica cum[211] multis Belgarum, duodecim cohortes ordinat. Cum quibus iter arripiens, usque Lemovicas procedit. Ibique[212] legionibus dispositis, cum pyratae, regium equitatum[213] non sustinentes, profugio eripi niteren-

56

The Death of Charles

Afterward Charles's health began to decline from fatigue   929
and anxiety and he lapsed into a chronic illness. He was afflicted with noxious humors and after a long period of de-
bility he died.[125] When King Radulf learned from messen-   930
gers that pirates had invaded Aquitaine and were rampaging
wildly and plundering the region, he decided to take action
against them.

57

The Battle Between the King and the Pirates; the Rout of the Latter

He therefore issued a royal decree mustering all the
available men of the warrior class from Celtic Gaul and
many from Belgica, putting twelve cohorts at his command.
Setting out with these forces, he proceeded all the way to
Limoges. There he put his legions into the field, and because
the pirates could not withstand the king's knights, they tried
to take flight and escape, but they were driven back by the

tur, ab Aquitanorum legione repulsi sunt. Rex vero cum cohortibus prosecutus, gravi cede[214] pene omnes fudit, paucis
fuga lapsis. Suorum vero nonnulli sauciati ex vulnere conva-
luere. Aliqui etiam interfecti. Itaque factum est ut Aquitani,
gratias regi reddentes, multa ei benivolentia subdi voluerint,
ac iure sacramenti in fidem firmissimam concesserint. Quibus utiliter patratis, rex exercitum reduxit procinctumque
solvit.

58

Hugonis et Heriberti[215] dissensio

Dum haec gererentur, inter Hugonem et Heribertum de
prelaturae dignitate lites agitantur, efferatique sese predis et
incendiis afficiunt. Rex in Heribertum indignans, eo quod
perfidiae promtum esse cognosceret, Hugonis partibus favebat,[216] unde et Heriberti oppidum[217] Donincum nomine,
Hugone ascito, aggressus expugnat ac captum diruit. Nec
minus et Atrabatum obsidione adhibita cepit civesque victos ac iuratos sibi annexuit. Rex inde digressus, cum quietum sese arbitraretur, Heribertus, Germanis qui Rheni litora incolunt eductis, in regem fertur ac execrabili furore

legion of the Aquitainians. The king pursued them with his troops, however, and destroyed almost all of them in a tremendous slaughter, although a few managed to escape.[126] A number of the king's men were wounded but recovered from their injuries. Some were also killed. The end result was that the Aquitainians, giving thanks to the king, voluntarily submitted to him with great goodwill and swore an oath of steadfast fealty to him. At the successful conclusion of this campaign, the king led his army back home and laid down his arms.[127]

58

The Quarrel Between Hugh and Heribert

While this was going on, Hugh and Heribert were quarreling over the office of archbishop,[128] despoiling and burning each other's property in their fury.[129] The king was angry at Heribert because he had come to realize how prone to treachery he was, and he took Hugh's side. Consequently, after summoning Hugh, he marched on and assaulted one of Heribert's strongholds called Denain, which he captured and destroyed. He also besieged and captured Arras and bound the defeated townsmen to himself with an oath. The king departed from there, but while he thought that he

931

incendia rapinasque exercuit. Insuper et Hugonis oppidum, quod secus torrentem Vitulam situm Braina dicitur, occupat, capit, ac diruit.

59

. . . eratio in regem[218]

Huius vero contumeliae causam rex se constituisse intelligens, eius potentiam minuere quaerebat. Remensibus ergo civibus legatos mittit ac ut pontificem eligant precipit. Quod etiam ni faciant, alium preter eorum velle eis sese impositurum mandat. At cives, regiae legationis mandatum excipientes,[219] quid ipsi inde velint ac sentiant per suos legatos referunt. Sese videlicet regio iussu Heriberti filium, licet adhuc puerum, suscepisse atque pontificem elegisse. Inde etiam fidem ei factam accommodasse; quapropter inpossibile esse ut fide inviolata ab eo sic deficere possint. Rex partibus Heriberti cives favere intelligens, collecto exercitu, urbem repentinus aggreditur, ingredique prohibitus, obsi-

would have peace, Heribert took some Rhinelanders and moved against him, plundering and burning with detestable fury. He also invaded, captured, and destroyed a stronghold of Hugh's called Braine located on the Vesle River.[130]

59

. . . Against the King[131]

Realizing that he himself had brought about the occasion for this strife, the king set about trying to diminish Heribert's power. For this reason, he sent envoys to the townsmen of Reims instructing them to elect an archbishop and declaring that if they were unwilling to do so, he would impose someone else on them against their will. But after the townsmen had listened to the message brought by the royal envoys, they sent their own messengers to make their opinions and wishes known to the king. Specifically, they declared that it was by the king's orders that they had received Heribert's son and elected him bishop, despite the fact that he was still a child. They had already pledged their faith to Hugh, and for this reason it was impossible for them to abandon him like this without violating their word. When he realized that the townsmen were taking Heribert's side, the king assembled an army and made a sudden march on the city. When he was prevented from entering, he laid siege

dionem applicat ac urbanos resistentes fervidus adurget. Qui multa expugnatione vexati, tercia tandem ebdomada portas victi et supplices aperuere. Ingressusque urbem, rex, post nonnulla disposita, collato cum suis consilio, cives accersit.[220]

60

Oratio Rodulfi regis ad cives Remenses pro se suasoria

Coramque sic contionatus ait: 'Quantum,' inquiens, 'caedis, quantum etiam rapinarum res publica factione malorum nuper passa sit, optime, ut puto, nostis. Non enim fieri potuit ut tot malis ubique grassantibus intacti penitusque immunes relinqueremini. Nam cum vestra necessaria sepe direpta, sepe combusta sint, eorum calamitatem tolerastis. Et non solum publica exterius, at hic privata bona intrinsecus a sevissimo exactore Heriberto cotidie imminuuntur. Unde et vobis consulendum arbitror ut pastorem vobis commodum conibentia communi eligatis, cum ille tiranni filius, adhuc

to the city and bore down fiercely on the townsmen, who were holding out against him. Finally, during the third week, after suffering through an intensive siege, they admitted defeat and opened the gates in submission to him. Thereupon the king entered the city, and after attending to some business and taking counsel with his men, he called the townsmen together.[132]

60

King Radulf's Persuasive Speech to the Townsmen of Reims on His Own Behalf

He addressed them as follows: "You know well, I think, how much slaughter and rapine the kingdom has endured lately because of the factions of evil men. It was not possible that with so many evils everywhere running riot you would remain untouched and wholly unharmed. For when the things that you needed to survive were frequently plundered and burned, you were forced to endure their destruction. Nor is it only public property outside of the city, but also private property here within the walls that is every day diminished by the cruel exactions of Heribert. For this reason I think you should take counsel and come to a common agreement to elect a bishop who is suitable to you, since the tyrant's son is still a child and not fit for office, and canon

infantulus, vobis idoneus non sit, ac canonica auctoritas vacare aecclesiam pastore tanto tempore non permittat. Nec dedecoris quicquam in vos redundabit, cum militari violentia victos et captos alia sequi necessitas[221] adurgeat. Nec vos fateor tantum quantum ego in hoc negotio oberravi. Itaque fecisse me penitet. Peniteat et vos vestrarum rerum dispendium peraegisse. Reducite in mentem quanta vos calamitas affecerit. Considerate etiam quanto secundarum rerum successu provehi possitis, si bono pastore regamini.'

61

Electio Artoldi

Cives ab rege suasi, iussis regiis concedunt. Artoldus itaque monachus, rege iubente, ex coenobio sancti Remigii omnium consensu mox assumptus, per impositionem manuum episcoporum tempore constituto regali donatione consecratur episcopus. Qui prudenter ac strenue omnia gerens, satis suis profuit atque ex benefactis omnium et maxime suorum benivolentiam habuit.

law does not permit a church to go without a bishop for so long. No dishonor will redound against you, because necessity compels those who have been defeated and captured in war to change course. I admit that you have not erred to the same degree that I have in this matter, and for this reason I repent of what I have done. You, too, should repent that you are responsible for the destruction of your own property. Recall how much this disaster has affected you. Consider as well the good fortune and prosperity that would attend you[133] if you were ruled by a good bishop."

61

The Election of Artald

The townsmen were persuaded by the king's speech and complied with his orders. And so, at the behest of the king and with universal consent, the monk Artald[134] was quickly brought from the monastery of Saint-Rémi, and at the appointed time he was ordained bishop by virtue of the laying on of hands of the bishops and the dispensation of the king.[135] He was an energetic and prudent administrator who greatly benefited his followers, and his generosity won him the goodwill of all men, especially his own.

62

Captio Bovonis Catalaunici episcopi Laudunique arcis[222]

Quae dum gererentur, Bovo Catalaunensium episcopus fortuita peragratione a regiis stipatoribus captus, eo quod et ipse desertor ab rege defecerat, regi oblatus est. Qui apud regem, prodentibus sui facti consciis,[223] convictus, ergastulo mancipatur. Quo peracto, a pernicie Heriberti non desistens, Hugone ascito, cum $\overline{\text{VIII}}$ Laudunum appetit. Ubi cum Heribertus multa obsidione urgeretur, egrediendi locum ab rege postulat, eo quod copias militum ciborumque sufficientes non haberet. Quo ab rege obtento, cum suis ab urbe exivit, uxoremque in arce quam exstruxerat relinquens, cum copiis sese subventurum in proximo ratus. Rex vacuam urbem ingressus dolosque penitus advertens, arcem diuturna expugnatione vexat eamque circumquaque vallat, ac omnem egrediendi aditum obcludit, pugnam diutina congressione adhibens. At tanto certamine vires resistentium impares, armis depositis, cedunt ac pro vita supplicant. Tiranni vero

62

The Capture of Bovo, Bishop of Châlons-Sur-Marne, and the Citadel of Laon

While this was going on, Bovo, the bishop of Châlons-sur-Marne,[136] was captured by members of the king's retinue as he chanced to be traveling and delivered up to Radulf because he too was a traitor who had deserted the king. Betrayed by his accomplices, he was convicted before the king and confined to a prison cell. Subsequently Radulf did not cease from his efforts to destroy Heribert, and he summoned Hugh and marched on Laon with eight thousand men. When Heribert began to come under strain from the duration of the siege, he asked the king for the opportunity to come out, on the grounds that he did not have sufficient forces or supplies of food. When the king gave him leave to do so, he withdrew from the city with his men, but he left his wife[137] behind in the citadel that he had constructed, intending to return shortly with more troops to help her. When the king entered the empty city and realized that Heribert had deceived him, he began a continuous assault on the citadel, surrounding it on all sides, shutting off every avenue of escape, and launching constant attacks upon it. Because the forces of the defenders were unequal to a contest of this magnitude, they laid down their arms in submission and begged for their lives. The wife of the tyrant surrendered at the same time and came to the king with her

uxor simul victa, pro se petitura ad regem cum suis properat, arcem reddens ac egrediendi tantum locum petens. Rex vero feminam retinere dedignans, cum suis digredi permisit ac arcem exinde cum urbe obtinuit.

63

Interfectio Adelelmi comitis, a quodam clerico episcopium Noviomense expetente seducti

Ubi postquam[224] urbi tuendae necessaria ordinavit,[225] de episcopio etiam Noviomensi cui esset dandum deliberabat, cum tunc Ayrardus episcopus obisset. Nam Walbertus Corbeiensium abbas ei succedere petebatur,[226] vir strenuus ac liberalis et cui totius honesti decus admodum placuit. Nec minus et predictae urbis quidam clericus ab rege sese fieri successorem postulabat, vir barbarus, manu atque audatia nimius, et cui solitum erat rerum alienarum surreptionibus laetari. Hic ab rege civibusque abiectus, cor ad dolos convertit. Adelelmum itaque Atrabatensium comitem, cuius casus

followers to plead on her own behalf, handing over the citadel and asking only for the chance to leave. The king thought it beneath him to hold a woman in captivity and he allowed her to depart with her household. Thereupon he took control of the citadel along with the city.[138]

63

The Death of Count Adelelm, Who Was Led Astray by a Cleric of Noyon Who Desired the Bishopric

After he had made the arrangements necessary to secure the city, the king considered who should receive the bishopric of Noyon, since Bishop Ayrard[139] had recently died. Walbert,[140] the abbot of Corbie, an energetic and honorable man who delighted in the propriety of all that was virtuous, was canvased as his successor. At the same time a certain cleric of Noyon also asked the king to succeed to the bishopric. He was a barbarous man, steeped in violence and impudence, who was accustomed to take joy in pilfering other people's property. When this man was rejected by the king and the townsmen, he turned his thoughts to treachery. He went to Adelelm, the count of Arras (whose fate inspired sadness in many people), in the hope of corrupting him, humbly beseeching him for his help and prom-

932

merorem multis incussit, seducturus petit, eius auxilium
suppliciter petens ac suum pollicens. Sese ab rege contemptum penitus supprimens, 'Si,' inquit, 'per te episcopatus dignitate potiar, per me efficaciter comitatus honorem conse-
queris. Quod etiam sic fieri valebit, si nocturnus urbis muros
conscendas et me interius procurante tuos introducas. Ego
etiam cum pluribus adero, collectique in agmine, urbem
pervademus. Itaque fiet ut cives aut capiamus aut propulse-
mus.' Horum Adelelmus credulus, dictis suadentis favet.
Scelus ergo attemptaturus, urbem nocturnus cum ingentibus copiis petit. Clericus nulli in urbe male credulus, facinus
patrandum in loco opperiebatur. Quo Adelelmus accedens,
ab eo cum suis exceptus est. Densatique in unum, tubis ac
clamore ac armorum strepitu in noctis caligine urbem ex-
turbant. Unde cives excitati, cum sese dolo pervasos adver-
tissent, fuga ab hostibus erepti sunt. Nullus captus, eo quod
hostes in unum iuncti per urbem dispergi formidaverint.
Unde et omnibus profugium patuit. Cives itaque abducti, a
vicinis arma ac reliquas suppecias accipiunt et die quinta
magnanimes in urbem feruntur. Suburbani etiam feliciter
subveniunt. Pugnam ergo promptissime adhibent. Adelelmus vero clericusque cum suis acerrime renituntur. At vul-
gus qui in urbe remanserat eisque fidem sacramento fecerat,

ising his own in return. Concealing entirely the fact that he had been rebuffed by the king, he addressed him: "If," he said, "you help me to obtain the episcopacy, I can assure you that through my good offices you will soon become count. And indeed, this can be accomplished if you climb the walls during the night and bring some of your men into the city while I take care of things on the inside. I will be there to meet you with many men, and once we have joined together, we will spread throughout the city. In this way we will either take the townsmen captive or drive them out of the city." Believing what he had been told, Adelelm agreed to the proposal that was being urged upon him. And so, in an attempt to carry out this crime, he came to the city at night with a large force. The cleric, who was not so foolish as to trust anyone in the city, was waiting in place for him to carry out what they had planned. Adelelm approached and was received by the cleric and his men. Joining together in a single band, they threw the town into disorder in the blackness of night with horns, shouting, and the din of arms. When the townsmen awoke and realized that they had been treacherously overrun, they fled from the enemy. None of them were captured because, in their fear of being dispersed throughout the city, the enemy stayed together in one group, allowing all the townsmen to escape. Having stolen away, they received arms and other aid from their neighbors, and on the fifth day they mounted a valiant attack on the city, aided by the timely assistance of the suburban residents. They gave battle without any hesitation. Adelelm and the cleric, along with their followers, fought back fiercely, but the townspeople who had remained inside the city and had sworn an oath of fealty to them broke their agreement and began to cut

fidem abrumpit ac a tergo duriter eos cedit.[227] Facti autem hostium medii, in aecclesiam fugere coacti sunt. Urbani vero ab interioribus recepti, Adelelmum ac clericum persequi non desistebant. Portisque aecclesiae concisis, hostes appetunt ac secus altare utrosque cum pluribus aliis crudeliter trucidaverunt. Urbemque possidentes, sua recepere. Quibus patratis, ac legali repurgio aecclesia emundata, Walbertus Corbeiensis monachus et abbas, ab rege donatus, per metropolitanum Artoldum Noviomensium consecratur episcopus.

64

Aquitaniae atque Vasconiae principes regi Rodulfo militaturi occurrunt

Interea Gothorum principes Ragemmundus et Ermingaudus super Ligerim fluvium regi obvenienti militatum occurrunt eiusque manibus suas inserunt. Militiam spondent ac inde fidem, prout rex iubet, concedunt. Rex inde digressus, in Aquitaniae exteriora se contulit. Quo etiam et Lupus Acinarius Vasco, qui equum ferebatur habere annorum plus quam C et adhuc toto corpore validissimum, regi militatu-

them down from behind without mercy. They were surrounded by their enemies and forced to flee into a church. Meanwhile, the townsmen were admitted into the city by those inside the walls, and they pursued Adelelm and the cleric relentlessly. They cut down the doors of the church and attacked them, cruelly slaughtering both of their enemies next to the altar, alongside many of their followers. And after taking possession of the city they recovered their property. When this had been accomplished and the church had been liturgically purified, Walbert, the monk and abbot of Corbie, was invested with the episcopal office by the king and ordained as bishop by Archbishop Artald.[141]

64

The Leading Men of Aquitaine and Gascony Become Vassals of Radulf

The leading men of Gothia, Raymond[142] and Ermengaud,[143] came to the Loire to meet the king and become his vassals. Placing their hands between his, they pledged their military service to him and swore faithfully to do as he commanded. The king departed from there and went to the border of Aquitaine, where the Gascon Lupus Aznar (who was said to possess a horse that was more than one hundred years old and still in perfect health) came to meet him to be-

rus occurrit, ac provinciae[228] procuratione reddita, rex liberaliter reddidit atque a se principari concessit.

65

Futurorum malorum prodigia[229]

Hac quoque tempestate igneae Remis in caelo acies visae et flammae sanguineae quasi iacula aut serpentes discur-
rere. Mox quoque subiit et pestis, papulis erysipilatis innu-
meros enecans. Nec multopost et regis defectus subsecutus.
Nam cum autumnali tempore melancolia in patientibus redundaret, cacocexia, quod Latini malam corporis habitudi-
nem dicunt, toto autumno detentus est. Victusque humoris
superfluitate, defecit hominemque exivit. In basilica sanctae Columbae virginis apud Senonas multa amicorum ambitione[230] suorumque obsequio tumulatur. De regni amminis-
tratione nihil disposuit, at primatibus eam reliquit, eo quod
filios non habuerit, qui regnorum rerum potirentur.

come his vassal.[144] After he had handed over control of his province, the king generously restored it to him and granted him rule over it.[145]

65

Portents of Future Misfortunes

At this time fiery armies were seen in the sky at Reims, and flames the color of blood that darted back and forth like javelins or serpents. Soon afterward there was an outbreak of pestilence that left countless people dead from pustules caused by erysipelas.[146] The death of the king followed shortly thereafter. He was taken ill by cachexia (what the Latins call "a bad condition of the body") for the whole of the autumn; for it is at this time of year that excessive quantities of black bile accumulate in those who suffer from it.[147] Overcome by an excess of this humor, he succumbed and departed his mortal body. He was laid to rest in the church of the Holy Virgin Columba at Sens,[148] amidst a throng of friends and a retinue of his kinsmen.[149] He made no arrangements for the governance of kingdom, leaving it instead to the magnates because he had no sons to take over the affairs of the realm.[150]

934

935

936

BOOK TWO

I

Gallorum deliberatio
de rege creando

Post cuius exequias principes in diversa ducebantur finemque petebant varium. Galli namque Celtae cum Aquitanis Hugonem, Rotberti regis filium, Belgae vero Ludovicum Karoli sequebantur. Quorum neutri commoditas aderat regnandi, cum Hugo patrem ob insolentiam periisse reminiscebatur et ob hoc regnare formidaret, et Ludovicus in partibus Anglicae moraretur, eo quod illuc delatus infans ad avunculum Adelstanum regem fuerit ob Hugonis et Heriberti insectationem, eo quod ipsi patrem eius comprehendissent ac carceri trusissent. Galli itaque in regis promotione liberiores videri laborantes, sub Hugone duce deliberaturi de rege creando collecti sunt.

I

The Gauls Deliberate Upon
the Election of a King

After Radulf's funeral there was a difference of opinion 936 among the leading men and they began to work at cross-purposes. Those from Celtic Gaul and Aquitaine took up the cause of Hugh, the son of King Robert, while the men of Belgica supported Louis,[1] the son of Charles. Neither one of them had an easy path to the throne, however. Hugh had not forgotten that overweening ambition had brought about the death of his father, and for this reason he feared to take the crown for himself, while Louis was still in exile in England, having been brought as a child to the court of his uncle King Aethelstan to escape the persecution of Hugh and Heribert, who had captured and imprisoned his father.[2] The Gauls, therefore, striving to appear more independent in the elevation of a king, assembled under Hugh's leadership to deliberate upon the election.

2

Oratio Hugonis ducis ad Gallos
pro Ludovico

Quorum medius dux, post multam consultationem ad multam benivolentiam animum intendens, sic prelocutus ait: 'Karolo rege miserabili fortuna defuncto, sive id eo promerente, sive nostris flagiciis ipsa divinitate indignante, si quid a patribus et nobis ipsis admissum est quo divinitatis maiestas laesa sit, multo conatu inprimis id erit abolendum atque ab oculis amovendum. Discordiarum itaque molimina absint, et communi omnium conibentia de preferendo principe deliberemus. Pater meus, vestra quondam omnium voluntate rex creatus, non sine magno regnavit facinore, cum is cui soli iura regnandi debebantur viveret et vivens carcere clauderetur. Quod credite deo non acceptum fuisse. Unde et absit ut ego patris loco restituar. Nec vero alieni generis quemquam post dignae[1] memoriae Rodulfum arbitror pro-

2

Duke Hugh's Speech to the Gauls on Behalf of Louis

The duke took his place among them and after lengthy deliberations he spoke, inclining to great goodwill: "After King Charles met his wretched end, whether he brought this on himself or whether God was outraged by our transgressions, if our fathers or we ourselves committed any offense against the majesty of God, then we must make every effort to blot it out and remove it from our sight. Therefore, let us put a stop to our incitement of discord and consider with one common accord whom we should elevate as the first among us. The reign of my father, who in former days was chosen king with all of your approval, was tainted by a serious crime, since the only man who had the right to be king was still living, and yet while he was alive he was shut up inside a prison. This, you may be sure, was not acceptable to God. Thus, let no one think that I should be restored to the position of my father. Nor, however, do I think that anyone from a different family should be elevated to the throne to succeed Radulf of divine memory, for during his reign we

movendum, cum eius tempore visum sit quid nunc innasci possit, contemptus videlicet regis, ac per hoc principum dissensus. Repetatur ergo interrupta paululum regiae generationis linea, ac Karoli filium Ludovicum a transmarinis partibus revocantes, regem vobis decenter create. Sicque fiet ut et antiqua nobilitas regiae stirpis servetur, et fautores[2] a querimoniis quiescant. Iam quod potius est sequentes, a maritimis horis[3] adolescentem revocemus.' Quibus dictis Gallorum principes mira benivolentia cedunt.[4] Dux itaque legatos oratores trans mare ad accersiendum Ludovicum dirigit, qui ei a duce Galliarum aliisque principibus reditum suadeant ac de itineris securitate fidem sacramenti iure faciant, principum adventum usque ad ipsas litoreas arenas denuntient. Qui mox digressi, Morinum[5] devenerunt. Cuius in portu naves ingressi, velis tumentibus prosperis ventis, raptim ad terram devexi sunt.[6] Adelstanus rex in urbe quae dicitur Eurvich regnorum negotia cum nepote Ludovico apud suos disponebat. Huc legati devenientes, regem adeunt ac a duce magnatibusque Gallorum decenter salutant.[7]

caught a glimpse of what could happen now, namely contempt for the king, giving rise to dissension among the leading men. Therefore, let us seek out once more the line of royal birth, which has been briefly interrupted. Recall Louis, the son of Charles, from the kingdom across the sea and rightly make him your king. In this way the ancient nobility of the royal line will be preserved, and partisans on both sides will cease their quarrels. Let us now choose the best course of action and call the young man back from the lands by the sea." The leading men of the Gauls yielded to his words with marvelous goodwill. And so the duke dispatched envoys skilled in speaking across the sea to summon Louis. On behalf of the duke of the Gauls and the other leading men they were to persuade Louis to return, to swear an oath guaranteeing his safe passage, and to announce that the leading men of the Gauls would be coming down to the shore to meet him. The envoys departed at once and arrived in Thérouanne.[3] They took ship in the port there, and with swelling sails and favorable winds they soon made landfall. King Aethelstan was with his nephew in the city of York, attending to the business of the realm with his men. The envoys arrived there and came before the king, greeting him with due courtesy on behalf of the duke and the magnates of the Gauls.[4]

3

Legatio Gallorum ad Adelstanum regem pro Ludovico

Legationem etiam promulgantes, 'Ducis,' inquiunt, 'benivolentia atque omnium[8] qui in Galliis potiores sunt huc per undas ignoti maris devenimus; tanta est omnium voluntas omniumque consensus. Dignae[9] memoriae Rodulfo orbi subtracto, dux Ludovicum succedere procuravit, cum id multi inviti concederent, eo quod de patris captione filium adeo suspectum haberent. Attamen duci elaboranti id ab omnibus iocundissime concessum est. Ludovico ergo omnes bene per omnia optant. Nec sibi quicquam maius aut carius est eius[10] salute. Illum itaque omnes reddi petunt, quem in Galliis utiliter regnare cupiunt. Tempus constitui volunt quo regnaturo ad ipsa maris litora dux cum principibus occurrat.' Adelstanus rex barbaris[11] non satis credens, ab eis fidem per sacramenta[12] super hoc quaerit et ad votum accipit. Tempus quoque colloquii habendi statuitur. Legati ab rege munerati atque digressi, in Gallias mari remenso redeunt, ab rege gra-

3

The Embassy of the Gauls to King Aethelstan on Behalf of Louis

They then announced the reason for which they had come: "Prompted by the good will of the duke and all the most eminent men of Gaul, we have crossed the waves of the unknown sea to come here; so great is everyone's desire and agreement. When Radulf of worthy memory was taken from this world, the duke saw to it that Louis would be the one to succeed him, in spite of the fact that many people were reluctant to agree to this because the imprisonment of Charles made them mistrustful of his son.[5] Nonetheless, thanks to the efforts of the duke, everyone happily acceded to his wishes. Consequently, everyone wishes Louis well in all that he does. Nothing is more important or dearer to them than his well-being.[6] Hence they all seek his return, desiring that he should rule over Gaul for their benefit. They would like a time to be appointed for the duke and the leading men to come down to the shore to meet their future king." Not entirely trusting these barbarous[7] men, King Aethelstan asked them to prove their trustworthiness on this point by swearing oaths, and this was done in accordance with his wishes. The time at which the meeting would take place was also determined. After receiving gifts from the king, the envoys departed. They crossed the sea and returned to Gaul, bringing thanks from the king to the duke

tias duci referentes ac pro regis creandi advocatione multam eius amicitiam pollicentes. Dux itaque cum Galliarum principibus dominum regem excepturi, Bononiam veniunt, ac secus ipsas litoreas arenas collecti, tuguriorum incendio presentiam suam[13] iis[14] qui in altero litore erant ostendebant. Ibi enim Adelstanus rex cum regio equitatu nepotem praestolantibus Gallis missurus aderat. Cuius[15] iussu domus aliquot succensae sese advenisse trans positis demonstrabant.

4

Hugo et reliqui Galliarum principes[16] Ludovicum ab exilio revocant,[17] eiusque fiunt, et regem creant

Rex ergo[18] Odonem episcopum,[19] post Canthorbricensium metropolitanum, Gallis ex adverso positis legatum dirigit, magnae aequitatis ac eloquentiae virum, Ludovicum sese[20] libenter missurum mandans, si tanto illum in Galliis

and promising him Aethelstan's steadfast friendship in return for his support in making Louis king. The duke and the leading men of Gaul subsequently went to Boulogne to await their lord king. There they gathered on the sandy beach and set fire to some huts to make their presence known to their counterparts on the opposite shore. King Aethelstan had come there with his horsemen to send his nephew off to the waiting Gauls. On his orders, several houses were set alight to inform the men on the other side that they had arrived.[8]

4

Hugh and the Rest of the Leading Men of Gaul Recall Louis from Exile, Become His Vassals, and Make Him King

The king, therefore, dispatched Bishop Oda (afterward the Archbishop of Canterbury),[9] a man of surpassing fairness and eloquence, as his envoy to the Gauls waiting on the opposite shore. He brought word that the king would be happy to let Louis go so long as they showed him the same honor in Gaul that he himself had received among his own people (since they were no less capable of doing so), and they swore an oath to that effect. If they were unwilling to comply with his wishes, then he would give Louis one of his

honore proveant quanto ipse a suis provectus est, cum illi etiam non minus[21] id facere valeant, idque iureurando se facturos confirment. Quod si nolint,[22] sese ei[23] daturum suorum aliquod regnorum, quo contentus et suis gaudeat et alienis non sollicitetur. Dux cum reliquis Galliarum magnatibus[24] id sese facturum asserit, si rex creatus a suis consiliis non absistat. Prosecutusque iurisiurandi sacramentum non abnuit. Legatus itaque rediens, regi prestolanti haec omnia refert. Unde et securus nepotem cum iis qui apud se potiores erant multa[25] insignium ambitione navibus dirigit. Velisque aura commoda turgentibus pelagus ingressi, per quietum spumantibus remis ad terram feruntur. Firmatis vero tergo arenae navibus, Ludovicus[26] egreditur ac ducem occurrentem cum reliquis excipiens, iure sacramenti sibi adcopulat. Dux inde accelerans, equum[27] insignibus regiis adornatum adducit. Quem cum ascensui aptare vellet, et ille impatiens in diversa sese tolleret, Ludovicus agili exilitione prosiliens, equo strepenti neglecta stapha repentinus insedit. Quod etiam fuit omnibus gratum ac multae gratulationis provocatio. Cuius arma dux suscipiens, armiger precedebat, donec iussus[28] magnatibus Galliarum contulit.

own kingdoms to rule, where he would be content and happy among his own people and would not be bothered by strangers. The duke, with the agreement of the rest of the magnates of Gaul, declared that he would do as Aethelstan wished, so long as Louis did not stand aloof from his counsel after he had been made king. And he followed this by agreeing to swear an oath. Oda then returned and reported all of this to the waiting king. With his mind now at ease, Aethelstan sent his nephew down to the ships in the company of some of his more important men, surrounded by the trappings of honor. They embarked upon the sea with a favorable breeze and swelling sails, and the foaming oars bore them across the still water to land. After they had secured their ships on the edge of the beach, Louis got out and greeted the duke, who had come to meet him along with the others, and bound the duke to himself with an oath. The duke then hastened to bring forward a horse that was adorned with royal insignia. While he was getting it ready for the king to mount, it shied and reared up in different directions, but with a graceful leap Louis jumped up and suddenly seated himself upon the whinnying horse without using a stirrup. This delighted everyone who was there and won him a good deal of praise. Taking up Louis's arms, the duke went before him as his weapon-bearer until the king commanded him to hand his arms over to the other magnates of Gaul.[10] With these men in military atten-

Quibus militantibus, cum multa ambitione et obsequio Laudunum deductus est. Ubi etiam et regnandi[29] iura quindennis[30] accipiens, omnibus faventibus per domnum metropolitanum Artoldum cum episcopis XX rex creatus est. Inde quoque deductus, in vicinis urbibus gratulanter excipitur. Universi ei applaudunt. Omnes letantur, tanta omnium fuit et eadem mens.

5

Rex cum duce Burgundiam petit ac urbem Lingonicam bello premit[31]

Nec minus et Burgundiam petere ac urbes sedesque regias lustrare a duce monetur. Rex hortanti consentiens,[32] Burgundiam duce comitante ingreditur. Ad quem urbium principes benigniter confluentes, magnifice exceperunt ac rogati fidem iure sacramenti dederunt. Hugo tantum, Rodulfi regis frater, Lingonicam urbem possidens, regi occurrere distulit, [iis] qui occurrerunt admodum iratus. Rex dum

dance upon him, Louis was brought to Laon with a great deal of pomp and a large escort. Here, at the age of fifteen, he took up the rights of kingship, and with everyone's support he was consecrated king by Archbishop Artald, assisted by twenty bishops.[11] From there he was taken to the neighboring cities, where he was welcomed joyously. All the people cheered him on and everyone rejoiced, so great was the unity of sentiment that prevailed among them.[12]

5

The King Goes to Burgundy with the Duke and Besieges the City of Langres

In addition, Louis was advised by the duke to go to Burgundy and make a tour of the cities and royal residences there. The king gave in to his urging and went to Burgundy, accompanied by Hugh. The leading men of the cities came to meet him courteously, receiving him in splendid fashion, and they swore oaths of fealty to him when they were asked to do so. Only Hugh,[13] King Radulf's brother, who held the city of Langres, put off coming before the king, and he was very angry at those who did so. As Louis made a tour of his holdings over the next several weeks, he became aware of the hostility of his enemy. Resolving therefore not to forgo visiting any of the cities of Burgundy before he left, he sent

per aliquot ebdomadas sua lustraret, inimici invidiam advertit. Proponens itaque ante discessum nullam preterire urbem, legatos Hugoni dirigit qui a pertinatia eum revocent
ac ei de fide sibi servanda persuadeant. Qui apud eum pero-
rantes, nihil pacis, nihil regii honoris acceperunt. Unde et
digressi, audita regi referunt. Hugo preter ius sese aegisse
dinoscens, urbi copias deputat, ipse in partes regni exteriores usque ad tempus secedens. Rex vero pertinaci indignans,
exercitum urbi applicat, a parte qua planiciem prefert
pugnam acriter ingerens. Altera enim parte, latere montis
educto, pene inaccessibilis est. In parte ergo quae obsidioni
aptior est milites urbi rex cum duce adhibet. Quibus in-
pugnantibus, hostes vehementissime resistunt, telisque ac
lapidibus aerem densant, atque impetentes atterunt. Non
tamen usque ad effectum repulsionis perstare potuerunt.
Nam regii equitatus infestationem non ferentes, a parte pre-
rupta quae obsidione non premebatur nocte egressi aufuge-
runt. Cives vero qui remanserunt regi mox portas aperuere,
eum cum suis absque refragatione in urbe gratulabundi exci-

envoys to Hugh to recall him from his stubbornness and urge him to preserve his fidelity to the king. But after delivering their speech to Hugh, they heard nothing in response about peace or respect for the royal office, so they departed and related what they had heard to the king. Hugh, realizing that he had acted unlawfully, assigned troops to the city of Langres and withdrew to the outer parts of the duchy for the time being. The king, meanwhile, in his anger at Hugh's recalcitrance, brought his army to Langres and mounted a fierce assault upon the city from the side where it provided level ground. For the other side of the city, where the face of the hill sloped away, was virtually inaccessible. For this reason, the king and the duke deployed their forces where it was more suitable for a siege. The enemy resisted the besieging army ferociously, filling the air with stones and projectiles and wearing away at their attackers. They could not hold out long enough to succeed in driving them away, however. Unable to withstand the attacks of the king's knights, they slipped away during the night and fled via the steep part of the city that was not under siege. The townsmen who remained inside, however, soon opened the gates to the king, receiving him and his men into the city joyfully and without any resistance. After the king had taken

pientes. Qua rex potitus, ab eius episcopo aliisque regni pro-
ceribus obsides accepit, atque sic cum duce Parisium iter
retorsit.

6

Rex ducis procurationem
a se amovet

Rex felicium rerum successu elatus, preter ducis procu-
rationem res suas ordinari posse cogitabat. Unde et[33] rei militaris administrationem absque eo iam disponebat. Laudunum itaque tendit ibique matrem suam Ethgivam reginam
ad urbis custodiam deputat, ac exinde quaecumque preter
ducem adoriebatur. Quod etiam fuit non minimae[34] labis
seminarium. Dux etenim regem suae procurationis dispositionem reppulisse advertens, Heribertum comitem sibi as-
ciscit, plurima apud eum in regis contumeliam pertractans.
Amicitiam inter sese mutuam conditionibus utrimque confirmant.

control of the city, he took hostages from the bishop of Langres[14] and the other magnates of Burgundy, and with that he and the duke went back to Paris.[15]

6

The King Removes Himself from the Duke's Supervision

Puffed up by the success of these felicitous events, the   937 king started to think that his affairs could be managed without the duke's supervision. As a result, he began to oversee the direction of military matters without him. Accordingly, he went to Laon and assigned the task of protecting the city to his mother, Queen Eadgifu, and from then on the duke played no role in any of his undertakings. In fact, this turned out to be the source of great misfortune. For when the duke realized that Louis had rejected the supervision he had arranged over him, he admitted Count Heribert to his counsels and plotted with him intently to worst the king. The two men agreed to terms and sealed a mutual pact of friendship.[16]

7

Heribertus castrum Teodericium dolo capit, ac proditorem in vincula conicit

Heribertus itaque Walonem, regis fidelem qui castro quod Theoderici dicitur preerat, in dolo adiit ac de transfugio illum alloquitur. Nec diu moratus, decepto[35] persuadet, maiora pollicens ac plura promittens. Ille mox de pollicitis iusiurandum postulat, postulata sese sic facturum spondens. Tirannus libenter annuit. Nec minus et transfuga iuratus, tempus patrando facinori demonstrat. Immo et tiranni manibus sese exinde militaturum committit ac ex militia fidem accommodat. Quo peracto, in sua discedunt. Tempus advenit; Walo, simulatis negotiis, milites regios qui secum preerant in diversa, acsi regis causam facturos, disponit. Ipse castro evacuato solus cum famulis relinquitur. Nec defuit cum cohorte tirannus. Qui a transfuga susceptus, castrum ingreditur atque occupat. Intuitusque transfugam, 'Putasne,' inquit, 'tuae curae oppidum hoc reservandum?' Cap-

7

Heribert Captures Château-Thierry Through Treachery and Puts Its Betrayer in Chains

Thereupon Heribert approached Walo, one of the king's faithful men and the castellan of Château-Thierry, with deceitful intent and spoke to him about deserting over to his side. Before long he had beguiled and convinced him by making grand promises and lofty guarantees. Straightaway the castellan asked Heribert to swear an oath to do as he had promised, pledging in turn that he would do what was asked of him. The tyrant happily agreed to this, and after the traitor had bound himself with an oath, he set a time for the wicked deed to be carried out. Walo also committed himself into the hands of the tyrant to become his vassal from that day forward, and he swore an oath to serve him faithfully. Afterward they both went home. When the time came, Walo pretended that there was some business to take care of and sent the royal troops who garrisoned the castle with him off in different directions under the pretext that they were acting on behalf of the king. Walo was left alone in the empty castle with his servants. The tyrant did not fail to appear with a cohort of his troops. He was welcomed by Walo, whereupon he entered and took control of the castle. Then, turning his gaze to the traitor, he said, "Do you suppose that this stronghold is going to remain under your control?" And

tumque mox in vincula conicit suisque castri custodiam donat.

PRESAGIUM ADVENTUS[36] HUNGARORUM

Et nocte diei succedente, caeli pars prodigiose flammis erumpentibus in septentrione ardere visa est. Qua etiam mox prosequitur et Hungarorum per Gallias repentina persecutio. Qui nimium sevientes,[37] municipia aliquot villasque et agros depopulati sunt; basilicas quoque quamplures combusserunt, ac indempnes redire ob principum dissidentiam permissi sunt, cum magna captivorum multitudine. Rex enim copias non habens, ignominiam pertulit, et utpote a suis desertus, sevientibus cessit.

8

Oppidum Montiniacum rex per cohortem expugnat eiusque principem capit

Quibus digressis, rex ad oppidum Montiniacum cohortem mittit quae illud occupet captumque diruat, eo quod Serlus quidam latrocinia exercens illic receptui sese habe-

with that he seized him and immediately put him in chains, after which he put his own men in charge of the castle.[17]

A Portent of the Coming of the Hungarians[18]

When day gave way to night, part of the northern sky could be seen blazing ominously with eruptions of fire. Soon afterward there followed a sudden onslaught of the Hungarians throughout Gaul. In their terrible savagery they ravaged a number of towns, villages, and fields. They burned a great many churches as well, but because of the dissension among the leading men, they were allowed to withdraw unscathed with a great haul of captives. For without forces at his disposal, the king was compelled to endure this disgrace, and because he had been abandoned by his men, he yielded in the face of their savagery.[19]

8

The King's Troops Besiege the Stronghold of Montigny and Capture Its Commander

After they had departed, the king sent a cohort to seize, 938 capture, and destroy the stronghold of Montigny, because a certain Serlo was operating as a brigand there and using it as

bat. Cohors ergo oppidum appetens, latrones impugnat. Nec morata vi capit, comburit, ac subruit. Latronem principem comprehensum, dimissis minoribus, regi deducit. Qui cum iussu regio gladiatori decollandus traderetur, Artoldi Remorum metropolitani interventu veniam[38] ab rege obtinuit, ac sese ulterius non latrocinaturum iuratus, abire permissus est. His ita gestis, rex in partes Belgicae mari contiguas concessit, oppidum in ipso maris portu exstruere nisus. Cui etiam loco Guiso est nomen. Exceptusque ab Arnulfo regionis illius principe, apud eum de oppidi erectione agebat. Ubi dum in agendo moras faceret, castrum Remensis aecclesiae nomine Causostem, secus fluvium Matronam[39] ab Artoldo presule editum, Heribertus proditione ingreditur ac capit. Castrensesque invadens, eorum potiores abducit. Rura circumquaque depopulatur ac ingentibus praedis oppidum implet et cum armis milites ibi deponit, aliorsum ipse secedens.

a base. The king's troops therefore marched on the stronghold and attacked the brigands. And in short order they
captured, burned and destroyed it. They took the leader of
the brigands prisoner, and after releasing his underlings,
they brought him before the king. At Louis's command he
was handed over to the executioner to be beheaded, but
through the intervention of Archbishop Artald of Reims he
won a pardon from the king, and after swearing an oath not
to engage in brigandage any more, he was allowed to depart.
After this, the king withdrew to the area of Belgica near the
coast and directed his efforts toward the construction of a
stronghold in a seaport there called Guines.[20] He was welcomed by Arnulf,[21] the leading man of the region, with
whom he discussed the building of the stronghold. While
the king was delayed in this activity, Heribert used treachery to seize control of the castle of Chausot, which belonged
to the church of Reims and had been built on the Marne
River by Archbishop Artald. He captured the garrison and
led away the most important members. After plundering
the surrounding countryside and filling the stronghold with
the spoils, he left weapons and troops there and left to go
elsewhere.[22]

9

Rex Lauduni arcem capit

Interea regi ab metropolitano per legatos ista suggeruntur. Qui mox coeptum negotium intermittens, suo auxiliaturus regreditur. Milites colligit ac exercitum parat. Cum quo Laudunum veniens, arcem ab Heriberto nuper ibi exstructam et a suis adhuc detentam obsidet. At qui in arce erant rebellioni sese parant. Rex ergo circumcirca sagittarios adhibens, missilibus evincere instabat. In quo tumultu hinc inde quam plures sauciati fuere, cum non minus qui in arce erant sagittis aliisque missilibus uterentur. Rex ergo cum finem oppugnandi viribus non fecisset, ingeniose eos capere cogitabat.

9

The King Captures the Citadel of Laon

When messengers sent by the archbishop brought word of this to the king, he set aside the task that he had undertaken and went back to help his ally. He mustered his fighting men and prepared his army for battle. Arriving at Laon with his troops, he laid siege to the citadel that Heribert had recently built there, which was still occupied by his men. For their part, those who remained in the citadel prepared to hold out against him. The king, therefore, surrounded them with archers and tried to overwhelm them with missile fire. In the ensuing battle there were a great many casualties on both sides, since the men inside the citadel were also using arrows and other missiles. Since the king could not bring an end to the fighting through force, therefore, he contemplated using strategy to capture the garrison.[23]

10

Machinae compositio

Fecit itaque ex vehementissimis lignis compactis machinam, instar longilaterae domus, duodecim virorum capacem, humani corporis staturae in alto aequalem. Cuius parietes de ingenti lignorum robore, tectum vero de duris ac intextis[40] cratibus exstruxit. Cui etiam intrinsecus rotas quatuor adhibuit, unde machina ab iis qui intrinsecus laterent usque ad arcem impelleretur. At tectum non aeque stratum fuit, verum ab acumine dextra levaque dependebat, ut iactis lapidibus facilius lapsum preberet. Quae exstructa, tironibus mox impleta est ac ad arcem rotis mobilibus impulsa. Quam cum a superioribus hostes rupibus opprimere conarentur, a sagittariis undique dispositis contumeliose repulsi sunt. Ad arcem itaque machina deducta, murus ex parte suffossus atque eversus est. Hostes multitudinem armatorum per hunc hiatum possibile introduci formidantes, arma deponunt ac regiam clementiam implorant. Rex ergo amplius tumultuari prohibens, intactos pene comprehendit, preter hos qui in militari tumultu sauciati fuere, suosque ad urbis tutelam in arce deposuit.

10

The Construction of a Siege Engine

And so he had a siege engine made out of stout, tightly bound timbers in the shape of a house with long sides. It was capable of holding twelve men and equal in height to a human body. The walls were made of very strong timbers and the roof of tough interwoven wicker lattices. Four wheels were placed inside so that the device could be rolled up to the citadel by the men who were hiding within. The roof was not laid smooth; instead the top sloped away from its peak to the left and right so that it could more easily deflect rocks that were hurled at it. When it was complete, it was filled with newly levied troops and rolled up to the citadel on moving wheels. The enemy tried to attack it from the hillside above, but they were beaten back in humiliating fashion by the archers who had been deployed all around it. After the siege engine had been brought up to the citadel, part of the wall was undermined and collapsed. Fearing that this breach would allow great numbers of armed men to enter, the enemy laid down their arms and implored the king for mercy. The king, therefore, called an end to the fighting and seized most of the garrison unharmed, save for those who had been wounded in the battle, and he put his own men inside the citadel to guard the city.[24]

II

Dolus Arnulfi atque oppidi Monasterioli captio

Haec dum gererentur, Arnulfus predictus Morinorum princeps Erluini oppidum secus mare situm Monasteriolum nomine suae parti addere cogitans, eo quod ex navium advectationibus inde plures questus proveniant, adipiscendi insidias componebat. Dirigit itaque quosdam suorum callidos in veste abiecta, dolos dissimulans, ad quendam eiusdem oppidi custodem, quem etiam in proditione non diffidebat facillimum. Qui ingressi, eum a domino salutant ac loquendi oportunitatem petunt. Secedunt ergo. Illi tantum esse negotium propter quod venerant simulantes ut a quo exordiri possent penitus ignorarent, aliquantisper herebant. Et tandem suspirantes, 'Eia te,' inquiunt, 'Rotberte! Eia te, Rotberte!' (sic enim vocabatur) 'Quantis malis elapsus, quantis periculis exemptus es, et quanti insuper secundarum rerum tibi debentur successus!' Et statim protulerunt duos anulos, alter aureum, alter vero ferreum. 'Et vide,' inquiunt, 'quid in his perpendi valeat.' Quo quid esset ignorante, illi prosecuntur: 'In auro dona egregia, in ferro vincula carceris puta. Instat etenim tempus quo et oppidum hoc in ius alterius

II

The Treachery of Arnulf and the Capture of Montreuil

While this was going on, Count Arnulf of Flanders set   939
about devising a plot to capture Montreuil, a coastal stronghold that belonged to Erluin,[25] intending to add it to his possessions because of the great profits it derived from mari-
time traffic. He sent some clever men of his, dressed up in
shabby clothes in an effort to disguise his trickery, to one of
the stronghold's guards, a man whom he was confident could
easily be persuaded to turn traitor. Entering the stronghold,
Arnulf's men greeted the guard on behalf of their lord and
asked for an opportunity to speak with him, whereupon
they withdrew in private. For a while they hesitated, pretending that the business for which they had come was so
important that they were quite at a loss as to where they
should even begin. At last with a sigh they said: "Come now,
Robert, come now, Robert! (for this was his name). How
many misfortunes you have escaped! How many dangers you
have survived! And above all, how much success and good
fortune are owed to you!" They immediately put before him
two rings, one made of gold and the other of iron. "Consider
the meaning of these objects," they said. When he professed
his ignorance, they continued: "Imagine that the golden ring
represents magnificent gifts and the iron ring the chains of a
prison. For the time has arrived when this stronghold, too,

concedat. Tacenda haec tuae fidei committimus. Res vobis nesciis disposita est. Nos quoque id ipsum penitus ignoramus. At rei summam scire non negamus. Mortem loquimur aut exilium. Unde et tibi Arnulfus comes consulens, futurae cladis calamitatem per sua indicia significavit, hortans ut ad sese transeas et ab eo auri et argenti insignia terrarumque copiam ac militum multitudinem accipias, cum dono regis in manus Nortmannorum, qua arte nescimus, in proximo sitis deventuri. Et quid super his tibi visum fuerit, amico per nos respondere ne differas.' Ille cupiditate ductus, proditionem[41] addubitat. Haerebat ergo stupens. Proponit sibi tandem proditionis dedecus ea posse necessitate purgari, quod omnes oppidanos in proximo aut exulaturos aut morituros sibi innotuit. Proditionem ergo spondet ac iuratus fidem dat. Nec minus et illi de pollicitis iurant. Tempus facinori datur ac sacramento firmatur. Legati digressi, sese persuasisse referunt.

must pass under someone else's control. We are trusting you to remain silent about this. Arrangements have been made that you are not aware of; indeed, we ourselves know nothing about it. But we do not deny that we know what the end result will be, and we shall tell you: it is either death or exile. It is for this reason that Count Arnulf, who is looking out for your interests, has shown you these signs as a warning of the disaster that is to come. He urges you to come over to his side, where you will be rewarded with gold and silver finery, abundant lands, and a multitude of men to serve you, since through the dispensation of the king you are all going to fall into the hands of the Northmen, though in precisely what manner we do not know. Do not delay sending word to your friend Arnulf through us to let him know of your decision in this matter." Driven by greed, Robert wavered over the betrayal. He hesitated, at a loss for what he should do. At last he told himself that this shameful act of treachery could be excused by the plight in which he found himself, since he knew that all the members of the garrison were soon going to be exiled or put to death. Therefore, he promised to betray the stronghold and pledged his faith by swearing an oath. Arnulf's men likewise swore to do as they had promised. A time was appointed for this wicked deed and confirmed with an oath. The messengers then departed and informed Arnulf that they had succeeded in persuading him.[26]

12

Ingressus Arnulfi in Monasteriolum

Arnulfus itaque militum electorum copiam colligit, facinus quaesitum patraturus. Iterque carpens cum duabus cohortibus, usque⁴² oppidum pene devenit. Sol iam occiderat. Proditor per portam quosdam emiserat, acsi aliqua utilia curaturos. Unde et ipse in muro stans, facem ardentissimam pretendebat, veluti famulis emissis lumen ministraturus, quo etiam luminis signo per legatos aditum significaverat.⁴³ Huc Arnulfus cum equitatu irruens, per portam patentem oppidum ingressus est. Eoque potitus, Erluini uxorem cum filiis capit ac eius thesauros diripit. Erluinus vero habitu immutato e medio hostium elapsus est. Arnulfus quoque, omnibus pervasis, oppido suos deputat. Erluini uxorem cum natis Aedelstano regi Anglorum servandos trans mare deportat. Sicque ad sua, oppido suis munito, rediit.

12

Arnulf's Entry into Montreuil

Arnulf then assembled a force of picked fighting men to carry out the criminal act that he had planned. He set out with two cohorts and got almost as far as the stronghold. By now the sun had set. The traitor had sent some men out through the gate, under the pretext that they were going to attend to some necessary business. He then stood atop the wall and held aloft a burning torch, ostensibly to provide light for the servants whom he had dispatched, whereas in fact he had sent word through the envoys that this would be the signal for them to approach. Arnulf and his knights charged forward and entered the stronghold through the open gate. Once he had it under his control, Arnulf took Erluin's wife and children prisoner and seized all of his valuables. For his part, Erluin managed to escape from the midst of his enemies in disguise. Arnulf ransacked everything and put his men in charge of the stronghold. He shipped Erluin's wife and children across the sea to Aethelstan, king of the English, for safekeeping, and after he had garrisoned the stronghold with his own men, he returned home.[27]

13

Conquestio Erluini apud Wilelmum ducem de castri uxorisque et natorum amissione

Erluinus vero vix mortis periculo liber, ad Wilelmum principem Nortmannorum sese contulit, plurimam de suis casibus querimoniam apud eum agitans, sese inquiens infeliciorem, cum oppido et militibus privatus, uxore filiisque orbatus, nihil preter corpus possideat. De oppidi amissione non se adeo affici, cum id sine spe aliqua recuperandi non sit, eo quod terra immobilis ac oppidum intransitivum sit. Uxoris vero ac filiorum privatio calamitatem interminabilem pretendere videntur, cum illis consumptis, ipse doloribus assiduis urgeatur, et non consumptis, at sub aliena dominatione detentis, ipse vana seducatur exspectatione. Quare quoque ad petenda solatia se venisse memorabat, ac gemebundus hec indesinenter petebat.

13

The Complaint of Erluin to Duke William Concerning the Loss of His Fortress, His Wife, and His Children

Erluin was scarcely out of danger of death when he went before Duke William of the Northmen and poured out a long tale of woe about his misfortunes, declaring himself a miserable wretch because now that he had been dispossessed of his stronghold and his fighting men and robbed of his wife and children, he possessed nothing but his own body. He was not quite as distraught about losing Montreuil, for there remained some hope of recovering it, since land was immovable and the stronghold was not going anywhere. But the loss of his wife and children seemed to spread before him an endless source of misery, because if they died, he would be oppressed by continual grief, whereas if they lived but remained under someone else's power, he would be the prey of idle hopes. For this reason he said that he had come seeking relief from his sorrows, and in his grief-stricken state he did not cease asking for help.

14

Erluinus oppidum expugnat
ac capit

Princeps his querimoniis motus, auxilium annuit ac militum copiam ei committit. Erluinus itaque ad oppidum properat ac tempestivius cum copiis appetit circumque vallat terra marique. Instat itaque atque acriter adurget. Tandem vero multa expugnatione attritum ingreditur totumque pervadit. Arnulfi milites omnes comprehendit. Quorum alios gladio enecat, alios uxori natisque repetendis conservat.

15

Congressus Erluini cum
militibus Arnulfi

Arnulfus, tanta suorum calamitate confectus, milites[44] colligit eosque in Erluinum mittit, qui eius terram usque ad oppidum depopulentur. Directique incendiis circumquaque

14

Erluin Assaults and Captures the Stronghold

Moved by his pleas, the duke agreed to help and provided him with force of fighting men. Erluin therefore hurried to Montreuil and made a timely assault upon the stronghold, encircling it by land and sea. He pressed the attack and kept up a fierce assault. At last, after he had worn the defenders down in a long siege, he entered and took control of the whole stronghold. He took all of Arnulf's men captive, putting some to the sword and keeping others to use in ransoming his wife and children.

15

The Battle Between Erluin and Arnulf's Men

Distraught at the disaster his men had suffered, Arnulf assembled his troops and sent them against Erluin with instructions to despoil his territory all the way to Montreuil.

ac rapinis admodum deseviunt, multaque rerum preda abducta, festinabant, cum legati ab Erluino affuerunt qui indicarent quod nisi totam predam sine mora redderent, sine mora eis esse congrediendum. Hostes legationem spernentes, capta abducere accelerabant. Legati regressi, sese abiectos referunt. Erluinus cum quadringentis armatorum mox processit ac festinantibus supervenit. Illi vero, preda relicta, conversi irruentibus obvertuntur. Signisque collatis, acriter dimicatum est. Predones fere omnes gladio occubuere, preter hos quos fuga belli violentiae exemit. Et tamen ii,[45] cum fuga eos exagitaret, ab Erluino post insectante atrociter fusi sunt. Erluinus, predis receptis, cum ingentibus hostium manubiis ad sua feliciter remeavit.

16

Belgicorum querimonia apud[46] regem super eius levitate

Quo tempore Belgicorum principes ad regem conveniunt ac Lauduni apud eum gravissime conqueruntur, eo quod inconsultus omnia appetat. Si eorum quoque consiliis ad-

Having been sent off, they savagely raided and burned the surrounding area, and after carrying off a great haul of plunder, they were hastening away, when envoys arrived from Erluin to inform them that if they did not return all of their booty immediately, he would meet them in battle at once. Scoffing at their message, the enemy hurried to make off with what they had taken. The envoys then returned and reported that they had been treated with contempt. Erluin immediately set out with four hundred armed men and overtook his enemies as they were hurrying to get away. Abandoning all of their loot, they turned to face their attackers. Battle was joined, and there was fierce fighting. Almost all of the raiders fell to the sword, except for those whom flight delivered from the violence of battle. Erluin, however, pursued these men as they fled and cut them down without mercy. After recovering what had been plundered and capturing a great deal of booty from his enemies, he returned home victorious.[28]

16

The Complaint of the Men of Belgica to the King Concerning His Immaturity

At this time the leading men of Belgica[29] went before the king at Laon and complained bitterly to him that he was undertaking everything without seeking counsel. They told

quiescat, in bonum exitum res suas deventuras memorant. Ad hoc etiam sese convenisse, ut quid velit eis iniungat, quod cupit ingerat. Si velit, consilio et armis, terra marique contra hostes sese congressuros. Rex, ab eis fide suscepta, cum multa benivolentia redire permisit, si fortuna quandoque postulet redire iubens. Nec multopost et ab Aedelstano Anglorum rege classis regi cum copiis missa est. Audierat enim illum ab iis[47] qui maritima incolebant loca exagitari, contra quos classis dimicaret regique nepoti auxilium ferret. Comperto vero contra regem illorum neminem stare, ipsumque regem in partes Germaniae prosperum secessisse, mari remenso ad propria remeat.

him that if he followed their advice, then all of his affairs would prosper. Indeed, it was for this reason that they had come before him, so that he might impose upon them whatever tasks he wished and burden them with whatever responsibilities he desired. If it was his will, they would employ their counsel and their arms to meet his enemies in battle on both land and sea. The king accepted their profession of loyalty and allowed them to depart with great goodwill, ordering them to return should circumstances ever demand it. Not long after this, King Aethelstan of England dispatched ships and men to the king. For he had heard that Louis was being troubled by the inhabitants of the coastal regions, and the fleet was intended to do battle with his enemies and bring help to his nephew.[30] But when it was discovered that none of these people were contesting Louis's authority and that the king himself had departed for Germany in good order, the fleet crossed back over the sea and returned home.[31]

17

Rex in Belgica suos sibi sociat et Ottonis fautores ultra Rhenum fugat

Rex[48] in pago Elisatio cum Hugone Cisalpino principe locutus, Belgicos exteriores qui ad se nondum venerant sibi asciscebat. Et qui partibus Ottonis favebant ultra Rhenum fugere compulit. Presenserat enim Ottonem velle in suum ius Belgicam transfundere. Unde et equo ei non ferebatur animo. Truculentius ergo contra illum agitans, suos de regno exturbavit. Qui vero sibi consentiebant[49] asciscens, Gislebertum videlicet Belgicorum ducem, Theodericum quoque atque Isaac comites, cum eis consilium confert, ac pro fide habenda iusiurandum ab eis accipit, post haec Laudunum rediens. Ibique eiusdem urbis episcopum Rodulfum, proditionis evidentissime insimulatum, ab urbe pellit suosque simul eicit. Quorum etiam res suis contulit.

17

The King Brings His Followers in Belgica Over to His Side and Drives the Supporters of Otto Back Across the Rhine

After speaking with Duke Hugh of Burgundy in the county of Alsace, the king brought over to his side the men of outer Belgica who had not yet come over to him. Those who supported Otto[32] he forced to flee across the Rhine. For he had discovered that Otto intended to assert control over Belgica, and he did not suffer this calmly. For this reason, he moved against him aggressively and drove his followers out of the region. Summoning to his side those who supported him, namely Duke Gislebert of Belgica and counts Thierry[33] and Isaac,[34] he took counsel with them and received oaths of fealty, after which he returned to Laon. He expelled from the city Bishop Rodulf (who had been accused of treason on very credible grounds) and his followers and bestowed their possessions upon his own men.[35]

18

Otto Belgicam devastat

Otto interea Belgicos comperiens regis partes sustentare et a se penitus defecisse, Rheno transmisso, Belgicam[50] ingressus, eius loca plurima incendiis ac ingentibus predis devastat, eo quod ex collatione paterna princeps[51] fieri Belgicis dedignantibus contenderet, cum eius pater Saxoniae solum propter[52] Sclavorum improbitatem rex creatus sit, eo quod Karolus, cui rerum summa debebatur, adhuc in cunis vagiebat. Multam itaque predam abducens, Rhenum transmeat.

19

Impetus Gisleberti in Germania, eiusque ac suorum fusio

At Gislebertus dux dedecoris iniuriam ultum ire volens, omnem Belgicam lustrat ac tirones lectissimos in unum cogit, senes tantum emeritos patriae linquens. Factoque exer-

18

Otto Ravages Belgica

Meanwhile, when Otto learned that the men of Belgica had taken the king's side and abandoned him completely, he crossed over the Rhine and entered Belgica. There he plundered and burned widely, attempting on the basis of a grant from his father[36] to assert his lordship over the area against the wishes of the men of Belgica—this despite the fact that his father had only been made king of Saxony in order to deal with the treachery of the Slavs, because Charles, who had the title to the throne, was still bawling in his cradle.[37] And so, after hauling off a great deal of plunder, Otto crossed back over the Rhine.[38]

19

Gislebert Invades Germany;
He and His Men Are Defeated

Eager to avenge this insult to his honor, Duke Gislebert traversed all of Belgica, assembling a highly select body of new recruits and leaving at home only the old men who were

citu, Rhenum transmeat ac patriam solotenus incendiis ingentibus vastat. Armentorum etiam pecudumque predam nimiam exercitus congregat abducitque. Iam vero flumen ingredi parabat, cum Otto exercitum accelerantibus induxit. Belgici renitentes, cum Germanis secus fluvium congressi sunt atque in parte utraque nimium fusi. Qua die Germanorum victoria aegre sustentata est, et licet innumerabilibus suorum stratis, tamen enituit. Nam Gislebertus dux suorum fusione exercitum defecisse advertens, fuga periculum evadere nitebatur. In fluentum itaque cum equo prosilit. Qui cum fluminis pelagus enatare non posset, vi undarum victus periit atque sessorem inmersit.[53] Belgicorum vero alii fluvio enecati, alii ferro caesi, alii capti, nonnulli vero profugio erepti[54] sunt. Ludovicus rex Gislebertum extinctum comperiens, multam in eius casu commiserationem habuit. Atque in Belgicam profectus, eius uxorem Gerbergam, Ottonis sororem, coniugio duxit eamque secum reginam in regnum coronavit.

no longer fit to serve. When he had assembled his army, he crossed over the Rhine and devastated the entire area down to the very soil with widespread burning. In addition, his men gathered together and led off an enormous haul of cattle and other livestock. They were preparing to enter the river, when Otto sent his army against them in their haste. The men of Belgica fought back, engaging the Germans in battle near the river, and on both sides the losses were heavy.[39] The Germans just managed to eke out a victory that day, and although countless numbers of their men were killed, it shone forth nonetheless. When Duke Gislebert realized that his men had been routed and his army was lost, he tried to escape and save himself. He plunged into the flowing river on horseback, but his horse could not swim against the powerful current. Overcome by the force of the waves, it drowned, dragging its rider down to the bottom along with it. As for the men of Belgica, some drowned in the river, some were cut down by the sword, others were captured, and a number fled and managed to escape. When King Louis learned of Gislebert's death, he grieved sorrowfully for his untimely end. He subsequently departed for Belgica and married Gislebert's widow, Gerberga (a sister of Otto), and had her crowned with him as queen over the realm.[40]

20

Wilelmus dux piratarum regi contra omnes fidem iurat

Dum haec Lauduni gererentur, Wilelmus piratarum dux legatos regi dirigit qui sese satis ei fidelem indicent; quo rex iubeat, sese occursurum, fidemque contra omnes polliciturum. Quorum legationem rex multa benivolentia excipiens, in pagum Ambianensem sibi occurrendum constituit, eo quod ibi specialiter utilia quaedam per illos determinanda forent. Legatis itaque abductis, rex ad locum condictum tempore statuto devenit. Cui etiam dux predictus obvius venit. Exceptusque a rege decenter, provinciam quam ei pater Karolus rex contulerat ab eo etiam accepit. Unde et regis

20

Duke William of the Pirates[41] Swears Fealty to the King Against All Men

While this was going on at Laon, William, duke of the pirates, sent envoys to profess his loyalty to the king, declaring that he would come to meet him wherever the king should command it and swear fealty to him against all men. The king received the embassy with great goodwill and determined that William should come to meet him in the county of Amiens, where there were some matters of particular importance that they needed to pronounce judgment upon. After the envoys had been led away, the king came to the place that they had agreed upon at the appointed time. The aforementioned duke came to meet him there as well. After receiving a fitting welcome from King Louis, he received from him the province that Louis's father, King Charles, had previously bestowed upon him. Having thus became the king's vassal, William was bound to him with

940

factus, tanto ei consensu alligatus est ut iam iamque aut sese moriturum aut regi imperii summam restituturum proponeret.

21

Artoldus archiepiscopus Causostem munitionem expugnat et capit

Huiusque rei negotio utiliter peracto, rex in Burgundiam secessit. In cuius absentia Artoldus metropolitanus, ne suae rei putaretur inopia, absque regiis[55] copiis Causostem munitionem appetit eique obsidionem circumquaque adhibet. Quam continua oppugnatione[56] exagitans, quinto tandem die ingreditur capitque. Illos quoque qui sibi surripuerant comprehendit. Sed utpote vir bonus nulliusque vitae aemulus, indempnes abire permisit. Oppidum etiam funditus subruit sicque ad sua rediit.

such affection that he declared then and there that he would either restore the whole of the king's dominion to him in short order or else perish in the effort.[42]

21

Archbishop Artald Assaults and Captures the Stronghold of Chausot

When this business had been successfully concluded, the king departed for Burgundy. While he was gone, Archbishop Artald, lest anyone should think his resources wanting, marched on the stronghold of Chausot without any of the king's troops and invested it on all sides.[43] After subjecting it to a continuous assault, he finally gained entry and took possession of it on the fifth day of the siege. He also seized those who had usurped the stronghold from him. As a good man, however, he begrudged no one his life, and he allowed them to depart unharmed. Then he razed the stronghold to the ground, and with that he returned home.[44]

22

Heribertus et Hugo Remos obsident et capiunt, presulemque pellunt

Heribertus malorum[57] occasionem nactus, acsi suorum oppidum dirutum dolens, apud Hugonem ducem qualiter Remos invadat atque episcopum expungat vehementissime agit. Cui mox Hugo utpote tiranno tirannus consentiens, sese auxiliaturum pollicetur. Collecto itaque agmine, ambo in urbem feruntur, multa eam circum obsidione vallantes. Urbani Heriberto faventes, eo quod regio iussu eius filium ante Artoldum delegissent, bello cedunt presulemque relinquunt atque ad suae poenae cumulum desertores ad tirannos transeunt. Apertis vero portis sexta obsidionis die, tirannos in urbe excipiunt. Artoldus pulsus, ad coenobium sancti Remigii proficiscitur, suam ibi deo conspectori omnium querimoniam fundens. Ubi[58] mox episcoporum aliquibus ac quibusdam magnatibus stipatus, rogabatur ut Avenniacensi abbatia sanctique Basoli rebus contentus, episcopii dignitate sese abdicaret. Atque multis minarum terroribus

22

Heribert and Hugh Besiege and Capture Reims and Expel the Archbishop

Having now acquired a pretext for mischief, Heribert pretended to be aggrieved that a stronghold held by his men had been destroyed and forcefully urged Hugh to attack Reims and get rid of the archbishop. As one tyrant dealing with another, Hugh soon came to see things his way and promised to help him. After mustering an army, they both marched on the city and invested it with an extensive siege. The townsmen, who were sympathetic to Heribert because they had chosen his son as archbishop at the behest of King Radulf prior to the election of Artald, yielded in the face of the assault and abandoned their archbishop. And to complete their guilt, they deserted the king and went over to the side of the tyrants. On the sixth day of the siege they opened the gates and welcomed the tyrants into the city. Artald was driven from Reims and fled to the monastery of Saint-Rémi, where he poured forth his complaints to God, who oversees all things. Some of the bishops and magnates crowded around him there and demanded that he renounce the office of bishop and content himself with the abbacy of Avenay and the patrimony of Saint Basil.[45] Afflicted with many terrors by their threats, Artald agreed, and he reportedly

affectus, consentit, iuratus etiam, ut fertur, repudium. Et tandem canibus satisfaciens, ad sanctum Basolum ibi moraturus abscessit.

23

Hugo ac Heribertus in regis absentia Laudunum inpugnant

Hugone ergo diacono tiranni filio Remis relicto, iam pridem etiam ad episcopatum urbis ipsius evocato, ipse Heribertus atque Hugo Laudunum cum copiis aggrediuntur, obsidionem undique adhibentes, urbem militibus vacuam rati, eo quod rex in partibus Burgundiae exterioribus alia curaret. Et qua poterant oppugnantes, ingredi conabantur. At montis eminentia superioribus impares, non semel cedere coacti sunt. Instabant tamen, ac regi ingressum preripere conabantur.

swore an oath to renounce his see as well. When at last he had satisfied those dogs, he retired to Saint-Basle to take up residence there.[46]

23

Hugh and Heribert Besiege Laon While the King Is Away

Therefore, Hugh the Deacon,[47] the son of the tyrant, was left at Reims, the city to which he had earlier been called to take up the office of bishop, while Heribert and Hugh marched on the Laon with their forces. They besieged the city on all sides, reckoning that with the king in outer Burgundy attending to other business, it would be empty of fighting men. They attacked wherever they could and tried to force their way inside, but the steepness of the hill put them at a disadvantage compared to the defenders above,[48] and on more than one occasion they were forced to retreat. They kept up their attacks however, in an effort to gain entrance to the city before the king arrived.[49]

24

Rege adveniente obsidio solvitur

Iamque ebdomadas septem obpugnaverant, cum rex huius rei accitus nuntio, in Campania Remensi tempestivus affuit. Et licet cum paucis, fluvium tamen Axonam permeat et sic in hostes fertur. Quo comperto, tiranni,[59] regis quoque animum simulque et aequitatem perpendentes, ab obsidione discedunt. Rex vero ingressus, victus necessaria suis paravit ac quaeque commoda ordinavit, sicque alia dispositurus Burgundiam repetit. In cuius discessu Wido Suessorum episcopus a desertoribus suasus, eo quod et ipse eorum partes latenter tueretur, Remos veniens, Heriberti filium Hugonem presbiterum ordinavit. Unde et eum pater sacerdotali dignitate ampliare cupiens, ut Artoldus pontificatus apice legaliter privaretur instanter quaerebat. Cuius rei rationem cum Hugone duce contulit ac in effectum redigi admodum petiit.

24

The Siege Is Broken Off by the Arrival of the King

The siege had been going on for seven weeks[50] when the king, summoned by news of what was happening, made a timely arrival in the region of Champagne around Reims. Although he only had a few men with him, he crossed the Aisne River and advanced against his enemies as he was. When the tyrants learned of this, they carefully weighed the courage and fairness of the king and raised the siege. After entering the city, Louis furnished his men with the necessary provisions and made some suitable arrangements. And with that, he went back to Burgundy to deal with other business. During his departure, some of those who had deserted the king persuaded Bishop Wido of Soissons[51] (since he secretly supported their faction) to come to Reims and ordain Hugh, the son of Heribert, as a priest. Thereafter Heribert, in his desire to further advance his son in the priesthood, sought insistently to have Artald legally deprived of the office of bishop. He discussed his plan with Duke Hugh and strove earnestly to have it put into effect.[52]

25

Artoldus a comprovincialibus episcopis repudiatur et pro eo Hugo eligitur

Disposita ergo rationum summa, Remensis dioceseos episcopos convocant, qui inter Artoldum et Hugonem controversiam determinent obiectorumque finem constituant. Collecti ergo apud urbem Suessonicam, in basilica sanctorum martirum Crispini et Crispiniani, civium Remensium querelam excipiunt, dicentium sese diutissime pastore destitutos, cui subdantur et obsequantur suppliciter expetere. Artoldum iam se nolle, eo quod sacramento episcopium repudiaverit, at Hugonem, quod omnium unione electus, omnibusque acceptissimus sit. Quorum querimoniis episcopi annuentes, sacerdotio dignum Hugonem asserunt, eo quod non solum carnis nobilitas, sed et animi mores pudici plurimum eum commendarent. Ratum etiam fore si tanti honoris culmen personae nobilitate adornetur. Hugonem itaque pene omnium conibentia attollunt, ac Remos deductum, in coenobio monachorum sancti Remigii metropolitanum sollempniter consecrant atque in urbe decenter exceptum, multo obsequio ac reverentia honorant. Rex in partibus

25

Artald Is Repudiated by the Bishops of His Province, and Hugh Is Elected in His Place

When all of their plans had been arranged, they called 941
together the bishops of the province of Reims to settle the
dispute between Artald and Hugh and put an end to the re-
criminations. The bishops therefore assembled in the basilica of the holy martyrs Crispin and Crispinian at Soissons,
and there they heard the complaint of the townsmen of
Reims, who said that because they had been without a shep-
herd for so long, they had come to petition humbly for a lord
whom they could serve and obey.[53] They no longer wanted
Artald, because he had taken an oath to renounce his see;
instead they preferred Hugh, who had been elected
with unanimous consent and was acceptable to everyone.
The bishops heeded their complaints and declared Hugh
worthy of episcopal office because not only his nobility of
blood but also his chaste habits of mind strongly recommended him. Indeed, they said, it was only proper that a position of such eminence should be dignified by someone of
his nobility of character. And so, with virtually unanimous
consent, they agreed to elevate Hugh to the see of Reims,
and after bringing him to the city, they solemnly consecrated
him archbishop at the monastery of Saint-Rémi, after which
he was given a fitting welcome in the city of Reims and hon-

Burgundiae viatorum relatu patratum negotium advertens, mox Laudunum rediit. Arnoldum quoque ac eius fratrem Landricum proditionis insimulatos, nec tamen penitus convictos, cum in hac re promptissimi viderentur, ab urbe expulit.

26

Rex in partibus Burgundiae exercitum contra tirannos colligit

Rex cum rei militaris inopia contra tirannos nihil moliri valeret, Burgundiam repetiit, ut exercitum inde sumeret Remisque induceret. Admodum etenim id attemptabat, ut Heribertum ab urbe pervasa pelleret. Dum ergo in colligendis militibus moram faceret, tiranni[60] multo equitatu Laudunum appetunt atque circumdant, spem proditionis in quibusdam habentes. Haec dum aguntur, ad regis aures tempestive feruntur. Qui, sumptis quos undecumque colligere valuit, in pagum Porcensem devenit. Ubi cum rem militarem ordinaret ac hostibus bellum inferre pararet, tiranni, Lauduni[61] obsidione relicta, in regem vadunt, ac insperatum

ored with great obedience and reverence. When the king, who was in Burgundy, learned what had happened from the reports of travelers, he returned immediately to Laon. He expelled from the city Arnold[54] and his brother Landry, who had been accused of treason but not actually convicted of it, because they had appeared all too eager in this regard.[55]

26

The King Raises an Army in Burgundy Against the Tyrants

The king was prevented by a lack of troops from taking any action against the tyrants, so he went back to Burgundy to raise an army to lead to Reims. Indeed, he was making a strenuous effort to do so, so that he might drive Heribert out of the city that he had captured. Therefore, while the king was taking time to gather his men together, the tyrants marched on Laon with a great number of knights and surrounded the city, expecting that it would be betrayed to them by certain men. While this was going on, the news was quickly brought to the king. Gathering men from whatever quarter he could, he advanced into the county of Porcien. As he was putting his troops in order and preparing to do battle with the enemy, the tyrants abandoned the siege of Laon and marched against the king. Catching his army off

invadentes eius exercitum, nonnullos sternunt, reliquos vero in fugam cogunt. Rex a suis eductus, vix cum duobus comitibus vim mortis evasit, oppido quod Altus mons dicitur sese recipiens. Tiranni spe proditionis frustrati, obsidionem solvunt atque in sua concedunt.[62]

27

Tiranni a papa monentur ne regem suum persequantur

Interea a domno Stephano papa vir clarus nomine Damasus legatus in Gallias directus est, apostolicae sedis litteras afferens, iussionem apostolicam continentes ut principes provinciarum[63] regem suum Ludovicum recipere non differrent nec gladio ultra hostili eum insectarentur. Et ni cessent, anathematis telo omnes esse figendos. Quo episcopi cognito Remorum dioceseos in unum mox coacti, de anathemate in sese habendo nisi resipiscant vehementer[64] pertractant. Mittendum enim ad Heribertum disponunt et ab eo suppli-

guard, they killed a number of men and put the rest to flight. The king was taken away by his men and just managed to escape death with two of his companions,[56] taking refuge in the stronghold of Omont. The tyrants, having been thwarted in their expectation of taking Laon through treachery, raised the siege and withdrew to their own territories.[57]

27

The Tyrants Are Warned by the Pope Not to Persecute Their King

In the meantime Pope Stephen[58] sent a distinguished man   942
by the name of Damasus as his legate into Gaul. He brought with him a letter from the apostolic see containing a command from the pope to the leading men of the provinces to the effect that they should not put off receiving Louis, their king, and that they should persecute him no more with the sword of enmity. If they did not cease to do so, then they would be transfixed with the shaft of anathema. When the bishops of the diocese of Reims learned of this, they gathered together and held impassioned discussions about the anathema that threatened them if they did not come to their senses. They determined to send to Heribert and hum-

citer petendum quatinus ipse ducem adeat atque apud eum
pro regis receptione agat, ostendentes anathematis periculum et quanta iis debeatur ruina[65] qui dominorum contemp-
tores ac persecutores esse non formidant. Quae suasio nullum effectum habuit. A predicto etiam papa mox alia legatio
directa est per Remensis aecclesiae legatos, qui a papa eodem sacerdotale pallium Hugoni metropolitano detulere,
dicentes apostolicae iussionis hanc esse sententiam, ut Galliarum principes regem suum persequi parcant et insuper illum magnifice attollant. Quod nisi intra prescriptum diem
efficiant, horribili anathemate huius faccionis auctores ac
cooperatores sive fautores gravissime esse multandos. Si
vero apostolicae iussioni gratanter oboediant, legatos Romam dirigant qui suam benivolentiam erga regem suum papae referant. Et nec sic quidem tirannis quicquam persuasum est. A quibus cum regi incessanter quaereretur ruina, in
contrarium res eorum tota relapsa est.

bly entreat him to go before the duke and try to persuade him to be reconciled with the king, pointing to the danger of excommunication and the terrible ruin that awaited those who did not scruple to reject and persecute their lords. Their efforts to persuade him came to naught, however. A short time later Pope Stephen sent another message via the envoys of the church of Reims, who were bringing back the episcopal pallium[59] for Archbishop Hugh. The envoys reported back that it was the judgment of the Holy See that the leading men of Gaul should cease to persecute their king and that they should honor him in a manner befitting his station. If they failed to comply with these instructions before the appointed time, then the instigators of this rebellion, as well as those who had cooperated with and supported them, would be severely punished with a terrible anathema. If, on the other hand, they were willing to submit to his apostolic command, then they should send envoys to Rome to inform him of their goodwill toward the king. Even after all of this, however, the tyrants could not be swayed. Yet while they continued to try to bring about the downfall of the king, it was their own fortunes that suffered a complete reversal.[60]

28

Rex per Rotgerum comitem Wilelmum ducem sibi conciliat

Etenim rex, bonorum usus consilio, Rotgarium virum clarum Wilelmo pyratarum principi pro se locuturum direxit. Qui apud eum pro rege optime functus legatione, ibi rebus humanis excessit. Ante tamen principi usque ad effectum suasit. Nam non multopost suorum legatione regem fideliter accersit, exceptumque Rodomi ingentibus donis[66] dignissime accumulat.[67] Unde et factum est ut alii hinc formidantes ad regem[68] tempestivius sese contulerint. Wilelmus itaque Aquitanorum dux Brittanorumque Alanus, piratas regiam rem curare comperientes, accessum maturant, regem adeunt, atque fidem pacti miliciam iurant. His itaque rex collectis, predictis tirannis Hugoni et Heriberto[69] secus fluvium Isaram locuturus procedit. Tiranni regium equitatum suspectum habentes, prevenerunt atque pontes precipitaverunt, naves circumquaque in aliud litus abducentes. Sicque cum suis in adverso fluminis litore consederunt. Dua-

28

The King Wins Over Duke William Through the Agency of Count Roger

Following the advice of good men, the king sent Roger,[61] a person of distinction, to speak to Duke William of the pirates on his behalf. After successfully carrying out this mission on behalf of the king at William's court, Roger departed from mortal affairs in that same place. Prior to this, however, he succeeded in persuading the duke. For not long afterward William sent some of his own men to summon the king in good faith, after which he received him at Rouen and heaped generous gifts upon him in a most worthy fashion. The result of this was that others grew fearful and hurried to do homage to the king in a more timely manner. Thus, when Duke William of Aquitaine[62] and Alan of Brittany[63] learned that the pirates had taken up the king's cause, they hastened their approach, went before the king, and pledged fealty to him, swearing to serve him as his vassals. Taking these men with him, the king went to speak with the afore-mentioned tyrants Hugh and Heribert by the River Oise. Because the tyrants were suspicious of the king's knights, they came to the river in advance, destroyed the bridges, and took all the boats in the area over to the far side of the river. After this, they set up camp with their men on the

bus tantum naviculis hinc inde cursitantibus, per internuntios controversia inter illos agitata est. Tandem sub pace sequestra obsidum iure a sese discedunt.

29

Ludovicus et Otto reges in amiciciam conveniunt, ac per Ottonem Hugo

Rex, principibus in pace dimissis, cum paucis iter in Belgicam retorquet, Ottoni, cuius sororem coniugem sibi addixerat, ad loquendum obveniens.[70] Quorum consilio multa concordia firmato, amiciciam mutuo conditionibus statuunt. Ac fine negotii facto, rex Laudunum rediit. Otto vero Hugonem in regis gratiam reducere satagebat. Quem multis verborum stimulis familiariter ac levi furore redarguens, eo quod regi suo contrairet dominumque insectari non formidaret, ad regem redire effecit. Et tempore oportuno, prudentium legationibus premissis, regi ducem reducit sibique conciliat.

bank of the river opposite the king. The dispute between the two parties was negotiated by intermediaries, with just two small boats going back and forth from one side to the other. At last they parted from one another, with peace having been negotiated through the surety of hostages.[64]

29

King Louis and King Otto Come Together in Friendship; Otto Reconciles Hugh and the King

After sending the leading men away in peace, the king took a few men and went to Belgica to speak with Otto, whose sister he had taken to wife. Their deliberations were strengthened by the great harmony that prevailed between them, and they agreed to terms on a pact of friendship. When their business was complete, the king returned to Laon. Meanwhile, Otto strove to bring Hugh back into the king's favor. By rebuking him gently with many pointed words and mild anger because he continued to oppose his king and did not scruple to persecute his lord, he successfully persuaded him to return to the king. After delegations of wise men had been sent out in advance, he brought the duke before the king at a suitable time and reconciled them with one another.[65]

30

Principum apud regem conventus, ac Wilelmi in eorum contione tumultuatio

Duce ergo in pristinam gratiam revocato, cum ipse virtute et copiis antecelleret, alii consequenter reducti sunt. Omnibus itaque ad regem reversis, in fisco regio Atiniaco principibus ab rege post dies triginta colloquium habendum indicitur. Et die constituta rex ibi cum provinciarum principibus affuit, Hugone videlicet[71] cognomento Magno, Arnulfo Morinorum, Wilelmo piratarum ducibus, ac Heriberto tiranno. Nec defuit Saxoniae rex Otto. Ludovicus rex cum in conclavi sese cum Ottone rege ac[72] principibus recepisset, consilio incertum an fortuitu,[73] solus Wilelmus dux admissus non est. Diucius ergo afforis exspectans, cum non vocaretur, rem animo irato ferebat. Tandem in iram versus, utpote manu et audatia nimius, foribus clausis vim intulit ac retrorsum vibrabundus[74] adaegit. Ingressusque lectum conspicatur gestatorium[75] in quo etiam a parte cervicalis Otto editior, rex vero in parte extrema humilior residebat. In quorum prospectu Hugo et Arnulfus duabus residentes sellis, consilii ordinem exspectabant. Wilelmus regis iniuriam non

30

A Meeting of the Leading Men Before the King, and the Disturbance Caused by William During Their Discussions

The duke was thus recalled to the favor that he had for-merly enjoyed, and because he was foremost in power and military might, others followed his lead and went back to the king as well. Now that everyone had been reconciled to the king, he announced to the leading men that a coun-cil would be held at the royal palace of Attigny thirty days hence. On the appointed day Louis was present, along with the leading men of the realm: the dukes Hugh the Great, Arnulf of Flanders, and William of the Pirates, and the ty-rant Heribert. Nor was King Otto of Saxony absent. When King Louis withdrew behind locked doors in the company of King Otto and the other magnates, Duke William alone was not admitted (it is not known whether this was inten-tional or not). As a result, he waited outside for a long time and began to grow irritated when he was not summoned. At last he became angry, and being as bold as he was strong, he applied force to the locked doors and flung them open, quiv-ering with rage. When he entered, he saw a couch upon which Otto was reclining higher up near the pillow, while the king sat below him down at the end. Hugh and Arnulf were seated before them on two chairs, waiting for the meeting to proceed according to order. William could not

passus, 'An,' inquit, 'his interesse non debui? Desertorisne[76] dedecore aliquando sordui?' Fervidusque[77] propinquans, 'Surge,' inquit, 'paululum, rex.' Quo mox surgente, ipse resedit dixitque indecens esse regem inferiorem, alium vero quemlibet superiorem videri. Quapropter oportere Ottonem inde amoliri regique cedere. Otto, pudore affectus, surgit ac regi cedit. Rex itaque superior, at Wilelmus inferior consederunt.

31

Otto iniuriam sub specie fidei habendae dissimulat, eiusque conquestio

Otto penitus iniuriam dissimulans, baculo innixus coepto negotio finem dare stando satagebat. Ac rationibus determinatis, rex cum consultoribus surgens egreditur. Otto iniuriam Wilelmi vehementissime dissimulans,[78] apud eum de fidei constantia inter sese servanda plurimum consultat. Unde et conceptum facinus variis verborum coloribus obve-

endure this insult to the king. "Was I not to be included in these deliberations?" he asked. "Have I ever been tainted by the dishonor due to a traitor?" He drew near, seething with rage, and said, "Rise up a little, my king." The king got up immediately and William sat down. He declared that it was unseemly for the king to be seen in a position of inferiority while someone else was positioned above him. For this reason Otto should get up and yield his place to the king. Stricken with shame, Otto stood up and gave way to Louis, who now sat at the head with William below him.

31

Otto Pretends Not to Have Taken Offense by Making a Show of Loyalty; His Complaint

Otto gave no indication at all that he had taken offense, but stood leaning on a staff and endeavored to bring an end to the proceedings. When the issues under discussion had been resolved, the king arose and left with his counselors. Making a strenuous effort to hide the fact that he had been insulted by William, Otto spoke to him at some length about the need to preserve the steadfast trust between them, all the while using various figures of speech to conceal the crime that he was planning. Afterward, the king returned

lat. Quibus peractis, rex cum Wilelmo ad sua remeat. Otto vero cum Hugone et Arnulfo consilium conferens, de iniuria irrogata apud illos[79] amplius conquerebatur, ultra aequum et ius sese spretum memorans, ac coram amicis a sedibus amotum. Amicos ergo compati oportere et amici[80] iniuriam suam debere arbitrari. Ab eis quoque tantam insolentiam summopere repellendam aiebat, cum ea facilius ad eos pervenire valeat. Nam qui sibi regi non indulsit minus illis indulturum.[81] Quae oratio plurimam invidiam paravit ac amicos in odium Wilelmi incitavit, cum et ipsi quamvis latenter ei admodum inviderent. Otto rex ad sua rediit.

32

Deliberatio Hugonis et Arnulfi de morte Wilelmi

Hugo et Arnulfus quid facturi Wilelmo essent deliberabant. Si eum gladio occidant, ad omnia sese fieri expeditiores aiebant. Regem etiam ad quodcumque volent facilius in-

home with William. Otto, meanwhile, taking counsel with Hugh and Arnulf, complained at considerable length to them about the insult that he had suffered, declaring that he had been dishonored beyond what was fair or lawful and forced to give up his seat in the presence of his friends. As his friends, therefore, they ought to sympathize with him and treat the insult that had been done to him as though it had been directed at them. Moreover, they should make every effort to put a stop to heavy-handed behavior of this sort, since it could very easily end up affecting them; for a person who did not for himself pardon the king would pardon them even less. This speech aroused great animosity and stirred up hatred of William among Otto's friends, since they themselves secretly viewed him with considerable hostility. King Otto then returned home.

32

Hugh and Arnulf Deliberate Over the Murder of William

Hugh and Arnulf debated what they should do about William. If they put him to the sword, then they would have more freedom to act as they wished. Moreover, with the duke gone, they would have an easier time bending the king to their will, since as long as Louis had William to rely on, he

flexuros, si is solum pereat quo rex fretus ad quaeque flecti nequeat. Si autem non occidant, discordias atque lites sine dubio proventuras, ac his occasione emersa, multorum stragem futuram. At horum utrumque perniciosum censebant, cum in occisione homicidii reatus redundaret, et in reservatione tirannis futura appareret. De occisione tandem persuasi, patraturos facinus accersiunt, vim negotii explicantes, atque in Wilelmum coniurare faciunt. Cuius interfectionis series mox apud coniuratos ita disponitur, ut ab Arnulfo legati mitterentur, qui pro colloquio multa necessitate in proximo habendo apud Wilelmum idonee legatione fungerentur; de tempore[82] quaererent quando[83] sibi obveniendum foret;[84] locum vero secus fluvium Summam peterent, qua ipse a terra sua[85] egredi et collocuturis obvenire dignaretur. Qui postquam adveniret et ab amico[86] exceptus esset, de amicicia[87] plurimum, multum etiam de fide proponerent. Et quia tunc suis stipatus pervadi non posset, ictus differrentur donec navim repeteret, si forte navigio eum advenisse contingeret. Cumque iam navigaret per pelagus, per coniuratos multo clamore revocaretur, acsi aliquid precipuum oblivione pretermissum auditurus. Navicula ergo advectus[88] cum paucis, aliis in pelago expectantibus, coniurati gladiis eductis incautum adorirentur. Si vero equester adveniret, post con-

could never be coerced into doing anything. On the other hand, if they did not kill him, then disagreements and quarrels were sure to crop up, and a great many deaths would follow as soon as an opportunity arose for such behavior. Both of these options seemed dangerous to them. If they killed William, then they would incur the guilt for his murder, whereas if they spared him, then tyranny would arise in the future. In the end they agreed that he must die. Summoning men to carry out this crime, they explained to them the importance of their mission and made them swear an oath against William. Then they arranged the events of the murder with the conspirators. Arnulf would dispatch envoys to William to deliver the message that there was a pressing need for talks between them in the near future. They would ask him to set a time for a meeting, and they would request a location near the Somme, so that William would agree to leave his own territory and go in person to meet the people who were coming to speak with him. When William arrived and had been received by his friend, they would say a great deal about friendship and much also about loyalty. And because at this point he would be surrounded by his own men and would not be vulnerable to assault, the attack would have to be delayed until he returned to his ship (if he happened to have come by water). Then, as he was sailing down the river, the conspirators would raise a great shout to summon him back, under the pretext that they had forgotten to mention something important that he needed to hear. The duke would then be brought over to them in a little boat with a small escort, while the rest of his men waited for him on the river, and the conspirators could then draw their swords and fall upon him while he was unsuspecting. If, on

silii finem Arnulfo digresso illoque recedente, coniurati
identidem eum repeterent, magnum quiddam sese afferre
simulantes,[89] quibusdam etiam seriis accitum detinerent,
donec cunctis preeuntibus extremus retrorsum incederet.
Quem adorsi gladiis non minus transverberarent. Insurgen-
tium vero piratarum vim evaderent, si equis velocibus rapti,
ad dominum cum copiis prestolantem[90] transfugere tempestivius accelerarent.[91] Piratas etiam tunc nihil aliud quam aut
fugam acceleraturos aut domini exsequias procuraturos.[92]
Sicque factum esset ut Arnulfo ignorante, eo quod absens
esset, tantum facinus patratum videretur.

33

Wilelmi ducis interfectio

Legati itaque directi, colloquium petunt et optinent.
Tempus post dies XXX datur. Locus quoque in pago Ambia-
nensi secus fluvium Summam ubi est insula Pinchinea conceditur. Negotioque peracto, legati redeunt. Tempore ergo

the other hand, he came on horseback, then after the meeting was over and Arnulf had left, the conspirators would call him back in the same way while he was leaving and pretend that they had something important to bring to him. When he arrived, they would keep him occupied with serious business of some sort until everyone else had gone ahead and he was just starting to follow after them. Then the conspirators would attack him and likewise run him through with their swords. They could escape revenge at the hands of the attacking pirates if they rode away on swift horses and made haste to flee to their lord, who would be waiting for them with his troops. At that point there would be nothing the pirates could do except speed them in their flight or else go back and attend to the body of their lord. In this way, because Arnulf was not there, it would be made to appear that the crime had been carried out without his knowledge.

33

The Murder of Duke William

The envoys were thus dispatched, and they asked for and 943 were granted a meeting. The time was set for thirty days hence, and it was agreed that it would take place in the county of Amiens on the Somme River, where the island of Picquigny is. When they had completed their mission, the

constituto, Arnulfus terra, Wilelmus aqua in locum destina-
tum conveniunt. Ac de amicitia multum, plurimum de fide
utrimque servanda collocuti sunt atque post nonnullos ser-
mones a se soluti. Arnulfus reditum simulans, aliquantisper[93]
digreditur. Wilelmus vero ad classem rediit. Naviculamque
ingressus, dum per pelagus navigaret, a coniuratis multo
strepitu[94] inclamatus, proram obvertit, remigansque ad litus, quid vellent sciscitaturus rediit. Illi mox quiddam preti-
osissimum[95] se deferre asserunt, quod a domino suo oblivione suppressum fuit. Dux, navicula litori appulsa, illos
excipit, a quibus etiam mox gladiis eductis[96] interimitur.
Duobus quoque puberibus qui cum eo inermes aderant et
nauta sauciatis, a navicula facinorosi exiliunt ac post conscium dominum in fugam feruntur. Qui autem iam per pelagus navigabant, conversi litus relictum repetunt ac dominum interemptum duosque puberes et nautam sauciatos

envoys returned home. At the appointed time, therefore, Arnulf and William met at the location that they had agreed upon, the former coming by land, the latter by water. They made many protestations of friendship and mutual loyalty, and after talking for some time, they parted from one another. Arnulf pretended that he was leaving and went off for a little while, while William returned to his ships. He embarked on a little boat and was traveling down the river, when he was summoned by a great deal of shouting from the conspirators. At this he turned the boat around, and rowing back to the shore, he came back to ask them what they wanted. They immediately declared that they had something valuable to bring to him that their lord had forgotten. When his boat had been brought up to the shore, the duke welcomed them on board, whereupon they immediately drew their swords and slew him. After wounding in addition two unarmed boys and a sailor who were with him, the perpetrators of this crime leapt out of the boat and fled back to their lord and fellow conspirator. The men of the duke's party, who by now were sailing back down the river, turned around and headed back for the shore. There they found their lord slain and the two boys and sailor wounded.

inveniunt. Sumptumque domini corpus lamentabili obsequio sepulturae deportant.

34

Rex filio Wilelmi Richardo terram patris concedit

Nec multopost et eius filium de Brittanna concubina,
nomine Richardum, regi deducunt, gesti negotii ordinem
pandentes. Rex adolescentis elegantiam advertens, liberaliter excipit, provinciam a patre pridem possessam ei largiens.[97] Potiores quoque qui cum adolescentulo accesserant
per manus et sacramentum regis fiunt. Multaque regis liberalitate iocundati, recedunt Rodomum.[98] Alii vero Nortmannorum Richardum ad regem transisse indignantes, ad
Hugonem ducem concedunt.

Taking up the body of their lord, they carried him away for burial in a mournful funeral cortège.[66]

34

The King Grants Richard, the Son of William, the Lands of His Father

Not long after this they brought Richard,[67] William's son by a Breton concubine,[68] before the king and recounted the whole series of events to him. Taking note of the young man's dignified bearing, the king received him generously and granted him the province formerly held by his father. In addition, the magnates who had accompanied the boy became the king's men by giving him their hands and swearing oaths. Afterward they returned to Rouen, delighted by the king's generosity. Some of the other Northmen, however, were resentful of the fact that Richard had gone over to Louis, and they gave their allegiance to Duke Hugh instead.[69]

35

Rex a suis Rodomum accersitur ac cum piratis dimicat

Qui autem regis partes tuebantur per legatos eum accersitum Rodomi decenter suscipiunt. Ubi cum ei referretur regem piratarum Setrich cum classe copiosa[99] fluvium Sequanam ingressum, ac eius ducem Thurmodum[100] consequenter navalibus copiis advenisse, ut absque regis dono omnia pervadant atque defuncti ducis filium ad idolatriam suadeant ritumque gentilem inducant, rex copias unde congrediatur colligit. Deumque propitiaturum confisus, alienigenis cum DCCC occurrit. Et quia cum paucis erat, ad hostes concludendos acies in diversa disponere nequivit. Suis itaque stipatus, erectis signis ac densato agmine procedit. Gentiles quoque ordine pedestri incedebant. Propinquantesque patrio more in primo tumultu enses iaciunt. Quorum densitate equites territos ac sauciatos rati, cum clipeis et telis prosecuntur. At regius equitatus,[101] ensium nube dilapsa, clipeorum obiectione tuti, in pedites feruntur. Ac densati,[102] acies sternendo atque interimendo indivisi penetrant egrediunturque. Rursusque regressi, penetrant ac disrumpunt.

35

The King Is Summoned to Rouen by His Subjects and Does Battle with the Pirates

Those who supported the king, however, sent envoys to summon him and gave him a fitting welcome at Rouen. While he was there, he was informed that the pirate king Sihtric[70] had entered the Seine with a large fleet, and that his captain Turmod had subsequently arrived with naval forces. Their intention was to take over the whole area without a grant from the king, to convert the son of Duke William to the worship of idols, and to bring back pagan rites. When he heard this, the king mustered his forces to meet them in battle. Trusting in God's favor, he went to meet the foreigners with eight hundred men. Because he had so few troops, he was unable to extend his lines widely enough to envelop the enemy. So he marched into battle surrounded by his men, with the standards raised and the army packed tightly together. The pagans likewise marched forward in a line of infantry. As they approached, they hurled their swords at the outset of the battle, in accordance with their native custom. Then, reckoning that the king's knights had been frightened and injured by the dense fire, they pressed the attack with shields and spears. But the king's troops held their shields in front of them for protection, and once the hail of swords had dissipated, they advanced toward the enemy foot soldiers. Crowding together, they charged forward

Regem quoque Setrich cum violentia belli in fugam cogeret, in dumeto mox repertus, tribus lanceis a palantibus transfixus est. Thurmodus vero cum adhuc in certamine totis viribus ageretur, ab Ludovico equi impetentis pectore est deiectus. Quem cum rex impetu preteriret, nec eum dinosceret, et ab hostibus impetitus in loco staret comminusque confligeret, Thurmodus, suis stipatus, regem a tergo appetit, factusque ei dexter, per loricae manicam pene usque ad sinistri lateris ypocundriam lancea sauciat. Rex multa cede ab eo impetu paulisper dimotus, sauciantem respicit. Ictuque in dextram obliquato, provocantis caput cum humero sinistro obtruncat. Tanta quoque caede gentiles fusi sunt, ut eorum $\overline{\text{VIIII}}$[103] cesa ibi referrentur. Reliqui vero, paucissimi tamen, navali profugio erepti sunt. Rex a deo victoria potitus est, suorum tamen paucis fusis, nonnullis vero sauciatis. Post quorum curam redire disponens, Rodomum Erluino commisit, ipse Compendium rediens.

into their ranks, slaughtering and killing, and emerging in an unbroken formation. Then they turned around and drove through them once more, shattering their lines. The ferocity of the fighting drove King Sihtric to take flight, but he was discovered hiding in a thicket by some men ranging over the battlefield and run through with three spears. Turmod, for his part, was still in the thick of battle, fighting with all of his might, when he was struck head-on by Louis's charging horse and thrown down onto the ground. The king careened past him without recognizing who he was, whereupon he was set upon by his foes, but he stood his ground and fought them hand to hand. Turmod, surrounded by his men, came up from behind him, flanked him on the right side, and struck him with his spear through the armhole of his hauberk, delivering a blow that reached almost as far as his left lung. The king, whose attention had been briefly diverted from this attack by the slaughter around him, turned to look at the man who had just wounded him. Then he struck a blow crosswise to his right and cut off the head and left arm of his attacker. The pagans were put to rout with such tremendous bloodshed that nine thousand of them were said to have been killed there, although a very small number of survivors did manage to escape by ship. By God's hand the king had prevailed, although a few of his men had been struck down and some wounded. After attending to them, he made arrangements to return home, entrusting Rouen to Erluin, while he himself went back to Compiègne.[71]

36

Artoldus archiepiscopus tirannos dimittit et ad regem transit

Quo eum advenisse dinoscens, Artoldus, qui in coenobio sancti Basoli confessoris ab urbe pulsus morabatur, mox quicquid a tiranno sibi relictum erat abiciens, ad regem sese contulit, mallens apud eum parvo contentus morari quam insaciabilis tiranni beneficiis detineri. Rex metropolitanum[104] quo ipse rex consecratus fuit iniuste precipitatum dolens, ne diffidat hortatur, summum sacerdotium sese ei redditurum pollicens.

37

Interitus Heriberti

His ita sese habentibus, cum Heribertus quaeque pernitiosa pertractaret ac de quorundam calamitate multa disponeret, cum inter suos in veste preciosa sederet atque apud illos extensa manu concionaretur, maiore apoplexia ob super-

36

Archbishop Artald Renounces the Tyrants and Goes Over to the King

When Artald, who had been driven out of Reims and was residing in the monastery of Saint-Basil the Confessor,[72] learned of the king's coming, he immediately abandoned what had been left to him by the tyrant and went to the king, preferring to stay with him and be content with very little rather than be held hostage by the favors of an insatiable tyrant.[73] Aggrieved that the archbishop who had consecrated him had been unjustly deposed, the king urged Artald not to despair and promised to restore him to his see.[74]

37

The Death of Heribert

In the meantime, Heribert was plotting all sorts of mischief and making detailed arrangements to bring about the ruin of certain people. As he was sitting among his men, dressed in his finery and holding forth to them with an outstretched hand, he was struck with severe apoplexy brought

fluitatem humorum captus, in ipsa rerum ordinatione constrictis manibus nervisque contractis, ore etiam in aurem distorto, cum multo horrore et horripilatione coram suis inconsultus exspiravit. Susceptusque a suis, apud sanctum Quintinum sepultus est. Quo sepulto, eius filii mox regem adeuntes, ab eo benigne excepti sunt. Patris iniuriarum[105] nihil sibi reducens. Excipitur et Hugo episcopus, ea tamen conditione, ut tempore congruo ratiocinari pro se de episcopatus adeptione non differat. Cum quibus quoque rex Ambianum digressus est. Ubi cum non sine suorum potioribus quaeque precipua disponere vellet, Erluinum Rodomi morantem per legatum accersit.

38

Congressio Arnulfi et Erluini

Quod cum malivolorum relatione Arnulfus comperisset, insidias pretendit obvenientique, rege ignorante, cohortem inducit. Quod Erluinus mox dinoscens, signis collatis congreditur. Congressus utrimque non modicus. Arnulfus suis

on by an excess of humors, and at the very moment when he was giving orders, his hands contracted and his sinews grew tight, his mouth twisted up on one side to his ear, he shuddered and his hair stood up on end, and right in front of his men he suddenly dropped dead.[75] He was taken up by his men and buried at Saint-Quentin.[76] Shortly after the funeral, his sons went before the king and received a gracious welcome, since Louis did not impute to them any of the wrongs done to him by their father.[77] Archbishop Hugh was also received by the king, but only on the condition that at an appropriate time he would not hesitate to come and present arguments on his own behalf regarding his acquisition of the see of Reims.[78] The king departed for Amiens with them, and because he wished to attend to some matters of particular importance there with the most prominent of his men, he sent a messenger to summon Erluin from Rouen.

38

The Battle Between Arnulf and Erluin

When Arnulf learned of this from the reports of malicious men, he set a trap for Erluin and came to intercept him with a cohort of troops, unbeknownst to the king. Erluin was quick to perceive the ambush and battle was joined. The fighting was heavy on both sides. Arnulf's men were

fusis profugiens, vix urgentem evasit. Erluinus victoria potitus, alios enecat, alios capit, alios in fugam cogit. In quo
etiam certamine interfectorem Wilelmi, qui cum Arnulfo
sibi vim[106] intulerat, militari insectatione comprehendit.
Cuius manus obtruncans, in ultionem amici Rhodomum
misit. Ac cesorum ereptis manubiis, ad regem[107] concessit.

39

Quo tempore Hugo dux in magna gratia regi habitus,
eius filiam ex sacro lavacro suscepit. Unde et eum rex[108] omnium Galliarum ducem constituit. Quo duce rex equitatum
parans, cum Gerberga regina in Aquitaniam proficiscitur.
Ac urbem Nivernicam deveniens, Gothorum ducem Rage-
mundum Aquitanorumque precipuos illic obvios excepit.[109]
Apud quos de[110] provinciarum cura pertractans, ut illorum[111]
omnia sui iuris viderentur, ab eis provincias recepit. Nec distulit earum administrationem eis credere. Commisit itaque
ac suo dono illos principari constituit, regia hilaritate hilares

routed and he fled, just managing to escape his pursuer. In the aftermath of his victory Erluin killed some of the enemy, took some prisoner, and forced others to flee. During the battle some of his troops hunted down and captured William's murderer, who had taken part in Arnulf's attack on the duke. Erluin cut off his hands and sent them to Rouen to avenge the murder of his friend William.[79] Then, after stripping the spoils from the dead men, he went to meet the king.[80]

39

At that time Hugh, who was held in great favor by the king, raised Louis's daughter from the baptismal font.[81] As a result, the king made him duke over all of Gaul.[82] Under his 944 leadership the king assembled his knights and set out for Aquitaine with Queen Gerberga. When he arrived in the city of Nevers, he received Duke Raymond of Gothia[83] and the chief men of Aquitaine, who had come to meet him there. The king discussed the governance of the provinces with them, and to make it clear that everything that they possessed rightfully belonged to him, he received their lands back from them and lost no time in entrusting them once more to their administration. After investing them with these territories and confirming their authority over them, he permitted them to depart, heartened by his good humor.

redire permittens; ac cum duce iter ipse in Galliam retorquens, Lauduni sese recepit.

40

Arnulfus et Erluinus regis suasione in amiciciam redeunt

Ubi suorum precipuos preter ducem colligens, apud eos agebat quatinus viri illustres Arnulfus atque Erluinus factarum iniuriarum inmemores fierent ac in benivolentia unirentur, suis rebus prosperiorem eventum deberi ratus suorum concordia. Convocatis itaque de amicicia suadet, sese inter eos iudicem penitus aequitatem utrique parti facturum pollicens. Concedunt itaque ac iussis regiis parent.[112] Datisque vadibus, equitatis iura exsecuntur. Rex cum utrisque faveret, quamlibet utrique liberalitatem conferre meditabatur. Qui cum Arnulfum de recompensatione rerum ereptarum nutare ac Erluinum instantius amissa repetere adverteret, Arnulfum quoque maiora restituturum, eo quod ipse ampliore rerum dispendio Erluinum affecerit, Erluino Ambia-

Louis himself went back to Gaul with the duke and installed himself at Laon.[84]

40

Arnulf and Erluin Are Reconciled at the Urging of the King

Having assembled there the most important of his vassals save for the duke, he endeavored to persuade them that those illustrious men Arnulf and Erluin ought to forget the wrongs that had been done in the past and be reconciled to one another in a spirit of mutual goodwill, reckoning that a happier outcome would attend all of his affairs if there were harmony among his subjects. And so, after calling them together, he urged them to be friends, promising that he would serve as an arbiter between them and render absolutely impartial justice to both sides. They assented and yielded to his commands, and after providing sureties, they submitted to arbitration. Because the king favored both sides, he considered bestowing on each of them some sort of boon. When he saw that Arnulf was reluctant to provide recompense for the property that he taken, while Erluin was all the more insistent on regaining what he had lost, and that Arnulf would have to make greater restitution because he had inflicted a greater loss upon Erluin, he himself granted

num in recompensatione amissorum pro Arnulfo concessit. Sicque factum est ut Erluino sua restituerentur, et Arnulfo sua non minuerentur.[113] Regis itaque industria in amiciciam revocati, regia negotia exinde curabant.

41

Prodigiosa demonstratio cladis Brittannorum

Quo tempore ferebatur Parisii turbo repente exortus tanta vi discucurrisse ut parietes multa lapidum mole fundati in Monte Martium funditus eversi fuerint; demones quoque equitum specie visos basilicam quandam non procul sitam evertisse eiusque trabes memoratis parietibus tam valide incussisse ut eos subruerint; evulsisse etiam eiusdem montis vineta ac sata devastasse. Mox viso prodigio, Brittannorum pernicies subsecuta est. Qui Berengarii atque Alani principum dissidentia discordes, a Nortmannis cum quibus pactum egerant pervasi multaque cede attriti sunt. Necnon et civitas Namtarum capta est. Cuius episcopus,

Amiens to Erluin on Arnulf's behalf in order to compensate him for his losses.[85] In this way it happened that Erluin regained what belonged to him, while Arnulf did not lose anything.[86] Thus, through Louis's efforts they were recalled to friendship, and from that time forward they attended to the affairs of the king.[87]

41

A Portent of the Disaster That Befell the Bretons

At that time it was reported that a storm arose suddenly at Paris and struck with such violence that walls on Montmartre whose foundations had been laid with solid blocks of stone were completely overturned. In addition, demons in the guise of horsemen were seen demolishing a nearby church and dashing its wooden beams against the aforementioned walls with such force that they knocked them down. They also uprooted vineyards and destroyed the crops on the hillside. Shortly after the appearance of this portent, a disaster befell the Bretons. While they were quarreling amongst themselves because of the enmity between the magnates Berengar[88] and Alan,[89] they were attacked by the Northmen with whom they had made a truce and subjected to great slaughter. The town of Nantes[90] was also captured,

cum supervenientium hostium metu territus in aecclesiam
fugere cogeretur, suorum densitate oppressus ac suffocatus
est. Brittanni in ipso impetu viribus resumptis, hostes ab
urbe vehementi conamine reppulerunt illosque adorsi gravi
caede fuderunt. At Brittanni[114] prosperiore fortunae successu confortati, tertia itidem die classem pervadunt congre-
diunturque. In parte utraque innumeri fusi. Brittanni vero,
adversariorum copias non passi, in fugam feruntur. Nortmanni autem victoria potiti, Brittannorum alios gladio
occidunt, alios in fluctus cogunt, alios vero a Brittanniae
finibus eliminant, preter hos qui servitutis iugo subdi non
recusavere.

42

Rex terram Nortmannorum
pervadit capitque

Quo ad regis aures perlato—presenserat etenim nonnullos a fide defecisse Hugonique cessisse—Arnulfum ac Erluinum comites simulque et Burgundiae episcopos aliquot rex
accersit ac cum exercitu in eos fertur. Arnulfus cum suis re-

and the bishop, in his terror of the oncoming enemies, was forced to flee into the church, where he was suffocated amid the crush of his parishioners. In the midst of the assault the Bretons managed to regroup and drive the invaders out of the city with a forceful effort, attacking them and putting them to rout with tremendous bloodshed. Heartened by their success, the Bretons attacked the enemy fleet on the third day and engaged them in battle. Countless men were killed on both sides, but the Bretons could not withstand the forces of their enemies and they fled. Having obtained the victory, the Northmen put some of the Bretons to the sword, drove others into the sea, and banished the rest from the land of Brittany, save for those who were willing to submit to the yoke of servitude.[91]

42

The King Invades and Seizes the Territory of the Northmen

When the news reached the king (who had already gotten wind of the fact that a number of the Northmen had abandoned him and gone over to Hugh), he summoned counts Arnulf and Erluin and several bishops from Burgundy and marched against the Northmen with his army. Arnulf and his men went ahead of him, successfully engaging and

gem precedens, Nortmannos qui custodias observabant utiliter congressus apud Arcas fudit ac regi incessum expedivit.
Rex Rhodomum veniens, ab iis qui fidei servatores fuere exceptus est. Desertores vero mare petentes amoliti sunt; municipia vero copiis munita[115] reliquere. Rex malorum nimias
esse copias considerans, ab Hugone duce suppetias congre-
diendi per legatos postulat. Et ut ipse cum sufficientibus
copiis veniat, Baiocarum urbem, ita[116] si eam cum reliquis
expugnet, accommodat. Dux donum regium excipiens, suppetias parat[117] regique subvenit. Cum suis itaque ac quibusdam Cisalpinorum potentibus trans Sequanam fluvium iter
faciens, Baiocas pervenit. Quam aggressus, multa obsidione
premit. Inter haec, a regiis stipatoribus persuasi, Nortmanni
ad regem redeunt. Dux autem Baiocences urgebat. Rex
duci[118] obsidionem solvere per legatos iubet. Ille autem, utpote ab rege datum, amplius oppugnat. Rex quoque iterum
mandat quod nisi cito discedat, sese in eum cum copiis iturum. Dux regiis iussis contraire non valens, ab obsidione
coactus discedit. Rex urbem consequenter ingreditur. Cuius
ad se civibus revocatis, Ebrocas petit ac nullo resistente in-

defeating the Northmen who were guarding Arques-la-Bataille, and clearing the way for the king's approach. When he arrived at Rouen, the king was received by his loyal followers. Meanwhile, the rebels took to the sea and departed, leaving their strongholds garrisoned with troops. Realizing that the forces of his enemies were too strong for him, the king sent messengers to ask Duke Hugh for aid in battle. And to encourage Hugh to come in person with a sufficient number of troops, he agreed to turn over the city of Bayeux to him if he could capture it along with the rest.[92] Accepting this royal gift, the duke mustered reinforcements and went to bring aid to the king. He crossed the Seine with his men and some of the magnates of Burgundy and arrived at Bayeux, which he assaulted and subjected to an extensive siege. Meanwhile, the Northmen were persuaded by members of the king's retinue to be reconciled with the king. The duke, however, was still attacking Bayeux, so the king sent messengers to order him to raise the siege. Hugh intensified his assault on the city, however, on the grounds that it had been granted to him by the king. Louis then sent word to the duke again, this time threatening to march against him with his forces if he did not withdraw at once. The duke was not in a position to disobey the king's orders, so he was forced to abandon the siege. Shortly thereafter the king entered Bayeux. After receiving the submission of the townsmen, he departed for Évreux, which he entered without any

greditur. Nec minus et ab Ebrocensibus acceptis obsidibus, reliqua absque contradictione obtinuit.

43

Dux suos in regis iniuriam hortatur

Dux apud suos hanc iniuriam sepissime memorans, de regis pernicie petractabat, fideles et amicos hortans ut hoc ultum iri accelerent. Quod[119] etiam multis querimoniis amplificans, suos in regem provocat. Bernardus itaque Silletensis atque Teutboldus Turonicus conquerenti[120] satisfacientes, Montiniacum regis oppidum in ipsis paschae diebus pervadentes, capiunt diruuntque. Compendium quoque regiae sedis aulam repentini penetrant ac quaeque regalia insignia diripientes asportant. Nec multopost et idem Bernardus regis venatores canesque capiens, cum equis ac venabulis abduxit.

resistance. He likewise received hostages from the towns-men there, and he took control of the rest of the area with-out opposition.[93]

43

The Duke Exhorts His Men to Take Up Arms Against the King

The duke frequently reminded his men of the wrong that had been done to him and plotted with them to bring about the ruin of the king, urging his friends and faithful men to lose no time in exacting revenge on his behalf. And by dilat-ing upon it with frequent complaints, he incited his men against the king. In an attempt to assuage his anger, Bernard of Senlis[94] and Theobald of Tours[95] attacked, seized, and de-stroyed Montigny, one of the king's strongholds, during Eas-ter week. They also made a surprise attack on the royal pal-ace at Compiègne, plundering and carrying off all of the king's finery. Not long after this, the same Bernard seized the king's huntsmen and dogs and took them away, along with his horses and hunting spears.[96]

945

44

Rex urbem Remorum obsidione premit

Rex Rhodomi talia comperiens, Nortmannorum exercitum colligit copiosum, ac collecto, redit, pagum Veromandensem ingrediens penitusque depopulans. Accitis quoque Arnulfo, Erluino, Bernardo alio, Theoderico comitibus, in urbem Remorum fertur. Eamque disposita circumquaque obsidione cingit, eo quod Hugo eiusdem urbis episcopus, quia ducis partibus favebat, regi ingressum negabat.[121] Primo ergo impetu graviter dimicatum est. Nam sagittariis hinc inde dispositis, qui in muro resistebant missilibus sauciantur. Quibus amotis, alii intacti succedunt, vices pugnae ingerentes. Sed et extra telis ac lapidibus iactis nonnulli afficiuntur ceduntque. Sepe tumultus reparantur, sepe ad portas, sepe ad murum comminus congressi. Animo utrimque feroces nullomodo cedere parant; numquam sibi usque ad internetionem cessuri, nisi intercedentium supplicationibus obsidio soluta discessisset.

44

The King Lays Siege to the City of Reims

The king was at Rouen and when he learned what had happened, he raised a sizeable army of Northmen and returned home, passing through and thoroughly devastating the county of Vermandois on the way. After summoning counts Arnulf, Erluin, Bernard (a different one),[97] and Thierry,[98] he marched on Reims. He invested the city on all sides because Hugh, the archbishop of the city, supported the duke's party and refused to allow him to enter. During the initial assault there was heavy fighting. The king had deployed archers in various locations, and the men defending the walls were wounded by their arrows. Yet as soon as they withdrew, fresh troops stepped in to take their place and keep up the fight. Outside the walls many men were struck by projectiles and rocks hurled from above and forced to retreat. There were repeated clashes and frequent hand-to-hand combat at the gates and at the wall. The men on both sides fought ruthlessly and showed no signs of backing down, and neither side would have yielded until they had both been wiped out, had the siege not been broken off through the entreaties of intermediaries.[99]

45

Dux regi per legatos suadet ut ab obsidione discedat

Dux namque in ipsa obsidione per legatos petiit ut Ragenaldus comes, sumptis a sese obsidibus, locuturus sibi occurrat. Quod et fieri ab rege concessum est. Directus itaque
sub obsidum iure ad ducem venit. Apud quem dux diu deli-
berans, tandem agit ut rex ab episcopo et urbanis obsides
accipiens, ab urbis oppugnatione discedat, quatinus quocumque et quando rex velit idem episcopus rationem redditurus accedat. Ragenaldus ducis animum regi perferens ac
consilium approbans, id fieri suadebat. Obsidibusque sumptis idoneis, rex obsidionem XV die solvit tempusque audien-
dae rationis post dies XL sub ipsa Kalendarum Iuliarum die
constituit. Aliis ergo interim curatis, dies habendi colloquii
advenit. Et dux de superiore negotio locuturus, obvius regi
affuit. Declamatis autem eorum causis, vix sibi consentiebant. Rationibusque non satis utiliter procedentibus, nihil

45

The Duke Sends Envoys to Persuade
the King to Break Off the Siege

For in the midst of the siege the duke sent messengers to ask that Count Reginald[100] be allowed to come and speak with him if he gave hostages. The king granted this request. And so Reginald was sent off and came to the duke under the surety of hostages. After deliberating with him for a long time, the duke eventually proposed that the king take hostages from the archbishop and the townsmen and raise the siege, in return for which the archbishop would come to render an account of his conduct wherever and whenever the king wished. Reginald brought the duke's proposal back to the king, and by lending his approval to the plan, he persuaded him to agree to it. After the king had received suitable hostages, he raised the siege on the fifteenth day and set the time for his audience with the archbishop forty days hence, on the first of July.[101] Other matters were attended to in the interim, and the day of the meeting arrived. The duke came to meet the king to discuss the aforementioned business, but after they had each stated their position, they could scarcely agree on anything. The discussions were not getting anywhere, and no progress toward peace was made,

paci commodum constitutum est, preter quod sub pace sequestra usque ad medium Augusti rationem distulere.

46

Obitus Theotilonis
Turonensium episcopi

Quo tempore, cum beatae memoriae Theotilo Turonicae
urbis presul de renovanda inter principes pace vehementissime certaret, atque his admodum occupatus studiis Lauduno discederet, peripleumonia in ipso itinere corripitur.
Quae cum pulmonibus tumorem ac fervorem incuteret, die
quarta nati morbi hac vita migravit. Cumque adhuc in noctis tempesta spiritum efflaret, mox luminis globus per aera,
ut fertur, emicans, vigilantibus visus est. Cuius lumine ad
noctis depellendas caligines sufficienter usi, qui eius corpus
exanime deferebant per CL miliaria usque urbem Turonicam huius lucis solamine corpus beatissimum detulere, in
basilica sancti Iuliani martiris, quod idem vir sanctus summa
instruxerat religione, multa reverentia deponentes.

except that they agreed to observe a truce until the middle of August, when they would resume negotiations.[102]

46

The Death of Bishop Theotilo of Tours

At that time Archbishop Theotilo of Tours[103] of blessed memory was exerting himself to the utmost to restore peace among the magnates, and while he was actively engaged in these efforts, he was stricken with pleurisy during the course of a journey from Laon. His lungs were afflicted with swelling and burning, and he departed from this life on the fourth day of his illness.[104] In the dead of night, as he was breathing his last, it is said that those who were still awake could see a ball of light shining in the air. Its illumination allowed the men who were carrying his lifeless body to ward off the darkness of night, and with the solace of the light they carried his most blessed body 150 miles, all the way to Tours, where they deposited him with great reverence in the basilica of the monastery of Saint-Julien, which this same holy man had organized according to the highest standards of monastic observance.[105]

47

Captio regis a Nortmannis

Quo sepulto, cum adhuc inter regem ducemque pax nulla composita esset, atque rex dolos simulatorum nondum perpenderet, Erluino suisque aliis sumptis, Rhodomum rediit, nil veritus cum paucis illic immorari, cum idem consueverit. Dolus apud ducem a transfugis paratus qui ante latuerat, orta oportunitate ex raritate militum, in apertum erupit. Nam dum tempestivus adveniret, ab Hagroldo qui Baiocensibus preerat per legationem[122] suasoriam accersitus, Baiocas cum paucis ad accersientem, utpote ad fidelem quem in nullo suspectum habuerat,[123] securus accessit. Barbarus vero militum inopiam intuitus, cum multitudine armatorum regem incautum aggreditur. Cuius satellitum alios saucians, alios interimens, regem in fugam cogit. Et forte cepisset, nisi ab eius armigero resistente et[124] ibi mox interfecto ali-

47

The King Is Captured by the Northmen

After the burial of Theotilo, when as of yet no peace had been established between the king and the duke, and Louis was not contemplating the schemes of duplicitous men, he took Erluin and some of his other vassals and went back to Rouen. He was not in the least bit fearful about staying there with such a small escort, because he had become accustomed to doing so. Now the traitors at the duke's court had concocted a scheme to betray the king, and it had remained secret up to this point, but when an opportunity arose because the king had so few men with him, their plan saw the light of day. As Louis made a timely arrival at Rouen, envoys came to present him with an invitation on behalf of Harald, who was in charge of Bayeux.[106] The king took a small escort and went to meet him without any apprehension, since he viewed him as a loyal follower whom he had no reason to mistrust. But when the barbarian saw how few soldiers the king had with him, he ambushed him with a large group of armed men, wounding some members of the his retinue, killing others, and forcing the king to flee. Harald probably would have captured Louis, had he not been briefly held up by the king's squire, who fought back but was

quantisper detentus esset. Qua mora rex equi velocitate per devia raptus, Rhodomum solus pervenit. Urbemque ingressus, a civibus, eo quod cum Baiocensibus conspirassent, captus ac tentus est.

48

Rex a Nortmannis per obsides dimittitur et iterum dolo a duce capitur

Hugo dux regem Rhodomi captum comperiens, Baiocas devenit pro regis captione gratias redditurus ac ut sibi captus committatur ratiocinaturus. Nortmanni vero[125] iustis conditionibus id agendum respondent, ut si dux regem excipiat, ipsi regis filios omnes sub iure obsidum accipiant; nec sub alia lege regem sese dimissuros. Dux captionem dissimulans, acsi regis causa rem ordinaturus, ad reginam Gerbergam pro filiis regis legatos mittit. At regina rem necessa-

quickly killed. Taking advantage of this delay, the king rode rapidly over side paths on a swift horse and arrived alone at Rouen. When he entered the city, however, he was seized and held captive by the townsmen because they had conspired together with the men of Bayeux.[107]

48

The King Is Released by the Northmen After Hostages Are Given, and He Is Once More Taken Prisoner by the Duke Through Treachery

When Hugh learned that the king was being held at Rouen, he went to Bayeux to express thanks for Louis's capture and to argue that the prisoner be turned over to him. The Northmen replied that they would only agree to his request if the terms were fair, so that if the king was to be delivered into the hands of the duke, they would have to receive all of the king's sons as hostages in return. They would not release the king on any other condition. The duke sent messengers to Queen Gerberga to ask for Louis's sons, con-

riam cognoscens, sub sacramento minorem dirigit, maiorem mittere evinci non valens. Nam duo tantum erant. Minore ergo obside oblato,[126] Nortmannis non satis fuit, maiorem admodum petentes.[127] Sed quia iis quibus fidelior mens inerat visum est regiae stirpis nobilitatem posse penitus absumi si desertoribus omnes filii cum patre teneantur, id sese non facturos responderunt; minorem tantum daturos, et pro maiore ex se ipsis quemcumque petant dimissuros. Widonem ergo Suessorum episcopum, quem inter omnes potissimum videbant, expetunt ac pro obside cum regis filio recipiunt. Rex itaque dimissus, cum a duce in sua deduci putaretur, ab eodem detentus est ac Teutboldo Turonico custodiendus deputatur. Unde et manifestatum fuit regiae lineae decus in absumptione patris et filiorum penitus abolere tirannum voluisse. Re autem in contrarium ducta, unus tantum regis filius a captione superfuit.

cealing the fact that the king had been taken prisoner and pretending instead that he was acting on his behalf. Recognizing that she had no choice, the queen sent her younger son[108] under oath, but she could not be prevailed upon to give up the elder; for she had only two sons. The younger son was thus offered to the Northmen as a hostage, but this did not satisfy them, and they continued to demand the older one. But because those who remained loyal to the king could see that the nobility of the royal line was at risk of being completely extinguished if Louis and all of his sons were held by the rebels, they refused to do so. They would only hand over the younger son, and in place of the elder they would send whichever one of themselves the Northmen asked for. The Northmen therefore demanded Bishop Wido of Soissons,[109] because they judged him to be the most important of all of them, and they received him as a hostage along with the king's son. Louis was thus released, but while it was assumed that he was being escorted home by the duke, he was actually taken prisoner by him and handed over to Theobald of Tours for safekeeping.[110] In this way it was made clear that the tyrant wanted to extinguish completely the glory of the royal line by doing away with the father and his sons. But things turned out quite differently, and one of the king's sons, at any rate, remained outside of captivity.[111]

49

Otto et Edmundus, reges Germanorum et Anglorum, in ducem pro rege moventur

Cuius rei ordinem regina mox per legatos oratores Edmundo Anglorum Ottonique[128] Transrhenensium regibus indicat, ac super hoc gravissimam querimoniam litteris habitam mittit. Otto regis ac sororis casum dolens, pro restitutione regis Hugoni mox legationem delegat, plurima postulans, aliqua etiam intentans. Edmundus quoque rex de sobrini miseriis adeo conquestus, eidem duci multam animi indignationem suorum legatione demonstrat, plurimum, si non reddat, contra illum sese facturum intendens, insuper et hostes ei terra marique inducturum ac terram eius penitus depopulaturum. Quod si quolibet claudatur municipio, obsidionem vehementi conamine adhibiturum atque amplius duce se a Gallis accepturum suppetias. Et nisi regem in proximo reddat, eum terra marique in proximo appetendum.

49

Otto and Edmund,[112] the Kings of the Germans and the English, Take Action Against the Duke on Behalf of the King

Soon afterward the queen dispatched envoys skilled in speaking to relate this series of events to King Edmund of England and King Otto of the Men-beyond-the-Rhine, sending in addition a letter in which she complained bitterly about what had happened. Otto was saddened to hear of the misfortune that had befallen his sister and the king, and he immediately sent envoys to Hugh to pressure him to restore Louis to the throne, making many demands and even some threats. King Edmund, too, was much aggrieved at the sufferings of his cousin,[113] and he sent a deputation of his men to make his displeasure clear to Duke Hugh, threatening that if he did not release Louis he would take action against him, and that in addition he would lead a hostile army against him by land and sea and thoroughly devastate his lands. If the duke were to shut himself up in one of his strongholds, then he would exert all of his energy to lay siege to it, and he would receive more help from the Gauls than the duke himself. And if the duke did not hand over the king in a timely manner, he would soon find himself threatened by both land and sea.[114]

946

50

Indignatio ducis in
Edmundum regem

Dux gravi legatione confectus, Ottoni pro parte dissentit,[129] pro parte favet. Regis vero Edmundi legatis id nec[130] in proximo nec preter rationem agendum respondit. Ob minas Anglorum nil sese facturum. Ipsos, si veniant, quid in armis Galli valeant promtissime experturos. Quod si formidine tacti non veniant, pro arrogantiae tamen illatione Gallorum vires quandoque cognituros et insuper poenam luituros. Iratus itaque legatos expulit. Consultumque[131] se conferens, apud suos partibus utitur deliberationis. Et post consultum, Ottonem expetit. Qui cum per legatos colloquendi oportunitatem quereret, infensus ei loqui non optinuit. Nimiumque iratus, in sua discedit,[132] ac suorum usus consilio, regem adit sicque alloquitur:

50

The Duke's Resentment
Against King Edmund

The duke was chastened by the seriousness of Otto's message, and while he continued to oppose him on certain points, he took his side on others. As for the envoys of King Edmund, he told them that their demands could not be carried out hastily or without consideration. Nor was he going to do anything in response to the threats that he had received from the English. If they came to attack him, then they would very quickly discover what the Gauls could accomplish in battle. If they stayed away out of fear, however, then for all their arrogant boasting they would one day come to learn the strength of the Gauls—and pay the penalty. With that he angrily sent the envoys away. Turning to consider what he should do next, he entered into deliberations with his men, and after taking counsel with them, he went to see Otto. But when he sent envoys to request an opportunity to meet with him, he was treated as an enemy and denied an audience. Furious at this, the duke returned home, and on the advice of his men he went to King Louis and spoke to him as follows:[115]

51

Proloquutio Hugonis ad regem

'Parvum te, o rex, adversariorum insectatio in partes transmarinas olim compulit. Meo vero ingenio et consilio inde revocatus, regnis restitutus es. Post, dum meis usus fuisti consiliis, rerum secundarum prosperis floruisti. Numquam nisi tui furoris pertinatia a te defeci. Infimorum ac imprudentium hominum dispositione usus, a sapientium consiliis plurimum oberrasti. Unde et rerum calamitas digne consecuta est.[133] Quomodo enim preter me necessaria tibi ac gloriosa provenire arbitrare? Multum, inquam, tibi in hoc derogatum est. Iam memineris te virum esse. Consideres quoque quid tuae rationi commodum sit. Sicque virtus redeat, ut[134] in benivolentiam nos revocet, te imperantem, et me militantem,[135] per me etiam reliquos militatum tibi reducat. Et quia rex a me creatus, nihil mihi largitus es, Laudunum saltem militaturo liberaliter accommoda. Quod etiam causa erit fidei servandae.' Rex, utpote captus, dictis prolo-

51

Hugh's Address to the King

"Long ago, my lord, while you were still a child,[116] the persecution of your enemies drove you to the lands beyond the sea. Yet thanks to my ingenuity and my counsel you were recalled from there and restored to the throne. Afterward, as long as you followed my advice, you met with success and prosperity. Nor did I ever desert you, except when driven to it by your stubborn madness. You let yourself be guided by lowborn and foolish men, and you strayed far from the advice of wise counselors. As a result, disaster befell you—and deservedly so. For without me how can you hope to achieve that which you require and that which redounds to your glory? Your behavior has diminished you greatly, I tell you. Recall now that you are a man and consider what is in your own best interest.[117] Let virtue return so that it may recall us to mutual goodwill, with you as the ruler and I as your vassal, and so that the rest of your men may be brought back into your service with my help. Now because I have received no reward from you, in spite of the fact that it was I who arranged to have you elected king, be so generous as to grant me Laon, at the very least, in exchange for my service. This will also be an incentive for me to remain faithful to you." Because he was still a prisoner, the king had no choice but to agree to the duke's proposal. He was subsequently released, and after handing Laon over to the duke,

quentis cessit. Unde et dimissus, data Lauduno, Compendii[136] sese recepit. Adest Gerberga regina multa virtute me-
morabilis. Adsunt quoque aliquot ex Belgica episcopi.
Confluunt etiam viri illustres nonnulli.

52

Querimonia regis apud privatos de Hugonis persecutione

Apud quos etiam rex his verbis conquestus est. Et 'Eia
tu,'[137] inquiens, 'Hugo! Eia tu,[138] Hugo! Quantis bonis a te
privatus, quantis malis affectus, quanto etiam merore nunc
detineor! Urbem Remorum pervasisti, Laudunum surri-
puisti. His tantum duobus recipiebar, his duobus claudebar.
Pater meus captus atque in carcerem trusus, has quae me
premunt aerumnas cum anima simul amisit. Ego vero in eadem precipitatus, ex regno paterno nihil nisi spectaculum
prebeo. Iam nec vivere libet, nec emori licet. Quo me itaque
conferam?' Paransque amplius conqueri, ab indignantibus

he took up residence at Compiègne.[118] Queen Gerberga, who is worthy to be remembered for her great virtue, was with him, along with some of the bishops from Belgica. A number of prominent men assembled there as well.[119]

52

The King's Complaint to His Council Concerning His Persecution at the Hands of Hugh

The king delivered a complaint to them in these words: "Alas, Hugh! Alas, Hugh! How many good things you have deprived me of! What great evils you have inflicted upon me! In what miserable conditions I am now held captive! You have taken Reims from me and snatched away Laon, the only two places where I could find refuge and security. My father was taken prisoner and thrown into a dungeon, but when he lost his life he also bid farewell to the miseries that now oppress me. I, on the other hand, who have been cast down into the same misfortunes, have nothing to show for my father's kingdom but a public spectacle. I do not care to live any more, but I am not permitted to die.[120] Where then shall I betake myself?" He was preparing to continue on in this vein, but he was prevented from doing so by the

inhibitus est. Deinde animum temperans, consilium cum suis confert.

53

Quo collato, Ottoni regi per legatos ereptionem suam demonstrat, antea sese captum, nunc autem omnibus bonis privatum memorans. Unde et amico auxilium conferat. Urbes amissas repetere iuvet. Si id faciat, gratiam multam sese inde recompensaturum. Otto benignissime legationem excipiens, cum copiis in regis auxilium se iturum spondet ac tempus edicit. Legati redeunt ac mandata referunt. Nec minus et ab rege Genaunorum Conrado copias petit et accipit.

54

Interea Otto rex, cum Rheno transmisso exercitum per Belgicam duceret, obviat regi Conrhado, qui tunc ab Alpibus egressus, cum multa expeditione Ludovico succurrere accelerabat. Iuncti ergo ambo, cum multo equitatu gradiebantur. Quorum accessum Ludovicus dinoscens, ocius oc-

indignation of his audience. Thereupon he regained his composure and took counsel with his men.

53

After conferring with them, Louis sent envoys to King Otto to inform him of his release, declaring that whereas he had formerly been a prisoner, he had now been deprived of all of his possessions. For that reason Otto should come to the aid of his friend and help him to recover the cities that he had lost. In return, the king would repay him with many tokens of his gratitude. Receiving the envoys graciously, Otto promised to bring his forces to help the king and fixed a time for it. The envoys returned and reported Otto's response. Louis also asked for and obtained troops from King Conrad of Burgundy.[121]

54

Otto had crossed the Rhine and was leading his army through Belgica when he encountered King Conrad, who had just emerged from the Alps and was hastening to Louis's aid with a large contingent of troops. Joining together, therefore, the two of them continued onward with a substantial force of knights. When Louis learned of their ap-

currit. Tres itaque reges in unum collecti, primi certaminis laborem Lauduno inferendum decernunt et sine mora illo exercitum ducunt. Cum ergo ex adverso montis eminentiam viderent et[139] omni parte urbis situm explorarent, cognito incassum sese ibi certaturos, ab ea urbe discedunt et Remos adoriuntur. Ubi quia planicies commoditatem exercitibus parabat, obsidio circumquaque disposita est. Et[140] primo certamine comminus pugnatum est. In quo tela ac lapides tam dense ferebantur quam densa grando quandoque dilabitur. Per integram ergo diem continuis motibus urbs inpugnata est. Post vero comminus septies dimicatum, atque hoc fere per dies sex.

55

Nec tamen[141] cives assiduis tumultibus victi ullo modo cedebant,[142] cum eorum presul Hugo quosdam principum qui sibi quadam cognatione conveniebant extra urbem[143] allocutus est, quaerens ab eis rationem, ut scilicet quid agendum, quid vitandum sibi dicerent; si aliquorum intercessione id medendum videretur, si opus foret precibus, si etiam pugnae instandum esset. Illi mox regum animositatem de-

proach, he hastened to meet them. The three kings, now united into one group, decided that their first order of business was to attack Laon, and they led the army there without delay. But when they saw the height of the hill before them and investigated the layout of the city on every side,[122] they realized that it would be pointless to contest Laon, so they left and marched on Reims. Because the level ground there was better suited to their troops, they invested the city on all sides. The initial assault issued in hand-to-hand combat. During the battle missiles and stones rained down as thick as a dense fall of hail. All throughout the day the city was subjected to continuous assaults by the besieging army. There were seven more close engagements after that, and this went on for about six days.[123]

55

Although the townsmen were getting the worst of the constant skirmishes, they refused to give in. At this point Archbishop Hugh spoke outside the city with several of the magnates who were related to him in one way or another,[124] asking their advice about what he should do and what he should not do, whether the situation could be resolved through intermediaries, and if he should resort to entreaties or press on with the battle. They, in turn, made clear to him

monstrantes, fixum in eis asserunt nullorum interventibus sese concessuros, at obsidioni usque ad effectum operam daturos. Quod si urbem vi capi contingat, ipsi presuli oculos effossuros, et hoc ita ordinatum fixumque. Unde et accelerandum ut egrediatur suosque ab regum indignatione eripiat. His presul territus, suis hoc monstrat.[144] Et consilio habito, die obsidionis sexta cum suis egreditur. Portae regibus panduntur.

56

Reges vero Artoldum resumentes, urbem consequenter introducunt. Duorumque metropolitanorum medius, Friderici Maguntini ac Rotberti Treverensis, ab eis per manus pristinae sedi restitutus est. Ubi etiam mox Gerbergam reginam cum aliquot illustribus custodiae deputantes, ipsi tres reges in Hugonem ducem cum exercitu feruntur. Silletum quoque vi irrumpere nitentes, considerato oppidi firmamento, inde amoliuntur, non tamen sine suburbii combustione et aliquorum nece; sicque ad fluvium Sequanam contendunt.

the anger of the kings and explained that they were determined not to yield to appeals from anyone, but instead to continue the siege until they were victorious. If they took the city by force, they were going to gouge out his eyes — this had been determined and settled. Hence, he needed to make haste to get out of the city and save his men from the wrath of the kings. Terrified at what he had heard, the bishop related the news to his men. And after taking counsel, they left Reims on the sixth day of the siege.[125] Thereupon, the gates of the city were opened to the kings.[126]

56

The kings then took Artald and brought him back into the city. Archbishops Frederick of Mainz[127] and Ruotbert of Trier[128] took him by the hand, one on either side, and restored him to his former see. After assigning Queen Gerberga to guard the city with several prominent men, these same three kings set out against Duke Hugh with their army. They tried to take Senlis by force, but when they realized the strength of the stronghold's fortifications, they abandoned the effort, although not before setting fire to the outskirts of the town and killing a number of people. After this they marched to the Seine.[129]

57

Quomodo pauci iuvenes naves a duce subductas per astutiam repetitas exercitui deduxerint[145]

Dux vero eorum impetum presentiens, a litore hostibus contiguo per XX miliaria omnes naves abduci preceperat, ne adversariis transeundi commoditas pararetur. At frustrato eius consilio, multo aliter provenisse notum est. Nam decem numero iuvenes, quibus constanti mente fixum erat omne periculum[146] subire, habitum militarem in peregrinum transformantes, reges prevenerant, obsecrationum vota simulantes.[147] Sportulis itaque ab humero dependentibus, ferratis baculis procedunt. Habitumque mentiti peregrinum, urbem Parisium cum Sequana pontibus pertranseunt. Nullus eis molestus extitit. Ac litora exteriora quibus naves tenebantur petunt. Sicque in hospitium farinarii cuiusdam divertentes, sese gratia visendi sanctorum loca ex citeriore

57

How a Small Band of Young Men Used Their Wits to Find the Boats That Had Been Confiscated by the Duke and Bring Them Back to the Army

When the duke got wind of their advance, he ordered all the boats within an area of twenty miles to be removed from the right bank of the river in order to deny his enemies any convenient way of crossing. His plans were thwarted, however, and it is known that things turned out quite differently. A band of ten young men who were unwavering in their determination to undergo any danger had exchanged their warlike garb for the habit of pilgrims and gone on ahead of the kings, pretending that they had taken vows of prayer.[130] They traveled with iron-tipped staves and hung baskets from their arms. And by employing this disguise they were able to cross the bridges over the Seine and pass through the city of Paris without anyone bothering them. They made for the left bank of the river, where the ships were moored. Stopping at the house of a miller, they told him that they had come over from the other side of the river to visit the shrines of the saints. When the miller looked upon these handsome young men, for all their shabby clothes he was glad to offer them lodging, and he carefully attended to their needs. As part of the scheme that they had

litore advenisse referunt. Farinarius iuvenes formosos in habitu licet abiecto considerans, hospitium gratanter accommodat et insuper eos mitius curat. Qui fraudem meditati, nummos dant, vinumque mercati, hospitem inebriant. Et sic totam diem convivii iocunditate consumunt. Iuvenes hospitem vino faciliorem advertentes, quod ei sit officium percunctantur. Ille farinarium sese[148] memorat. At illi prosecuti, si quid amplius possit interrogant. Ille etiam piscatorum ducis magistrum se asserit, et ex navium accommodatione questum aliquem sibi adesse. Illi vero, 'Quoniam,' inquiunt, 'humanissimum nobis te invenimus, ampliora etiam optamus. Unde et si quiddam nobis facias, X solidos nos allegaturos pollicemur, ut videlicet[149] trans fluvium nos evehas, eo quod ulterius procedere oratum nequeamus, itineris longitudine fatigati.' At hospite respondente ducis edicto naves ad interiora[150] litora raptas ne Germanis irrumpentibus pateat accessus, illi tempore nocturno absque calumnia id fieri posse prosecuntur. Ille pecuniae cupidus naulum accipit ac de patrando negotio fidem dat. Nox affuit. Iuvenes promissum fieri postulant. Ille mox, assumpto puero privigno, cum iuvenibus in noctis tempesta ad naves properat. Comitantur et iuvenes. Qui solitudinem videntes, puerum raptum in fluentum demergunt. Hospitem vero clamare nitentem gutture invadunt atque mortem ni quod volunt efficiat interminantur, ut videlicet naves solvat. Pervasus ergo ac territus, naves solvit. Consilioque inito, vinctum

devised, the young men produced some money to buy wine and got their host drunk. And so they spent the whole day eating and drinking together convivially. When the young men saw that the wine had loosened up their host, they asked him what his job was. When he replied that he was a miller, they followed up by asking him if he could do anything else. He said that he was also the master of the duke's fishermen and that he derived some income from renting out boats. Then they said, "Since we have found you so kindly disposed toward us, we have a further request to make. So now if you will do something for us—namely, carry us across the river—then we promise to pay you ten solidi. For we are worn out from the length of our journey and cannot go any further to pray." When their host told them that all of the boats had been seized and taken over to the left bank of the river on the orders of the duke to prevent the invading Germans from crossing, they replied that it could be managed at night without any problem. Eager to get his hands on their money, the miller took their fare and promised to arrange it for them. When night came, the young men asked him to go through with what he had promised. Taking along his young stepson, the miller hurried to the boats in the dead of night, accompanied by the young men. When they saw that they were in an out-of-the way place, they snatched up the boy and threw him into the river. Their host tried to cry out, but they seized him by the throat and threatened to kill him if he did not untie the boats as they wished. Terrified by this rough treatment, he did as they asked. Then, after conferring amongst themselves, they tied him up and threw him into one of the boats. Each one of them brought a single boat back to the shore. Then they

navi conitiunt ac naves singuli singulas ad litus deducunt. Eiecto vero hospite vincto, navim unam omnes ingressi, alias repetunt ac novem iterum deducunt. Octiesque fluvium remensi, naves numero LXXII abduxerunt.

58

Dum haec gererentur, regum exercitus in ipsa diei orientis aurora fluvio affuit navesque paratas cum remis invenit, quas tirones cum armis ingressi navigant ac exaquantur. Tum circumquaque palantes, nullo prohibente a diversis portibus alias rapiunt et exercitibus deducunt. Nam qui ruri degebant irruentium metu omnes auffugerant; dux vero Aurelianis sese receperat. Unde et qui resisteret[151] aberat. Navibus itaque conexis ac multo robore compactis, liburnas solidant. Quas ingressus, exercitus fluvium transit. Dein terra recepti, incendiis predisque vehementibus totam regionem usque Ligerim depopulati sunt. Post haec feruntur in terram pyratarum ac solotenus devastant. Sicque regis iniuriam atrociter ulti, iter ad sua retorquent. Ludovicus vero rex Remos redit.

tossed their host out of the boat, still bound, and all of them boarded a single vessel. They went back to the rest of the boats and brought back another nine. They crossed the river eight times and made away with seventy-two boats in all.

58

Meanwhile, the kings' army came to the river at dawn on the following day and found the boats ready and outfitted with oars. Young recruits bearing arms went on board, disembarked, and set off on the river. Then they ranged in different directions, taking more boats from various ports and bringing them back to the army without anyone stopping them; for the people who lived in the countryside had fled in fear of the invaders, and the duke had withdrawn to Orléans, so that there was no one to oppose them. They joined the boats together and bound them fast to create a solid bridge which the army marched over to cross the river. When they reached dry land, they pillaged and burned with fury, ravaging the whole region as far south as the Loire. After this, they moved into the territory held by the pirates[131] and devastated the land down to the very soil. Having exacted a brutal vengeance for the wrongs done to the king, they reversed course and headed home. For his part, King Louis returned to Reims.[132]

59

Qualiter Deroldus a quodam medico deceptus sit eumque deceperit

Quo tempore Ambianensium episcopus Deroldus ab hac vita decessit, vir spectabilis ac palatinus, et quondam Karolo regi admodum dilectus, in arte medicinae peritissimus. De quo etiam fertur quod cum adhuc in palatio regi serviret, a quodam Salernitano medico deceptus sit eumque deceperit. Etenim cum uterque in arte medicinae optime posset, et iste regi potior, Salernitanus vero reginae[152] peritior videretur, commento regis repertum est quis eorum[153] rerum naturas magis dinosceret. Iussit etenim coram se illos consedere convivas, causam rei penitus dissimulans ac sepe eis questiones proponens. Quisque ut poterat proposita solvebat. Deroldus quidem, utpote litterarum artibus eruditus, probabiliter obiecta diffiniebat. Salernitatus vero, licet nulla litterarum scientia preditus, tamen ex ingenio naturae multam in rebus experientiam habebat. Regio itaque iussu cotidie consident ac mensa regia continue una potiuntur. Et die quadam de dinamidiarum differentiis disputatum est, tractatumque uberius quid efficiat farmaceutica, quid vero

59

How Derold Was Deceived by a Certain Doctor, and How He Deceived Him in Turn

At that time Derold,[133] the bishop of Amiens, departed this life.[134] A distinguished courtier and onetime favorite of King Charles, he was supremely skilled in the art of medicine. It is also said that while he was still serving at the royal palace, he fell victim to the deceit of a certain doctor from Salerno, but that he deceived him in turn. While both of them were very capable in the art of medicine, the king preferred Derold, while the queen[135] judged the Salernitan to be the more skillful of the two; so the king devised a way to determine which one of them knew more about the properties of nature. He ordered both men to dine with him as his guests, and keeping his real motive hidden, he posed a number of questions to them. They each answered what was asked of them as best they could. For his part, Derold, who had been educated in the liberal arts, provided credible definitions, while the Salernitan, although he was not endowed with the knowledge of letters, nonetheless possessed a great deal of practical expertise as a result of his natural cleverness. And so, at the king's behest, they sat side by side every day, occupying the royal table together without interruption. One day there was a debate concerning the capacities of different kinds of medical treatments, and they had a lengthy

cirurgica, quid etiam butanica. At Salernitanus, peregrina
nomina non advertens, ab eorum interpretatione erubes-
cens quievit. Invidet ergo plurimum ac in eius mortem venenum parare meditatur, multam[154] dolose benivolentiam
simulans.[155] Parato vero maleficio, cum una in prandio resi-
derent, Salernitanus, ungue inpudici toxicato, liquorem pi-
peris quo cibum pariter intinguebant loetaliter inficit. Quo
Deroldus incaute sumpto, mox serpente veneno, deficere
coepit. Eductusque a suis, teriaca[156] vim veneni repellit. Et
triduo expleto coram rediens, Salernitano consuescebat. In-
terrogatus vero quid ei accidisset, fleumatis frigdore se leviter tactum respondit, quicquam fraudis se perpendisse dissimulans. Unde et hostem incautum efficit. Convivae itaque
redditi, Deroldus toxicum inter auricularem ac salutarem
occultatum eius cibo sumendo respersit. Quod mox venis
serpens, vitae calorem fugabat. Vexatusque a suis eductus
est. Qui veneno expellendo operam dans, nihil curae agebat.
Deroldum itaque magnificans summumque eum in medi-
cina predicans, eius curam vehementissime petebat. Qui regis iussu flexus, antidotis datis, a toxico per industriam non
ex toto purgavit. Nam sumpta teriaca, vis veneni in pedem

discussion about the relative efficacy of pharmacy, surgery, and botany. The Salernitan did not recognize these foreign words and to his chagrin could offer no explanation of them. As a result he was filled with envy, and while deceptively feigning great goodwill toward his rival, he pondered how he could concoct a poison that would bring about his death. He then prepared the drug, and as they were sitting at lunch together, the Salernitan applied some of the poison to the tip of his middle finger and put a lethal dose into the pepper sauce into which they were both dipping their food. Derold tasted some of it unknowingly, whereupon the poison quickly spread throughout his body, and he began to grow weak. He was led away by his companions and given theriac to counteract the poison. After three days, he returned to court and began to take up with the Salernitan again. When he was asked what had happened to him, he replied that he had suffered a mild touch of phlegmatic fever, giving no indication that he suspected any kind of foul play. This took his adversary off his guard. When they returned to the table together, Derold sprinkled some poison that he had hidden between his little finger and his index finger[136] into the food the Salernitan was about to eat. It quickly spread through his veins and began to chase the vital heat from his body, and he was taken away by his men in pain. When he tried to drive out the poison, he found his remedies to no avail, so he urgently entreated Derold for a cure, extolling him and proclaiming him to be supreme in the art of medicine. At the orders of the king, Derold was prevailed upon to administer the antidote, but he deliberately took care not to purge him of the toxin completely. Thus, when the Salernitan took the theriac, all the force of the venom concentrated itself in his

sinistrum penitus dilapsa est, in tantum ut apud domesticos eo familiariter agente, venenum, ut fertur, in modum ciceris a pede per venam surgens, ab antidoto obviante in pedem repelleretur. Quibus diutissime sic repugnantibus, pes in cutis superficie foratur. Factoque morbo, post a cirurgis miserabiliter absciditur.

60

Interea dux Neustriam combustam direptamque dolens, exercitum parat et in Arnulfum, cum in regem non auderet, truculentus effertur. Oppida quoque illius aliquot impugnat. At cum per dies sex nullum comprehendere posset, voto frustratus sua repetit. Quae dum a duce gererentur, rex obsidione Mosomum premebat, eo quod ducis nepos Hugo a pontificatu abiectus ibidem moraretur. Hunc itaque infestabat in ducis contumeliam. At ducem ab obsidione discessisse comperiens, ipse quoque Remos repetit. Qua etiam tempestate Bovo Catalaunensium episcopus hac vita decessit. Cui etiam mox successit[157] ab rege Gipuinus totius electione cleri, adolescens egregius, atque a domno Artoldo Remorum metropolitano consecratur episcopus.

left foot. The result was that that as he was going about his business among the men of his household, the poison reportedly rose up from his foot through a vein like a chickpea, only to be driven back down when it came into contact with the antidote. As a consequence of the prolonged struggle between these two forces, his foot developed holes on the surface of the skin. It became infected, and he had to endure a painful amputation at the hands of surgeons.

60

The duke, meanwhile, aggrieved at the burning and plundering of Neustria, raised an army and savagely attacked Arnulf, since he did not dare to move against the king. He also besieged several of Arnulf's strongholds. When he was unable to capture any of them after six days, however, he returned home, having been thwarted in his designs. While he was so engaged, the king was laying siege to Mouzon, since the duke's nephew Hugh was residing there after being deposed from his bishopric. Thus, he was harassing him in order to affront the duke. But when he learned that Duke Hugh had abandoned his siege, the king went back to Reims. At that time Bishop Bovo of Châlons departed from this life. Gibuin[137] was immediately chosen to succeed him by the king, and this outstanding young man was elected by all the clergy and consecrated as bishop by Archbishop Artald of Reims.[138]

947

299

61

Post haec vero rex in Belgicam concessit, ibique ei locuturus Otto rex[158] obviam venit. Ac quaeque necessaria ordinantes, ambo reges Aquisgrani pascha celebrant atque multa reverentia sese mutuo honorant, atque hoc ab Ottone amplius; a quo etiam Ludovicus regiis donis liberalissime honoratur.

62

Dux urbem Remorum[159] impugnat

Dum haec ita sese haberent, dux de regis iniuria apud suos agitabat, oportunitatem in regis absentia asserens qua urbem Remorum capiat, cum tunc urbs tam episcopo quam militibus vacua esset, rex etiam ipse alias occupatus alia quereret. Unde et possibile asserebat facili expugnatione urbem capi, idque attemptare sese plurimum velle. Quibus milites capti, in urbem mittendas cohortes censent. Quae collectae, cum duce gradiuntur. Urbem appetunt et circumquaque obsidione premunt. Diffunduntur quoque passim atque frumentum ex locis contiguis in usum pugnae convectant. Cas-

61

Thereupon the king withdrew into Belgica, where King Otto came to speak with him. After attending to some necessary business, both kings celebrated Easter at Aachen and each honored the other with great reverence, although Otto went somewhat further in this regard, honoring Louis very generously with royal gifts.[139]

62

The Duke Assaults the City of Reims

While this was going on, the duke was complaining to his men about the injustice he had suffered at the hands of the king. He declared that Louis's absence presented him with an opportunity to capture Reims, now that the city was empty of its bishop and its fighting men, and the king was occupied elsewhere with other business. As a result, he said, the city could be captured by a straightforward assault, and he was eager to make the attempt. His men were won over by his speech and they voted to send troops against the city.[140] When his army had assembled, they marched forth with the duke. They advanced to Reims and invested the city on all sides. Some of the men went off in different di-

tra fossis muniunt cratibusque circumdant. Pugnam ergo in dies aut semel aut bis inferunt. Nec minus et cives vehementissime resistunt. Iamque id diebus numero VIIII agitabant, cum regem adeo indignatum regredi ab observatoribus nuntiatur. Et mox obsidione soluta, duodecima die[160] ab urbe discedunt.

63

Nec diu moratus, rex urbem succurrendo ingreditur. Apud quem mox principes collecti, de eius ac communi salute consultant. Et quia rerum utilitas Ottonem consiliis interesse exigebat, diriguntur legati per quos ei necessitas demonstratur, ac colloquium exeunte mense Augusto sibi habendum secus fluvium Karam denuntiatur.

64

Cum haec sic sese haberent, dux nepotem ab presulatu pulsum dolebat. Suadebat itaque ut officio pontificali amplius insisteret, et ne privatus penitus dignitate videretur,

rections and brought in grain from the surrounding area to support the siege effort. His troops fortified their camp with ditches and surrounded it with bundles of brush. Every day they made one or two assaults upon the city, which the townsmen resisted fiercely. They had been at it for nine days when scouts announced that the king was returning in a state of great displeasure. Shortly thereafter they raised the siege, and on the twelfth day they departed from the city.[141]

63

Soon afterward Louis arrived in the city bringing help. A short time later the magnates assembled before him to deliberate over his welfare and that of the realm in general. Because it was necessary that Otto participate in these discussions if they were to be of any use, envoys were sent to tell him that his presence was needed, and it was announced that a meeting would be held between the two kings at the end of August,[142] beside the Chiers River.[143]

64

Meanwhile, the duke was aggrieved that his nephew had been expelled from his see. Consequently, he urged him to keep carrying out his duties as bishop and to promote some

aliquas ad gradus promoveret personas. Tetbaldum ergo
Suessonicae aecclesiae diaconum accersit presbiterumque
ordinat, ac post duce agente aecclesiae Ambianensium episcopum sacrat. In qua re favere visus est Wido tantum Suessorum episcopus. Quem quia post penituit sequentia de-
monstrabunt. Sed tempus colloquendi regibus advenit, ac
secus fluvium Karam sibi occurrunt. Nec defuit dux, qui et
ipse apud Duodeciacum vicum castra fixit, ut pro nepote
causam apud episcopos ageret.

65

Dux enititur ut causa pro suo nepote apud episcopos agatur

Regibus itaque rerum negotia agentibus, dux causam ne-
potis episcopis disponebat, penes quos etiam plurimam
habebat indignationem, iniuste et nullis evidentibus culpis
nepotem precipitatum memorans. Quod cum indicatum regibus esset, Ottone agente decretum est ut ibi ab episcopis
causa Artoldi atque Hugonis discuteretur, ita tamen ut et
dux tempore congruo regi satisfaceret. Episcopis itaque ra-

men into orders so as not to give the appearance that he had forfeited his office completely. In response, Hugh summoned Theobald, a deacon of the church of Soissons, and ordained him as a priest, and afterward, at the duke's bidding, he consecrated him bishop of Amiens.[144] Bishop Wido of Soissons was the only one who openly supported him in this. Subsequent events will make it clear that he came to regret this decision, however. The time for the meeting between the kings now arrived, and they met beside the Chiers River. The duke had also come (having set up camp at the village of Douzy) so that he might plead his nephew's case before the bishops.[145]

65

The Duke Tries to Have His Nephew's Case Heard by the Bishops

While the kings were conducting business, the duke laid out his nephew's case to the bishops, expressing outrage because, he claimed, he had been deposed unjustly and without any evidence of wrongdoing. When the kings had been informed of this, upon Otto's initiative it was publicly decreed that the bishops would discuss the dispute between Artald and Hugh there and then, provided that the duke made satisfaction to the king on a suitable occasion. And so

tionem excipientibus,[161] cum inter plurima quae ibi explicata
sunt illud constantissime refutarent, quod Hugo sacerdotio
privatus contra fas Ambianensium episcopum ordinasset,
regum sententia in aliam sinodum huiusmodi rationem
transferendam constituit. Videbatur etenim quod non ad
aequitatem satis commode haec altercatio determinari valeret, cum nec sinodus ad hoc convocata fuisset. Et decreto
regio XV Kal. Decemb. habenda denuntiatur. Interim vero
sedes Remensis Artoldo conceditur; Hugoni vero in castro
Mosomensi commorari permittitur. Pax quoque sequestra
Ottonis interventu regi ac duci ab alterutro datur et usque
ad tempus habendae sinodi sacramento firmatur.

66

Sinodus Virduni habita

Tempus advenit sinodusque episcoporum Virduni collecta est atque habita, presidente Rotberto metropolitano
Treverico, cum Artoldo Remensi, considentibus quoque
Adalberone Mettensi, Gauslino Tullensi, Hildeboldo Mime-
gardvurdensi, Israhele Brittigena, assistentibus etiam Bru-
none viro reverendo et abbate, cum aliis abbatibus et mona-

the bishops took the matter in hand, and because, among the numerous findings that were made there, they were united in rejecting Hugh's unlawful ordination of the bishop of Amiens after he himself had been deposed from office, the kings decided to postpone the proceedings to another synod.[146] For it was thought that it would be difficult for the dispute to be resolved fairly when a synod had not even been called for this purpose. It was then announced by royal decree that an assembly would be held on November 17.[147] In the meantime, Artald was given control of the see of Reims, while Hugh was permitted to stay in the fortress of Mouzon. Through Otto's mediation the king and the duke also agreed to observe a truce, and this agreement was confirmed with oaths up until the date of the synod.[148]

66

The Synod of Verdun[149]

When the time came, the bishops assembled at Verdun, where a synod was held under the leadership of Archbishop Ruotbert of Trier and Artald of Reims. Seated with them were Adalbero of Metz, Gauzlin of Toul, Hildebold of Münster, and Israel the Briton; also in attendance were the reverend abbot Bruno,[150] along with the other venerable abbots and monks Einold and Odilo.[151] Hugh had been summoned

chis venerandis Agenoldo et Odilone. Ad hanc sinodum Hugo vocatus, missis ad eum deducendum Adalberone et Gauslino episcopis, venire noluit. Unde et episcoporum sententia Artoldo tenere concedit episcopium. Sicque nullis rerum determinatis rationibus, sinodus soluta est.

67

Sinodus Mosomi habita

Indicitur vero habenda Id. Ian. Et evoluto tempore, in basilica sancti Petri[162] apud Mosomense castrum secunda sinodus habita est, presidente quoque predicto metropolitano Rotberto Treverico, cum fere omnibus suae dioceseos episcopis ac aliquibus Remensis; consedente etiam Artoldo, cuius causa discutienda erat. Nec[163] abfuit Hugo, at sinodum ingredi noluit. Epistolam vero nomine Agapiti papae signatam per suos sinodo legendam porrexit. Quae cum soluta et

to attend the synod, and Bishops Adalbero and Gauzlin had been sent to escort him there, but he had refused to come. As a result, the bishops decided that Artald should retain control over his see. And so the synod was dissolved, although no decision had been reached on any of the disputed issues.

67

The Synod of Mouzon[152]

It was then declared that a synod would be held on January 13. When the time came, this second synod was held in the church of Saint Peter at the fortress of Mouzon. Archbishop Ruotbert of Trier also presided over the council, which was attended by almost all of the bishops of his province and some from the province of Reims, in addition to Artald, whose case was going to be considered. Nor was Hugh absent, although he refused to appear before the synod. However, he had his men hand over a letter bearing the seal of Pope Agapitus[153] for the bishops to read. When the seal was broken and the letter was read aloud, it became apparent that it possessed no canonical authority and did not even present any argument to support Hugh's case apart from declaring that the bishopric should be restored to him.

948

lecta esset, nihil canonicae auctoritatis habere videbatur, nihil etiam pro eius causa significare, nisi ut ei episcopium redderetur. Qua perlecta, cum episcopi consulto sese contulissent, cassandam censuerunt, eo quod absque ratione rem quae in lite erat abdicato reddi iubebat. Et quia paulo ante ab ipso papa Agapito delegata erat epistola per Fredericum Maguntinum episcopum atque data Rotberto metropolitano Treverico coram regibus ac Galliae et Germaniae episcopis, quae erat continens auctoritatem apostolicae iussionis, partemque preceptorum eius iam exsecuti fuerant, communi mox consensu decretum est ut quod regulariter coeptum erat rationabiliter atque canonice pertractaretur. Simulque et mox a metropolitano iussum est ut recitaretur capitulum[164] XVIIII concilii Cartaginensis, quod constat de accusato et accusatore. Et recitato, secundum ipsius capituli sententiam constituere ut, Remensi parroechia Artoldo restituta, qui nullius sinodi rationes audire refugit, Hugo, qui ad duas iam sinodos accersitus venire contempserat,[165] a Remensis episcopii regimine abstineret donec in tertiam sinodum[166] purgandus de obiectis adveniret. Capitulum vero supra dictum litteris cartae mandatum est et ab episcopis cautum ac eidem Hugoni directum. In quo cum episcoporum cautionem subscriptam Hugo vidisset, motus in iram, Rotberto, qui sinodo preerat, contumeliose remisit,

After reading it through carefully and conferring amongst themselves, the bishops voted that the letter be declared invalid because it ordered them to restore the disputed see to the deposed party without advancing any supporting arguments. And because a short time earlier Pope Agapitus himself had sent a letter containing the authority of his apostolic command via Frederick of Mainz, a letter that had been handed over to Archbishop Ruotbert of Trier in the presence of the kings and bishops of Gaul and Germany, and because they had already carried out part of the instructions it contained, they decreed with unanimous consent that this matter, which had been undertaken in conformity with the rules of ecclesiastical law, should be handled in accordance with their own judgment and the canons. At the same time the archbishop ordered that the nineteenth chapter of the Council of Carthage concerning the accused and the accuser should be read aloud.[154] After it had been read out, they ruled, in accordance with the opinion contained in this chapter, that the province of Reims should be restored to Artald, who had never refused to hear the arguments presented before any council, while Hugh, who had been summoned to two synods already and had not deigned to appear before them, was to refrain from exercising any authority in the see of Reims until he appeared before a third synod to answer to the charges against him. The above-mentioned chapter was copied to parchment, confirmed by the bishops, and sent to Hugh. When Hugh saw the signatures of the bishops at the bottom of the page, he became furious and sent the letter back to Ruotbert (who had presided over the

episcoporum iudicio nihil sese facturum asserens. Et sic
causa penitus indiscussa, sinodus soluta est. Indicitur vero
tercia sinodus Kal. Aug. habenda.

68

His ita gestis, Artoldus epistolam ad sedem Romanam
dirigit commodissime continentem et suarum iniuriarum
seriem et regis incommodorum tenorem. Domnus itaque
Agapitus papa, ad multam benivolentiam animum intendens, mox accersit venerabilem Ostiensem episcopum Marinum, magnae aequitatis et prudentiae virum, vim epistolae
ei explicans et ad rerum correctionem illum vehementissime hortans. Mittitur ergo venerabilis Marinus, domni papae vicarius, ad Ottonem regem ob evocandam atque con-
gregandam universalem[167] sinodum. Diriguntur et epistolae
specialiter aliquot episcopis tam Germaniae quam Galliae
ad rerum aequitatem suasoriae.

synod) in a fit of pique, claiming that this decision of theirs would not make him do anything. And so the synod was dissolved without a resolution in the case. It was announced, however, that a third synod would be held on the first of August.[155]

68

At the conclusion of the proceedings Artald sent a letter to the see of Rome that conveniently laid out the series of wrongs that he had suffered and the nature of the difficulties endured by the king. Pope Agapitus, therefore, inclining to great goodwill, summoned Marinus, the venerable bishop of Ostia,[156] a man of great fairness and wisdom, explained the gist of the letter to him, and exhorted him in the strongest of terms to correct the situation. The venerable Marinus was subsequently dispatched as a papal vicar to King Otto with instructions to summon and call together a general synod. In several cases individual bishops from Germany and Gaul also received letters urging them to render impartial judgment.[157]

69

Item sinodus apud Angleheim habita

Interea statuto tempore sinodus universalis collecta est ex precepto Agapiti papae, sub Marino eius vicario, in palatio Angleheim, quod interpretatur angelorum domus, secus fluvium Rhenum, in basilica beati Remigii Francorum apostoli. Domno itaque Marino presidente, episcopi quoque qui ex diversis confluxerant iure aecclesiastico consederunt, Rotbertus videlicet Trevericus metropolitanus, Artoldus Remensis metropolitanus, Fredericus Maguntinus metropolitanus, Wicfridus Coloniensis metropolitanus, Adaldacchus Hammaburgensis episcopus, Hildeboldus Mimegardvurdensis episcopus, Gauslinus Tullensis episcopus, Adalbero Mettensis episcopus, Berengarius Virdunensis episcopus, Fulbertus Cameracensis episcopus, Rodulfus Laudunensis episcopus, Richoo Warmacensis episcopus, Reimboldus Spirensis episcopus, Boppo Wirzburgensis episcopus, Chounradus Constantiensis episcopus, Odelricus Augustensis episcopus, Thethardus Hildinesbeimsis[168] episcopus, Bernardus Alfureestedensis episcopus, Dudo Poderbrunnensis episcopus, Lioptacus Ribunensis episcopus, Michahel Radisponensis episcopus, Farabertus Tungrensis episcopus, Doddo Osnebruggensis episcopus, Euherus Mindensis episcopus, Baldricus Treiectensis episcopus, Heiroldus Salzburgensis

69

The Synod of Ingelheim[158]

At the appointed time[159] a general synod was assembled at the command of Pope Agapitus, under the authority of his vicar Marinus, in the palace of Ingelheim (which means "the home of angels") on the Rhine River, in the basilica of the blessed Remigius, apostle of the Franks. With Bishop Marinus presiding, the bishops who had assembled there from various places took their seats together in accordance with ecclesiastical law, namely archbishops Ruotbert of Trier, Artald of Reims, Frederick of Mainz, and Wicfrid of Cologne, and the bishops Adaldag of Hamburg-Bremen, Hildebold of Münster, Gauzlin of Toul, Adalbero of Metz, Berengar of Verdun, Fulbert of Cambrai, Rodulf of Laon, Richgowo of Worms, Reginbald of Speyer, Poppo of Würzburg, Conrad of Constance, Ulrich of Augsburg, Thiethard of Hildesheim, Bernard of Halberstadt, Dudo of Paderborn, Liafdag of Ribe, Michael of Regensburg, Farabert of Liège, Dodo of Osnabrück, Ebergis of Minden, Baldrich of

episcopus, Adalbertus Pazsoensis episcopus, Starchandus Eistetiensis episcopus, Borath Sleoswicensis episcopus, Wichardus Basiliensis episcopus, Liefdach Ripuensis episcopus.

70

De dispositione gerendorum et habendi[169] iuditii prelatura

Horum omnium cuique cum liceret ex canonibus vel decretis proferre quaecumque negotio commoda viderentur, disponendi[170] tamen facultas et rationum interpretatio domno Rotberto Treverico commissa est, eo quod divinarum et humanarum rerum scientia et eloquentiae efficatia insignissimus haberetur. Iudicii vero censura penes domnum Marinum domni papae vicarium mansit. Et considentibus cunctis, post premissas secundum ordinem celebrandi concilii preces, postque recitata decretorum sacra capitula,[171] serenissimi reges Ludovicus et Otto in sacram sinodum admissi sunt. Quibus etiam considentibus, domnus ac venerandus Rotbertus sic orsus cepit:

Utrecht, Herold of Salzburg, Adalbert of Passau, Starkand of Eichstätt, Horath of Schleswig, Wichard of Basel, and Liafdag of Ribe.[160]

70

On the Direction of the Proceedings and the Authority to Render Judgment

While each of those present was permitted by the canons and the decrees to bring up whatever he thought pertinent to the business at hand, the task of overseeing the proceedings and interpreting the arguments presented there was entrusted to Ruotbert of Trier because he was held in particular regard for his knowledge of divine and human affairs and for the power of his eloquence. The authority to deliver the council's verdict remained in the hands of Marinus, the papal vicar. Everyone took their seats, and after the opening prayers had been said in accordance with the rules of conciliar procedure, and the sacred chapters from the canons had been read aloud, the most serene kings Louis and Otto were admitted into the holy synod. After they had taken their seats in the council, the venerable Ruotbert addressed them as follows:[161]

71

Praelocutio Rotberti Treverici
metropolitani in sinodo

'Multa,' inquiens, 'sunt, patres reverendi, quibus hic apud serenissimos reges in unum coacti residemus; plurima etiam quae vestra probitate ordinanda videntur.[172] Totius pene Galliae rem publicam pravorum temeritate turbatam[173] magnisque subiacere periculis constat. Unde et leges divinae atque humanae indiscrete a malivolis contempnuntur, cum is cui regnorum Galliarum[174] iura debentur et imperandi potestas transfusione paterna credita est suorum insectatione captus ergastuloque immaniter trusus sit, suorum adhuc gladiis infestetur;[175] Remorum quoque metropolim absque pastore fures atrocissime insectentur; cultus divinus vilescat; religio canonica pro nihilo sit. His ergo, patres, vehementissime insistendum arbitror, multaque nobis diligentia enitendum, qui gratia sancti spiritus hic in unum confluximus,[176] quatinus res ante dissolutae sic in foedus redeant, ut et domno ac serenissimo regi libera regnandi red-

71

Archbishop Ruotbert of Trier's Address to the Synod

"There are many reasons, reverend fathers, why we have assembled here before the most serene kings; there are also many things that must be put right through the exercise of your probity. It is evident that almost the whole of the kingdom of Gaul has been thrown into turmoil through the audacity of wicked men and now lies exposed to great dangers. As a result, laws both divine and human are indiscriminately disregarded by evildoers, since the man who by rights should exercise authority over the kingdom of Gaul, and to whom the power of ruling was entrusted by virtue of paternal inheritance, was hunted down and taken prisoner by his own men and barbarously thrust into a prison cell, where he continues to be threatened by the swords of his own subjects. Brigands, moreover, make savage attacks upon the city of Reims, which is now bereft of its bishop. The worship of God is held cheaply. Canonical observance counts for nothing. Therefore, fathers, it is my judgment that these matters must be dealt with forcefully, and that those of us who have gathered here through the grace of the Holy Spirit must struggle earnestly to ensure that peace is restored to a realm that has been divided, so that the free exercise of royal power may be restored to his highness the most serene king,

datur potestas, et per eum ecclesiae Remensi debitus suus restituatur honor.

72

Responsio Marini Romanae sedis legati[177]

Ad haec domnus Marinus sanctae Romanae sedis vicarius: 'Optime', inquit, 'atque utiliter frater ac coepiscopus Rotbertus rerum seriem tenuit. Etenim cum divinas leges humanis preponendas ipse pernoscat, considerata tamen rerum fortuna, regiae dominationis imperium ante dixit restaurandum, ut eius vigore firmato eiusque potentia utiliter restituta, eius post liberalitate ecclesiarum dei honor consequenter recrescat, eius patrocinio agente, virtus bonis quibusque redeat. Quod ut deo annuente fieri queat, inprimis audienda atque strenuissime disponenda videtur causa domni ac serenissimi regis, si id quoque vestri iudicii paciatur censura.' Synodus dixit, 'Audiatur.'

and so that through him the church of Reims may regain its wonted honor."

72

The Reply of Marinus, the Legate of the See of Rome

In response to this Marinus, the vicar of the holy see of Rome, declared: "Our brother and fellow bishop Ruotbert has demonstrated an excellent and useful understanding of the course of recent events. For indeed, while he recognizes that divine laws must take precedence over the laws of man, nonetheless, after contemplating the circumstances in which we find ourselves, he has declared that the sovereignty of the king must first be restored, so that once his strength has been fortified and his power effectively reestablished, the honor of the churches of God may afterward flourish once more through his generosity, and all good men may be emboldened by his patronage and protection. In order that this may come about with God's help, we must first hear the case brought by his highness the most serene king and exert all of our efforts to bring it to a resolution, if your judgment allows it." The synod declared, "let the case be heard."

73

Conquestio Ludovici[178] apud Ottonem regem et sinodum regni

Tunc rex Ludovicus ab Ottonis regis latere surgens, stando conqueri modestissime petebat. At rogatus ab sinodo, huiusmodi residens effudit querelam: 'Quanto,' inquiens, 'Hugonis instinctu, quantoque eius impulsu conqueri cogor, testis est ille, cuius gratia vos hic congregatos paulo ante relatum est. Pater eius, ut a principio exordiar, patri meo regnum invidens, dum ei domi militiaeque servitium deberet, regno illum immaniter privavit et usque ad diem vitae eius supremum ergastulo trusum contrivit.[179] Me vero parvum in fasciculo farraginis a meis dissimulatum in partes transmarinas et prope in Rifeos fugere compulit. Patre autem extincto,[180] et me in exilium deportato, iste, cum reminisceretur sui patris ob insolentiam interfecti, regni curam suscipere formidabat. Nobis[181] itaque invidens, Rodulfum[182] promovit. Sed divinitas res illius sicut et cetera determinans, ei quando voluit finem regnandi dedit. Dum

73

Louis's Complaint Before King Otto and the Synod of the Realm

King Louis then rose from King Otto's side and very humbly requested leave to state his grievances while standing. At the request of the synod, however, he took his seat and poured out a complaint of the following sort: "He through whose grace you have assembled here (as someone mentioned a short while ago) can bear witness to how much Hugh's incitement and provocations have driven me to make this complaint before you. Hugh's father (to start from the beginning), begrudging my own father his kingdom in spite of the fact that he was duty-bound to serve him both at home and on campaign, cruelly usurped the throne from him and threw him into a prison cell, where he wasted away until the last day of his life. As for me, when I was just a small boy, he compelled me, having being hidden away by my people in a bundle of grain, to flee to the lands beyond the sea, almost as far as the Riphaean mountains. Yet although my father was dead and I had been carried away into exile, Hugh was still afraid to assume responsibility for the realm because he remembered his own father, who had perished on account of his overweening ambition. And so, out of envy toward me, he had Radulf made king. But God, setting the limits of Radulf's life as he does with everything, brought an end to his rule when it pleased him. With the throne now

item regnum vacaret, consilio bonorum me a partibus pere-
grinis exulantem revocavit, ac omnium conibentia in regnum
promovit, nihil mihi preter Laudunum relinquens. Promo-
tusque cum ea quae regii iuris videbantur repetere niterer, id
invidissime ferebat. Factus ergo latenter adversarius, amicos
si quos habebam, pecuniis subvertebat, inimicos in odium
amplius incitabat. Tandem urgente invidia, apud piratas
aegit ut ab eis dolo caperer, regnum in se posse refundi arbitrans, si id fieri contigisset. Nec defuit insidiis effectus. Captus fui carcerique[183] mancipatus. Ille vero me eripere simulans, filios[184] meos iure obsidum dandos petebat. At iis qui
mihi fide adiuncti erant omnes dari reclamantibus, dimisso
uno, a piratis me recepit. Iam libertatem sperans, quo animus impelleret ire volebam. Verum aliter provenisse manifestum est. Nam captum mox in vincula coniecit[185] ac an-
nuali carceri mancipavit.[186] Unde cum a cognatis et amicis
meis indignantibus sese impetendum adverteret, libertatem
spopondit[187] si Laudunum acciperet.[188] Hoc tantum claudebar, hoc solo cum uxore et natis recipiebar. Quid facerem?

vacant once more, Hugh, heeding the advice of wise counselors, recalled me from exile in foreign lands and established me on the throne with universal consent, although
he left me with nothing except the city of Laon. When I
later sought to regain what rightfully belonged to me as
king, he bore it with tremendous ill will. Therefore, having
secretly become my enemy, he subverted whatever friends I
had with bribes and incited my enemies to an even greater
hatred of me. Eventually his malice drove him to enter into
negotiations with the pirates to have me taken prisoner by
them through trickery, because he thought that if this were
to happen then the throne might revert to him. Nor were
his schemes unsuccessful. I was seized and confined to a
prison cell. Meanwhile, he sought to have my sons turned
over as hostages, under the pretext that he was working to
secure my release. Those who remained loyal to me, however, refused to allow all of my sons to be given up, and Hugh
received me back from the pirates after only one of them
had been sent. Expecting that I was going to be set free, I
was eager to go where my heart desired. But it is clear that
things turned out very differently. For as soon as I became
his prisoner, Hugh put me in chains and confined me to a
prison cell for a year. Then, when he realized that he was going to be attacked by my outraged relatives and friends, he
promised me my freedom in exchange for Laon. This was
the one place where I was secure, the one place where I
could take refuge with my wife and children. What was I to

Castro vitam preposui. Pro castro libertatem merui. Et en omnibus privatus, omnium opem deposco. His si dux contraire audeat, nobis tantum singulariter congrediendum sit.'

74

Oratio Rotberti pro Ludovico

Quibus palam promulgatis, Rotbertus metropolitanus subinfert: 'Quoniam,' inquiens, 'domni atque serenissimi regis satis breviter ac dilucide digestam optime, ut arbitror, conquestionem percepimus, consequens videtur ut eius causam in quantum fas est determinemus. Dux ergo quia omnia pene regni iura in sese transfudit, eique viribus reniti non valemus, mitius hoc attemptandum arbitror, ut qui deum non metuit et hominem non reveretur multa ratione multaque rerum consideratione ad normam deo iuvante reducatur. Igitur iuxta patrum decreta et canonum regulam inprimis ad satisfactionem fraterne monendus[189] est, verbisque suasoriis ad id modestissime revocandus. Quod si post

do? I chose my life over a fortress. In exchange for the latter I earned my freedom. And here I am, deprived of all that I have, asking everyone for their help. If the duke dares to contradict anything that I have said, then let him meet me face-to-face in single combat."[162]

74

Ruotbert's Speech on Behalf of Louis

After this public statement by the king, Archbishop Ruotbert replied: "Since I think that we all understood the complaint of his highness the most serene king perfectly well, delivered as it was with admirable brevity and clarity, it now seems appropriate that we should render a decision in his case, insofar as we have the power to do so. Therefore, because the duke has usurped authority over almost the whole of the kingdom, and we do not have the strength to oppose him, I think that we must try a gentler approach, so that through careful reasoning and a detailed examination of the circumstances, this person who neither fears God nor shows reverence to man may, with God's help, be brought back to the rule of right conduct. Thus, in accordance with the decrees of the fathers and the rule of the canons, let him first receive a brotherly admonition to make satisfaction, and let him be recalled to this mildly with words of persua-

blandam revocationis ammonitionem resipiscere noluerit,[190] omnium anathemate feriatur, hoc habentes presidio, quod iam a domno papa correctus sit iussusque a domini sui insectatione quiescere.'

75

Responsio Marini legati
pro eodem

Atque his domnus Marinus subiunxit: 'Reminiscor,' inquiens, 'domnum papam ante hunc annum anathema in reos misisse qui hunc dominum et regem Francorum insectabantur; epistolam quoque suasoriam ut ab eo non deficiant bonis quibuslibet delegatam, atque conquestionem de eadem re litteris expressam iis quibus sanior mens erat delegatam fuisse. Unde et opinor iustissime dictum, cum ante a papa vocatus atque correctus sit, nunc quoque caritatis gratia revocandus est et diligentissima suasione ut a malis quiescat commonendus; et post omnium anathemate dampnandus. Et non solum ille, verum omnes qui ei in malis favere faventque. Sed hanc solum a nobis accipiet opem. Numquid vero ab alio quicquam opis accipiet? Eius conquestio in sua clau-

sion. And if, after our gentle reminder to amend his ways, he still refuses to come to his senses, then let him be struck by an anathema from all of us, since we have in our defense the fact that he has already been reprimanded by the pope and ordered to cease persecuting his lord."

75

The Response of the Legate Marinus on Behalf of the King

To this Marinus replied: "I recall that before this year our lord pope directed an anathema against those who were guilty of persecuting his highness the king of the Franks. In addition, a letter was sent to all good men urging them not to abandon him, and a written complaint on the same subject was dispatched to those men who were of sounder judgment. Therefore, I believe that what has been said is eminently just: since Hugh was previously summoned and reprimanded by the pope, he must now be recalled with the grace of charity and advised with earnest entreaties to cease from his evil practices, and after this he is to be condemned with an anathema from all of us—and not only him, but all those who supported him and continue to support him in his wickedness. This is all the help that we can give to the king. Will he receive help from anyone else? At the conclu-

sula opem omnium postulat. Sed si a nobis ei succurritur, a domno Ottone rege quid accipiet? Et decretalia sancta acclamant, postquam tirannis anathema damnationis ab episcopis iniectum est, a bonis quoque potentibus vim[191] inferendam, ut si aecclesiasticis correctionibus ad normam redire nolunt, saltem potentium vehementi violentia ad bonum redire cogantur, ut vel invitis bona prestentur.'

76

Oratio Ottonis regis pro eodem

Ad haec rex Otto: 'Multa,' inquit, 'sunt, patres, beneficia quae a vobis[192] domno ac serenissimo regi Ludovico utiliter accommodari valebunt. Etenim si eius insectatores armis divinis adoriamini, consequenter aut facili tumultu devicti labascent, aut si quid impetendum relinquetur, facilius nostris armis infirmabitur. Vos ergo, iubente domni papae legato, vestri ordinis instrumenta exerite ac tanti regis adversarios anathematis gladio transverberate. Contra quae si

sion of the king's speech he asked that everyone render him aid. But if we come to his assistance, what help will he receive from King Otto? The sacred canons proclaim that when bishops have directed an anathema of condemnation against tyrants, all good men who have the power to do so should take up arms against them. In this way, if they are unwilling to return to the standard of right conduct after they have been punished at the hands of the church, then at least the application of brute force by the powerful will compel them to return to the good, so that some benefit may be done to them, even against their will."

76

Otto's Speech on Behalf of the King

In response to this King Otto declared: "There are many useful services, fathers, that you can perform on behalf of the most serene King Louis. For if you assail his persecutors with the armaments of God, then they will either be defeated and collapse after a short struggle, or, if there remains anything left to attack, it will crumble all the more quickly when confronted with our arms. Therefore, at the behest of the papal legate, unsheathe the tools of your order and transfix the enemies of so great a king with the sword of anathema. If they should dare to raise their necks in rebel-

cervicem posteá erigere audeant et dominicis interdictis resistere non formidant, nostrum exinde erit, quibus commis-
sum est in hac mundi parte sanctam dei aecclesiam tueri, ut
in tales arma sumamus, huiusmodi debellemus. Et si necessitas adurgeat, strictis gladiis usque ad immanissimam cae-
dem perditissimorum hominum deseviamus, habitá in illos
iustissimae indignationis causa, quod illicita aggrediantur,
et pro illicitis ammoniti non corrigantur. Vos itaque tantum
vestris insistite. Et post modestiam vestram virtus nostra
sequetur.'

77

Epistola a sinodo ad
Hugonem delegata

Quibus dictis, mox sinodi decreto epistola descripta est
palamque recitata, hanc verborum seriem tenens: 'Sancta sinodus in palatio Angleheim sub domnis atque orthodoxis
regibus Ludovico et Ottone utiliter habita, Hugoni duci.
Quantis malis quantaque persecutione vexaveris illam venerabilem Remorum metropolim, quanta quoque crudelitate

lion at some later date and show themselves unafraid to oppose a divine interdict, then it will be the duty of those of us who have been entrusted to watch over the holy church of God in this part of the world to take up arms against men such as these and vanquish them completely. And if necessity compels us to do so, then let us unsheathe our swords and go so far as to inflict a terrible slaughter upon these desperate men. Our righteous indignation against them will be completely justified because they are undertaking illegal acts, and even after being warned they do not accept correction for their crimes. Therefore, do only what is within your power, and our might will follow on the heels of your restraint."

77

The Letter Addressed to Hugh from the Synod

After this speech, a letter containing the following statement was immediately drafted and read aloud by a decree of the synod: "From the holy synod held to good effect in the palace of Ingelheim under the auspices of their highnesses the orthodox kings Louis and Otto, to Duke Hugh: The afflictions and persecution with which you have tormented the venerable see of Reims, and the cruelty with which you

debacchatus sis in dominum tuum regem, ora omnium lo-
cuntur; apud omnes id agitatur. Quod quam sceleratum et
quam pernitiosum sit, divinae atque humanae leges copiosissime produnt. Unde et tibi compatientes, ab talibus te
quiescere monemus, et ad dominum tuum multa mansuetu-
dinis humilitate quantotius reverti hortamur. Quod si con-
tempseris, priusquam in diversa referamur,[193] anathemate
sine dubio te perstringemus, donec aut satisfacias, aut Romam apud domnum papam ratiocinaturus petas, cuius litteris iam bis monitus es et a tanto facinore prohibitus. Unde
et nos post illum tercio iam te ad correctionem revocamus.'[194] Quae totius sinodi auctoritate roborata, duci per legatos mox directa est.

78

Causa Artoldi

Post haec surgens Artoldus[195] archiepiscopus, rerum ordinem sed et ipsius litis initium quae agitabatur inter sese et
Hugonem sibi subrogatum episcopum luculentissime disse-
ruit. Quin et epistolam profert, nuperrime a domno papa
sibi directam, per quam episcopatum sibi retinendum sig-

have raged against your lord the king are on everyone's lips and are spoken of by all men. Laws both human and divine amply testify to how wicked and pernicious your conduct has been. And so, in our compassion for you, we warn you to abandon these evil practices, and we urge you to return to your lord as soon as possible in a spirit of gentle humility. If you reject our admonition, be assured that before we depart to go our separate ways, we shall bind you with an anathema until such time as you either make satisfaction or go to Rome to answer to the lord pope. He has now warned you twice in letters and prohibited you from such criminal acts. And so, after him, we are recalling you to correction for the third time now." The letter was confirmed by the authority of the whole synod and immediately dispatched to the duke via messengers.

78

Artald Pleads His Case

After this Archbishop Artald arose and gave a very clear account of what had happened in the past and of the origin of the dispute between himself and Hugh, who had been installed as bishop in his place.[163] He also produced a letter recently sent to him by the pope, which declared that he was to maintain control of the bishopric.[164] After it had been

nificabat. Post cuius interpretationem, Sigeboldus quidam predicti Hugonis clericus aliam mox epistolam sinodo porrexit,[196] signo domni papae munitam et ab urbe a sese delatam. Quae etiam in conspectu episcoporum recitata atque diligentissime discussa est. In cuius textu id solum dicebatur, quod Rodulfus Laudunensis episcopus, Wido etiam Suessonicus, necnon et Hildegarius Belvacensis, ceteri quoque Remensis dioceseos episcopi ad sedem apostolicam pro restitutione Hugonis et abdicatione Artoldi epistolam miserint. Unde et domnum papam ad eorum vota eorumque petitionem omnia fieri velle. Post cuius recitationem, predicti mox consurgentes episcopi, epistolae sententiam penitus confutarunt ac calumniarum iniectorem hominem perditissimum adclamarunt. Quibus cum contraire non posset, quibusdam maledictis eos adortus, publice de perfidia criminabatur.

79

Calumniatoris episcoporum reprobatio

Tunc a domno Marino decernitur ut recitentur capitula de calumniatoribus prolata. Quibus mox lectis, cum calumniator reniti non posset, episcoporum iuditio diaconatus

translated,[165] a man named Sigebold, who was one of Hugh's clerics, immediately came forward and presented another letter to the synod[166] which he himself had brought back from Rome and which had been authenticated with the pope's seal. This letter, too, was read aloud before the bishops and subjected to careful scrutiny. The text said only that the bishops Rodulf of Laon, Wido of Soissons, Hildegar of Beauvais, and the other bishops of the province of Reims had sent a letter to the apostolic see supporting the restoration of Hugh and the removal of Artald, and that the pope had subsequently expressed his desire that everything would turn out in accordance with their wishes and their request. After the letter had been read aloud, the aforementioned bishops stood up and completely refuted its contents, crying out that this most depraved and wicked man was responsible for these slanders. Because Sigebold could say nothing to contradict the bishops, but could only hurl imprecations at them, he was publicly accused of treachery.[167]

79

The Condemnation of the False Accuser by the Bishops

Marinus then decreed that the canons concerning false accusers should be brought out and read aloud. When the reading was over and the perpetrator of these falsehoods

quo fungebatur officio privatur[197] et a conspectu sinodi contumeliose reprobatus exire compellitur. Artoldo vero pontificatus dignitatem secundum canonum instituta patrumque decreta sinodus habendam decernit atque corroborat, eo quod nullius concilii rationibus interesse refugerit. Atque haec prima consessionis die constituta sunt.

80

Secunda vero die, post recitatas sacrae auctoritatis lectiones et domni Rotberti allocutionem, a venerabili Marino constituitur ut, quoniam iuxta sacrae legis sententiam pontificalis dignitas Artoldo restituta est, in ipsius pervasorem sinodalis proferatur censura. Recitantur itaque decreta canonum et sanctorum instituta patrum Innocentii, Alexandri, Simmachi, Sixti, Celestini, Zosimi, Leonis, Bonefacii, aliorumque sanctae dei aecclesiae doctorum illustrium. Quorum decretis unanimiter anathematizant atque ab totius aecclesiae communione sequestrant Hugonem Remensis aecclesiae pervasorem, donec resipiscentem peniteat ac pro facinore offensis satisfaciat.

could offer no defense, he was stripped of his office of deacon by the verdict of the bishops and driven from the sight of the synod after being subjected to a humiliating condemnation. As for Artald, the council decreed and confirmed that he should maintain possession of the see of Reims in accordance with the ordinances of the canons and the decrees of the fathers, since he had not shrunk from taking part in the deliberations of any council. All of these things were decided on the first day of the synod.[168]

80

On the second day, after the readings of sacred authority and an address from Archbishop Ruotbert, the venerable Marinus laid down that because Artald had been restored to the office of bishop in accordance with the judgment of sacred law, the synod should now render a verdict against the usurper of his see. And so the decrees of the canons and the ordinances of the holy fathers Innocent, Alexander, Symmachus, Sixtus, Celestine, Zosimus, Leo, Boniface, and the other distinguished teachers of the holy church of God were read out.[169] By virtue of their decrees the synod unanimously excommunicated Hugh, the usurper of the church of Reims, and severed him from the communion of the Church until such time as he should come to his senses, repent, and make satisfaction for his crime to those whom he had wronged.[170]

81

Reliquis autem diebus decretum est de incestis et illicitis presbiterorum coniugiis, de presbiteris quoque eukaristiam indigne tractantibus, de aecclesiis etiam a laicis indebite usurpatis. Aliaque nonnulla ibi prolata[198] fuere, quae diligentissime investigata atque utiliter diffinita sunt. Sicque sinodus soluta est. Indicitur vero post dies XXX iterum habenda Lauduni in basilica sancti Vincentii martiris, ut ibi exeratur anathema in Hugonem tirannum.

82

Anathema episcoporum in ducem eiusque fautores

Quibus diligenter ac canonice peractis, Ludovicus rex ab Ottone rege militum copias duce Chonrado contra Hugonem tirannum accipit. Quae dum per dies XL colligerentur, episcopi supradicti tricesima die post peractam sinodum in basilica sancti Vincentii martiris apud Laudunum sub rege

81

Over the course of the remaining days rulings were made concerning incestuous and illicit priestly marriages,[171] priests who handled the Eucharist in an inappropriate manner, and churches that had been wrongfully taken away by laymen. Several other issues were also brought forward and resolved to good effect after careful investigation. And with that, the synod was dissolved. It was declared that they would meet again thirty days hence in the basilica of Saint-Vincent at Laon, so that there an anathema could be proclaimed against the tyrant Hugh.[172]

82

The Anathema of the Bishops Against the Duke and His Supporters

After all of this had been carried out scrupulously and in accordance with the canons, King Louis received a force of fighting men from King Otto under the command of Duke Conrad,[173] to be employed against the tyrant Hugh. During the forty-day period when the troops were mustering, the aforementioned bishops gathered together under the leadership of King Louis in the basilica of Saint-Vincent at Laon,

Ludovico collecti sunt. Et iterum presidente predicto Marino, post sacrae scripturae paginas quae ibi recitatae et multa consideratione discussae sunt, Hugonem tirannum anathemate damnant et a sancta aecclesia pellunt, nisi resipiscens domino suo satisfaciat, aut Romam pro sui absolutione apud domnum papam ratiocinaturus petat. In qua etiam sinodo agitur de episcopis qui cum duce evocati fuere et distulerunt venire, de iis etiam qui consecrationi Hugonis episcopi iam abdicati illicite interfuerunt, vel qui ab ipso pulso vel post abdicato contra fas videbantur promoti. Damnantur itaque duo pseudoepiscopi ab Hugone[199] ordinati, Tetbaldus scilicet et Ivo, quorum prior a pulso sacratus est Ambianensium episcopus, alter vero ab abdicato Silletensium. Damnatur et Adelomus Laudunensis aecclesiae diaconus, a Rodulfo suo episcopo[200] insimulatus, eo quod Tetbaldum excommunicatum in aeclesiam temerarius introduxerit. Hi enim in anteriore sinodo cum duce iam evocati,[201] satisfacere contempnebant. Vocatur vero Hildegarius Belvacensium episcopus domni Marini et episcoporum legatione, ut aut ad eos veniat aut sedem apostolicam pro suo facinore ratiocinaturus petat, eo quod interfuerit ordinationi supra iam dictorum pseudoepiscoporum. Vocatur et Heribertus,

thirty days after the conclusion of the synod.[174] Marinus again presided, and after the pages of sacred scripture had been read aloud and subjected to careful discussion, they condemned the tyrant Hugh with an anathema and expelled him from the Holy Church unless he should come to his senses and make satisfaction to his lord, or else go to Rome to give reasons to the pope why he should be absolved. At the same synod they also took up the matter of the bishops who had been summoned with the duke and had put off coming, as well as the bishops who had illegally taken part in the consecration of the now deposed Bishop Hugh and those who had been unlawfully promoted by him after he had been driven from Reims or deposed from office.[175] Two false bishops who had been ordained by Hugh were accordingly condemned, namely Theobald and Ivo, the first of whom Hugh had consecrated bishop of Amiens after he had been expelled from Reims,[176] while the second he had consecrated bishop of Senlis after his deposition from office. Adelelm, a deacon of Laon, was also condemned after being accused by Rodulf, his bishop, because he had recklessly brought the excommunicate Theobald[177] into his church. These men had been summoned along with the duke to appear before the earlier synod and had refused to comply. Bishop Hildegar of Beauvais was also summoned by envoys sent by Marinus and the bishops, and ordered either to appear before them or else to travel to the apostolic see to answer for the crime that he had committed, since he had taken part in the ordination of the aforementioned false

Heriberti tiranni filius, ob mala quae aecclesiis vel episcopis immaniter inferebat. Wido vero Suessonicus episcopus, cum a plurimis laceraretur, eo quod ipse Hugonem episcopum sacrasset, in sinodo reum sese confitens et multa penitentia reatum deplorans, intercedentibus apud sinodum Artoldo atque Rotberto archiepiscopis, absolvi ab eis obtinuit. Wicfridus quoque Morinensis episcopus, qui criminabatur interfuisse, immunis a crimine reperitur. Affuit vero Transmari Noviomensis episcopi legatus, Silvester presbiter, episcopum suum tanta vi febrium detentum asserens ut ad sinodum venire nequiverit, quod etiam in conspectu sinodi testibus approbavit. Post haec[202] episcopi in sua referuntur. Domnus vero Marinus, ab Ottone rege per legatos rogatus, in partes Germaniae secedit ibique aecclesiam Vuldensis monasterii dedicat et[203] hieme exacta Romam redit. His expletis,[204] Rodulfus Laudunensis episcopus, ultimo corporis dolore confectus,[205] hac vita decedit. Succedit ei vero frater regis ex concubina Rorico, omni rerum scientia inclitus.

bishops. In addition, Heribert,[178] the son of the tyrant Heribert, was summoned to appear on account of the cruel injuries that he was inflicting upon churches and bishops. And because Bishop Wido of Soissons was being harshly criticized by many people for having consecrated Hugh archbishop of Reims, he confessed himself guilty before the synod and wept over his guilt with deep repentance; and after archbishops Ruotbert and Artald intervened on his behalf at the synod, he obtained absolution from the bishops. Bishop Wicfrid of Thérouanne was also accused of having taken part in the consecration, but he was acquitted of the charge. In addition, a priest named Silvester was there as an envoy from Bishop Transmar of Noyon. He said that his bishop had been taken ill with a serious fever and was unable to come, and he brought witnesses before the synod to testify to this. Afterward, the bishops returned home. Marinus, however, at the request of envoys sent by King Otto, went to Germany, where he dedicated the church of the monastery of Fulda, and at the end of the winter he returned to Rome. After this, Bishop Rodulf of Laon was overcome with his body's final pains and departed from this life.[179] He was succeeded by Rorico,[180] the king's half-brother by a concubine, a man who was renowned for every type of learning.[181]

83

Rex cohortes Mosomum
mittit et capit

Interea[206] exercitu ex omni Belgica duce Conrado apud regem collecto,[207] tres cohortes rege iubente Mosomum mittuntur. Compererat etenim Hugonem abdicatum ibidem reclusum multaque rei militaris inopia eum haberi. Cohortes ergo oppidum in ipso crepusculo aggressae, repentina oppugnatione circumquaque infestant. Instant quoque magnanimiter capere. Et quia revera milites paucissimos armaque vix aliqua sciebant, indesinenter vires exerunt armisque adurgent. At aliis fatigatis, alii intacti succedunt; sicque sine intermissione paucissimos numerosi atterunt. Oppidani vero, assidua expugnatione attriti, die altera iam sole occiduo omnes cum domino ad deditionem coguntur.[208] In quo tumultu, quo genere fugae nescitur, Hugo abdicatus evadit. De militibus vero qui potiores videbantur capiuntur, ac oppido aliis deputatis, regi deducuntur.

83

The King Sends Troops to Capture Mouzon

Meanwhile, after an army drawn from all over Belgica and led by Conrad had assembled before the king, he ordered three cohorts to be sent to Mouzon. For he had learned that Hugh had taken refuge there after his removal from office and he was now trapped there with hardly any means of defense. The king's forces, therefore, approached the stronghold at daybreak, invested it on all sides in a surprise attack, and strove valiantly to capture it. And because they knew for a fact that there were very few men and scarcely any armaments inside, they were unflagging in their efforts and pressed the attack. Whenever men began to tire, they were replaced by fresh troops.[182] In this way the were able to use their superior numbers to wear down the defenders, giving them no chance to rest. For their part, the garrison were exhausted by the continuous attacks, and as the sun was setting on the next day, they were compelled to surrender along with their lord. The deposed Hugh managed to escape during the fighting, although it is not known how he did so. Those of the defenders who were deemed particularly important were taken prisoner, and after a new garrison had been installed, they were taken before the king.[183]

84

Rex Montem Acutum capit

Rex vero castrum quod dicitur Mons Acutus, quod etiam est Lauduno contiguum, cum exercitu oppugnabat. Et quia non satis adhuc murorum firmamento claudebatur, nec multitudo militum sufficiens commode ibi cohabitare poterat, urgenti obsidioni diutius resistere oppidani non patiuntur. Victi ergo, cedunt[209] ac resistere quiescunt. Oppido itaque capto, rex suos deputat et sic exercitum Lauduno inducit; obsidionem per loca commoda disponit, viresque admodum confert.[210] Saepissime eminus decertatum est. Comminus etiam dimicatum novies. Nullo vero prosperioris fortunae successu regius impetus eo tempore enituit. Imminebat etenim hiemis intemperies, unde et bellicae machinae in articulo temporis fabricari non poterant, sine quibus tanti montis eminentia expugnari non potest. Regis itaque iussu exercitus redit, hieme transacta rediturus. Rex vero Remis sese privatum recepit.

84

The King Captures Montaigu

The king and his army now assaulted the castle of Montaigu, which is located next to Laon. Because it was not protected by a strong circuit of walls and could not comfortably house a sufficiently large garrison, the defenders could not withstand the siege that was bearing down upon them for very long. Owning themselves beaten, therefore, they surrendered and abandoned their resistance. After taking the stronghold, the king put his own men in charge and led his army to Laon, where he deployed a siege at suitable points and mounted a fierce assault upon the city. There was frequent fighting from a distance. On nine occasions the opposing forces also clashed in hand-to-hand combat. But at that time the king's assault did not shine forth with the success of good fortune. For inclement winter weather was threatening, and in a short span of time it was not possible to construct siege engines, without which the heights of such a steep hill could not be taken. Thus, the army departed on the orders of the king, to return once the winter was over. The king, meanwhile, took up residence at Reims by himself.[184]

85

Hugo autem dux, episcoporum anathema vilipendens ac regi subdi contempnens, cum multis Nortmannorum copiis regiam urbem Suessonicam aggreditur multaque obsidione premit. Alios itaque adortus[211] gladio enecat, alios vero nube sagittarum ac balistarum loetaliter sauciat. Iniectisque iaculo ignibus, domum matris aecclesiae succendit. Claustrumque canonicorum ac partem civitatis maiorem ignibus solotenus combussit. Quam cum capere non posset, in pagum Remensem, ubi rex tunc privatus morabatur, iter truculentus reflectit.[212] Cuius adventum ii qui ruri degebant audientes, in aecclesias sanctorum cum suis rebus confugiunt. At tirannus, pauperum turbis inmisericors, eorum plus quam DLX[213] intra aecclesias succendisse traditur. Et sic ad sua refertur.

86

Rex vero Ludovicus Gerbergam reginam ad Ottonem fratrem suum dirigit ut[214] sibi copias acceleret.[215] Proficiscitur itaque imminente sollempnitate pascali et Aquisgrani palatio sanctum pascha cum fratre Ottone[216] concelebrat.

85

For his part, Duke Hugh, scorning the bishops' anathema and refusing to be subject to the king, attacked the royal city of Soissons with a large force of Northmen and subjected it to an extensive siege. His army attacked and cut down some of the defenders with swords and fatally wounded others with clouds of arrows and ballista shot. They also fired flaming missiles into the city and set fire to the cathedral church, and the cloister of the canons and the greater part of the city caught fire and burned to the ground. When Hugh proved unable to capture the city, however, in his fury he changed course for the county of Reims, where the king was staying without his army at the time. When those who lived in the countryside heard of the duke's coming, they fled into the churches of the saints with their possessions. But the tyrant took no pity on the throngs of poor people, and he reportedly burned more than 560 of them to death inside the churches.[185] And with that he returned home.[186]

86

Meanwhile, King Louis sent Queen Gerberga to her brother Otto to expedite the arrival of reinforcements for him. She set out as the paschal feast was drawing near and celebrated Easter together with her brother Otto at the pal-

949

Conveniunt ex Germania principes nonnulli; adsunt ex Belgica universi; nec desunt legati Grecorum, Italorum, Anglorum, atque aliorum plurimae legationes populorum. Regina ergo, cum fratre consilio habito et accepta ab eo auxilii pollicitatione, secura ad regem Ludovicum redit.

87

Ludovicus vero in tirannum iratus, nimio animi fervore Ottonis auxilium prevenire meditabatur. Arbitrabatur etenim quoniam in longa exercitus exspectatione iniuria inulta videretur. Confert itaque cum patre meo consilium, eo quod eius esset miles, consiliis commodus, facundia simul et audatia plurimus. Unde et rex admodum ei consuescebat et apud eum sepissime consultabat. Dictabat ergo pater meus apud regem et paucos qui intererant ordinem capiendi Laudunum ita. Primum sese observaturum oportunitatem aiebat, et an loci habitudo id ferret an etiam cives in observatione urbis cautissimi haberentur diligentissime exploraturum sese memorabat. Deinde dicebat efficaciter se adeo ordinaturum omnia et sic ad effectum utiliter reducturum, ut nulli post sese quicquam negotio inperfecto supplendum relinqueretur.

ace of Aachen. A number of the leading men of Germany
and all of those from Belgica were present. Envoys also came
from the Greeks, the Italians, and the English, as well as
many delegations from other peoples. The queen, therefore,
after taking counsel with her brother and receiving assur-
ances of aid from him, returned safely to King Louis.[187]

87

Louis, meanwhile, was furious at the tyrant, and in his
highly agitated state of mind he was contemplating taking
action against him before the arrival of Otto's reinforcements. For he thought that by waiting so long for the army's
arrival, it might appear as though the insult that had been
done to him was going to go unpunished. Therefore, he
sought the advice of my father, because he was one of his
vassals, a man useful in council and notable both for his eloquence and his daring. For this reason the king was on very
familiar terms with him and sought his counsel on many occasions. My father told the king and the few men who were
with him his plan for capturing Laon, which went like this:
first he would look for a suitable opportunity and then he
would carefully investigate whether the conditions on the
ground would allow his plan to work, and whether the
townsmen exercised sufficient vigilance in keeping watch
over their city. Then he said that he would plan everything
so effectively and carry it to completion with such success
that nothing would remain for anyone to do after him.

88

Rege ergo per dies aliquot Remis demorante, Rodulfus (sic enim pater meus dicebatur) commoditatem patrandi negotii per suos explorabat. Missisque exploratoribus, comperit agasones civium per dies singulos exire ab urbe tempore vespertino quinquagenos aut sexagenos et farraginis fasciculos equis in urbem deferre, capitibus ob solis ardorem obvolutis. Idque cotidie et tempore eodem. Quod cum ab observatoribus patri meo relatum fuisset, simili eos exercitio posse falli advertit. Refert[217] ergo sese ad regem et sic apud eum presentibus paucissimis concepta effundit.

89

'Magnum,'[218] inquiens, 'o rex, videretur, si hoc negotium solummodo armis viribusque esset attemptandum. Sed quia per astutiam eius principium utilitas aggredi suadet, prout mihi videtur, cohortes aliquot secus montem in abditis ponendae sunt. Exspectandum etiam qua tempestate equos educant agasones herbatum potatumque. Qui cum in suo tempore egressi fuerint, et ab observatoribus eorum egressus et numerus nobis referetur, mox ad eorum numerum

88

Thus, while the king remained at Reims for a few days, Rodulf (this was my father's name) sent some of his men to investigate the feasibility of carrying out his plan. He learned from the scouts whom he had sent out that every day the townsmen's grooms would leave the city at daybreak and bring fifty or sixty bundles of hay back to the city on horses, keeping their heads covered as protection against the heat of the sun. This happened every day at the same time. When the scouts reported this back to my father, he realized that it would be possible to trick the townsmen by mimicking the behavior of the grooms. And so he went before the king and revealed his plan to him in the presence of a very few men.

89

"It would be a noble thing, my lord," he said, "if we were to undertake this task through force of arms alone. But because our own interest urges us to proceed first through cunning, it is my opinion that we should place several cohorts in a concealed position near the hillside. Then let us wait for the moment when the grooms are taking out the horses to feed and water them. Once they have left the city at the usual time, and our scouts have notified us of their

lectissimi iuvenes eodem scemate eodemque numero, capitibus ut ipsi pilleatis,[219] farraginem in equis ad portam defe-
rant unde paulo ante agasones exierant, acsi ipsi agasones
redeant. Qui cum altitudine fasciculorum aspectum pro-
tegere possint, facili ingressu urbem penetrabunt. Et ne
quid impossibile a me dictum suspiceris, eorum ducem me
in hoc certamine offero. Animo tantum sint constanti. Successus vero deo volente prosperabitur. Si ergo tempestivius
cives insidias advertant bellumque nobis paucioribus inferant, fixum nobis animo sit aut portae ingressum tantum
tueri donec tubae clangore excitatae cohortes nobis subve-
niant, aut multa constantia in loco quem quisque possidebit
magnanimiter emori.'

90

Huiusmodi rerum dispositio omnibus apta videtur. Ob-
servatores itaque directi, agasonum consuetudinem eorumque habitum, tempus quoque et numerum promtissime referunt. Ad eorum quoque relatum cohortes in abditis secus
montem dispositae sunt. Pro numero etiam agasonum milites cum patre meo iurati[220] ad peragendum rei negotium di-

departure and their numbers, a picked group of young men, equal in number and dressed in the same garb as the grooms, with their heads covered just like theirs, should carry fodder back on their horses to the same gate from which the grooms left a short time earlier and enter the city as if they themselves were the grooms on their way back. The height of the bundles will serve to hide their faces, and they will be able to enter the city without any trouble. In case you think that anything that I have said is impossible, I hereby offer myself up as the leader of the men who take part in this mission. Only let them be unwavering in their determination. God willing, we shall succeed. But if the townsmen are quick to uncover our ruse and attack us while we are outnumbered, each man must be ready to defend the entrance to the gate until the blast of the trumpet summons reinforcements to our aid, or else to die bravely with steadfast resolve upon whatever spot of ground he holds."

90

This plan was deemed suitable by everyone. Scouts were dispatched accordingly, and they quickly reported back on the behavior and appearance of the grooms, their schedule, and their numbers. On the basis of this information, troops were placed in a concealed position beside the hill, while my father and a group of sworn fighting men equal in number

riguntur. Agasones itaque numero LX sumptis armis more solito per montis devexa capitibus pilleatis ad farraginem descendunt. Et circa carices colligendos occupati, moram regrediendi aliquantisper faciunt. At pater meus et ii qui iurati cum eo erant vehementi animo succedunt. Factoque agmine, pilleatis capitibus more agasonum, cum fasciculis farraginis tempestivius reditum accelerant, magnitudine fasciculorum vultus penitus abdentes. Quibus advenientibus porta patefacta est. Et indivisi urbem penetrant. Fasciculos itaque abiciunt et gladios educunt. Tubis personant magnisque clamoribus urbem conturbant. Urbani ergo insidias comperientes, cum armis in hostes feruntur. Instant omnes, et validissime plurimi paucos adurgent. At regii milites a leva quidem turri, a dextra vero domibus, a tergo autem muro urbis protegebantur, omnem vim belli ante habentes, unde et tutius congrediebantur. Nec ulterius in hostes audebant progredi, ne adversarii a tergo portam pervasam repeterent, et ne sic facti hostium medii interirent. Instat itaque quisque in loco quem possidet. Et iam nimium omnes sauciati pene deficiebant, cum regiae cohortes tubis excitatae ab abditis erumpunt multoque impetu iam prope victis subveniunt; portamque defensam ingrediuntur, atque urbanos

to the grooms were sent to carry out their mission. Sixty grooms bearing arms and wearing hats upon their heads descended the slope of the hill to go foraging, as was their custom. They put off returning for a little while because they were busy gathering sedge. Thereupon my father and the sworn men with him boldly took their place. They formed into a group, and with their heads covered just like the grooms, they hurried to get back to the city before them with their baskets of fodder, keeping their faces completely hidden behind their large bundles. When they arrived, the gate was opened for them, and they entered the city together. Thereupon they threw away their bundles and drew their swords. They sounded horns and threw the city into confusion with loud cries. The townsmen now realized that they had been tricked and took up arms against the invaders. They set upon them en masse, pressing the small group hard with their superior numbers. But the king's troops were protected by a tower on the left-hand side, by houses on the right-hand side, and by the city wall from behind, and they were able to keep the brunt of the attack in front of them, which allowed them to fight from a more secure position. They did not dare to advance any further against the enemy, however, for fear that their adversaries would retake the gate that they had come through and leave them to perish in the midst of their foes. And so each man fought hard upon the spot of ground that he occupied. Just then, at the moment when they were all grievously wounded and close to collapse, the king's troops, who had been summoned by the sound of the horns, burst forth from their hiding places and came to the aid of their comrades, who were now on the verge of defeat, with a tremendous charge. They entered

immani caede adoriuntur. Qui mox a cohortibus victi ac comprehensi sunt, preter paucos qui in turris presidium sese receperunt.

91

Ludovicus ergo rex urbe potitus, cum nulla expugnatione turrim evincere posset, ab urbe eam secludit, obducto intrinsecus muro. Quod factum dux comperiens, cum exercitu accelerat. At nihil virium exerere valens, non sine merore ad sua redit. Illud tantum fecisse fertur, quod arci copias demiserit.

92

Aderat tempus quo rex copias ab Ottone rege prestolabatur. Adest ergo Chonradus dux cum exercitu ex tota Belgica, ab Ottone rege missus. Ludovicus vero rex cum exercitu de Belgica ducis terram ingreditur. Primum vero urbem Silletum adit. Ibi autem primum certamen habere volens, impedimenta quaeque ab urbe amovet. Succendit itaque suburbium circumquaque, ac quidquid extrinsecus exstare

through the gate that was being defended and assailed the townsmen with terrible slaughter. The men of Laon were soon defeated and taken captive by the king's troops, except for a few who took refuge in the tower.[188]

91

King Louis had now taken control of Laon, but when his efforts to take the tower by assault failed, he shut it off from the rest of the city by throwing up an interior wall. When the duke learned what had happened, he hurried to Laon with his army. He was unable to exert any force against the city, however, and he returned home, not without sadness. Reportedly, the only thing he managed to accomplish was to send some troops into the citadel.[189]

92

The time had come when Louis was expecting the arrival of the forces sent by King Otto. Thus, Duke Conrad arrived, having been sent by Otto, with an army drawn from all over Belgica. Louis entered the duke's territory with these troops. He came first to the city of Senlis. Wishing to make this the site of his first engagement, he set about removing whatever obstacles stood between him and the city, setting fire to the

videbatur in planiciem redigit. Obsidionem deputat urbemque circumdat. Gravi congressu utrimque dimicatum est, utrimque quam plurimi sauciantur. Belgae vero, quia ab urbanis nimium arcobalistis impetebantur, resistere quiescunt. Nihil enim contra nisi tantum scutorum testudine utebantur. Unde et regio iussu ab ea urbe discedunt, non solum ob arcobalistarum impetum, verum etiam ob turrium plurimarum firmamentum.

93

Aliorsum itaque iter retorquent et usque ad fluvium Sequanam quidquid ducis visum est per XL miliaria immanissime insectati sunt. Sed cum fluvius equitatum regium ulterius prohiberet, rex[221] gratias exercitui reddit et secum usque quo a se dividerentur reducit. Dux autem evestigio exercitum collectum in pagum Suessonicum deducit.

suburbs on all sides and leveling anything that stood out beyond the walls.[190] Then he gave the order for a siege and invested the city. The battle was intense, with fierce fighting
on both sides and a great many casualties. Because the men
of Belgica were receiving such heavy fire from the crossbows
of the townsmen, however, they ceased trying to fight back.
For the only thing that they could do in response was to employ a shield wall. The king accordingly gave orders for the
army to abandon the siege, not only because of the attacks
from the crossbowmen, but also because of the protection
accorded the city by its many towers.

93

And so the army went off in another direction and for
forty miles all the way to the Seine they brutally ravaged
everything they could find that belonged to the duke. But
when the river prevented the king's knights from advancing
any further, he thanked his men and led them back with him
to the place from which they would go their separate ways.
Meanwhile, the duke hastily mustered an army and led it
into the county of Soissons.[191]

94

Ubi cum in regem conaretur, intervenientibus episcopis Widone Autisiodorense et Ansegiso Trecasino, iureiurando utrimque accepto sub pace sequestra usque in pascha ratio eorum dilata est. Quae omnia Iulio mense[222] gesta sunt.

95

Quo etiam tempore sinodus Romae habita est in basilica sancti Petri apostoli, presidente domno Agapito papa. In qua etiam ipse domnus papa concilium anteriore anno apud Angleheim habitum coram episcopis Italiae roboravit et ab eis roborari constituit. Hugonem quoque Galliarum ducem, in supradicta sinodo dampnatum, ipse etiam condempnat, donec regi suo satisfaciat aut Romam veniat inde ratiocinaturus. Moxque anathema descriptum et a sinodo roboratum episcopis Galliarum destinatur.

94

He was directing his efforts against the king there, when, through the intervention of bishops Wido of Auxerre and Ansegis of Troyes, both sides agreed to swear an oath to observe a truce until Easter and to defer further negotiations until then. All of this took place in the month of July.[192]

95

At the same time a synod was held at Rome in the basilica of Saint Peter the Apostle, with Pope Agapitus presiding. In the presence of the Italian bishops, the pope ratified the decisions made at the synod of Ingelheim the previous year and had them confirmed by the bishops. He also excommunicated Duke Hugh of Gaul, who had been condemned at the synod of Ingelheim, until such time as he should make satisfaction to the king or else come to Rome to plead his case there. Thereupon an anathema was drawn up and confirmed by the synod, after which it was dispatched to the bishops of Gaul.[193]

96

Episcopi itaque Galliarum anathemate moti, apud ducem colliguntur et inde gravissime conqueruntur, ex decretis patrum sacrisque canonibus duci demonstrantes neminem stare pertinaciter adversus dominum suum debere, nec temere in eum quicquam moliri. Illud etiam promptissime monstrant, secundum apostolum regem honorificandum, et non solum regem, verum omnem potestatem maiorem subiectis dominari debere asserunt. Preter haec quoque perniciosissimum esse apostolicum anathema pertinaciter vilipendere, cum id sit gladius qui penetrat corpus usque ad animam et sic mortificatos a regno beatorum spirituum repellat. Sibi etiam periculo esse memorant, si id quod animabus periculum ingerit neglegentes non innotescant.

97

Talibus dux persuasus, regi humiliter reconciliari deposcit eique satisfacturum sese pollicetur. Huius concordiae et pacis ordinatores fuere Chonradus dux et Hugo cogno-

96

The bishops of Gaul, dismayed by the anathema, went before the duke and remonstrated with him about it in the strongest of terms.[194] They informed him that according to the decrees of the fathers and the sacred canons no one was to persist stubbornly in opposing his lord or recklessly to plot against him. They were also quick to point out that according to the Apostle a king was to be held in honor, and they declared that not only the king but every higher authority had the right and obligation to rule over his subjects.[195] Apart from this, it was exceedingly damaging to persevere obstinately in ignoring an apostolic anathema, because excommunication was a sword that pierced through the body to the soul itself and drove those who were struck by it out of the kingdom of the spirits of the blessed. Moreover, they themselves were at risk if they failed to inform heedless men about a matter that put their very souls at risk.

97

Persuaded by such arguments, the duke humbly requested to be reconciled with the king and promised that he would make satisfaction to him. The men who arranged this rapprochement and peace were the dukes Conrad and Hugh

mento Niger, Adalbero quoque atque Fulbertus episcopi. Et die constituta rex et dux conveniunt, ac secus fluvium Matronam conlocuti, principibus predictis internuntiis, in summam concordiam benignissime redierunt. Et quanto vehementius ante in sese grassati fuere, tanto amplius exinde amicitia se coluere. Hugo itaque dux per manus et sacramentum regis efficitur ac turrim Laudunicam suis evacuatam regi reddit, multam abinde fidem se servaturum pollicens.

98

Iussus ergo ab rege, in Aquitaniam exercitum regi parat. Quo in brevi collecto, causis rerum exigentibus, ad interiores Burgundiae partes rex secum exercitum dirigit. Cum ergo in agro Matisconensium castra figeret, occurrit ei Karolus Constantinus, Viennae civitatis princeps, eiusque efficitur, fidem iureiurando pactus. Hic ex regio quidem genere natus erat, sed concubinali stemmate usque ad tritavum sordebat, vir grandevus et multis bellorum casibus saepissime attritus, et qui in superioribus piratarum tumultibus felici congressu insignis[223] multoties enituit. Affuit etiam Stepha-

the Black, and the bishops Adalbero and Fulbert.[196] On a fixed day the king and duke came together, and after holding talks by the Marne River, with the aforementioned magnates serving as intermediaries, they returned to a state of complete harmony in a spirit of mutual goodwill. From that time forward they cherished one another in friendship with a devotion equal to the hostility with which they had assailed one another in the past. By swearing an oath and giving his hands to the king, Duke Hugh became his vassal, and he returned the citadel of Laon to him after emptying it of his men, promising that he would remain completely loyal to the king from that day forward.[197]

98

On the orders of the king, therefore, Hugh raised an army for him to lead into Aquitaine. When the army had assembled a short time later, however, the king led it into inner Burgundy instead, to deal with pressing circumstances. While he was making his camp in the territory around Mâcon, Charles-Constantine, the count of Vienne, came to meet him and swore an oath of fealty to become his vassal. This man was actually of royal stock, but he was tainted by illegitimacy going back to his great-grandfather.[198] A man of long years who had been repeatedly worn down by the many hazards of war, he had distinguished himself with success in battle on several occasions in the earlier struggles with the pirates. Stephen, the bishop of Clermont, was also there and

951

nus Arvernorum presul[224] ac regi sese commisit. Necnon et
a Wilelmo Aquitanorum principe legati industrii affuere,
pro suo principe ex fide habenda sacramenta daturi. Quibus
postquam iussa regalia data sunt, rex in urbem Vesontium,
quae est metropolis Genaunorum, cui etiam in Alpibus sitae
Aldis Dubis preterfluit, cum duce exercitum deducit. Atque
ibi Letoldus, eiusdem urbis princeps, ad eius militiam sacramento transit.

99

Quibus feliciter atque utiliter habitis, cum autumno ma-
turante elementorum immutatio fieret, rex colerico vexatus,
in acutam febrem decidit. Cum ergo[225] aegritudine pressus
militaria curare non posset, dux ab eo iussus exercitum reducit. Letoldus vero princeps in ipsa regis aegritudine fidelissime atque humanissime regi famulatur. At die cretica
post febris initium impariter veniente,[226] firmiter et inreci-
dive convaluit. Transactisque diebus XXX[227] post corporis
reparationem, cum Letoldo principe in Franciam redit.

he committed himself to the king. In addition, diligent envoys had come from Duke William of Aquitaine to swear
oaths of fealty on behalf of their lord. After these men had
received instructions from the king, Louis led his army,
along with the duke, to the city of Besançon, the metropolitan see of Burgundy, which is located amid the Alps and is
washed by the River Doubs. And there Letald,[199] the leading
man of this same city, took an oath to become a vassal of the
king.[200]

99

These things had been arranged successfully and to good
effect, when, as autumn advanced and there was a seasonal
change in the air, the king began to be troubled by a bilious
humor and came down with an acute fever. Because he was
stricken with illness, therefore, and could not attend to military affairs, he ordered the duke to lead the army back
home. For his part, Count Letald tended to the king faithfully and compassionately in his sickness. When the day of
crisis following the onset of the fever arrived with diminished strength, the king's condition stabilized and he did
not experience a relapse. Thirty days after his recovery he
returned to Francia with Count Letald.[201]

100

Et cum iam Burgundiae extrema attingeret, viatorum relatu comperit quosdam qui latrociniis et discursionibus provinciam infestabant, Angelbertum scilicet et Gozbertum, munitionem quae dicebatur Briona exstruxisse, quo etiam post flagitiosa exercitia sese recipiebant. Hanc igitur rex aggressus, obsidione circumdat; pugnaque continua ac fame atterit; et tandem capit, solotenusque diruit. Latrunculos[228] vero, petente Letoldo, sub sacramento abire permittit.

101

Inter haec cum rex in partibus Burgundiae adhuc detineretur, Aethgiva mater eius regina, eo ignorante, Heriberto comiti nupsit, et relicta urbe Lauduno, ab eo deducta est. Quod rex vehementer indignans,[229] redire maturat et cum Gerberga regina uxore Laudunum ingreditur. Et a matre auferens predia et aedes regias, uxori[230] delegat.

IOO

He had just reached the border of Burgundy when he learned from the reports of travelers that certain men who had been harrying the region with pillaging and raiding (namely, Anglebert and Gozbert[202]) had fortified the stronghold called Brienne[203] and were taking refuge there after their depredations. The king therefore assaulted and laid siege to the stronghold, and after wearing the defenders down with continuous attacks and starvation, he eventually captured it and razed it to the ground. As for those petty thieves, he allowed them to depart under oath at the request of Letald.[204]

IOI

While the king was still detained in Burgundy, unbeknownst to him, his mother, Queen Eadgifu, married Count Heribert[205] and was taken away by him, abandoning the city of Laon. The king reacted to this with violent indignation, and he rushed back and entered Laon with his wife, Queen Gerberga. He took away his mother's estates and royal houses and bestowed them upon his wife instead.[206]

102

Interea Gerberga regina Lauduni geminos enixa est. Quorum alter Karolus, alter Heinricus vocatus est. At Heinricus mox post sacri baptismatis perceptionem in albis decedit. Karolus autem cum naturali virium robore educatur.[231]

103

Ludovicus vero rex Remos rediens, cum fluvio Axonae propinquaret, per campestria lupum preire conspicit. Quem equo emisso insecutus, per devia exagitat. Ad omnes ferae declinationes equum impatiens obvertebat. Nec quiescere paciebatur donec equestri certamine fugientem evinceret. Equus ergo per invia coactus, cespite offendit atque prolabitur. Rex vero gravissimo attritus casu, et a suis exceptus, cum multo omnium merore[232] Remos deportatur. Infestis itaque doloribus toto corpore vexabatur. Et post diutinam valetudinem, corruptis interius visceribus ob humorum superfluitatem, elefanciasi peste toto miserabiliter corpore

102

Meanwhile, Queen Gerberga gave birth to twins at Laon. One of them was named Charles,[207] and the other Henry. Shortly after Henry had received the sacrament of baptism he died, still dressed in his white baptismal garments. Charles, however, was blessed with natural physical strength and survived into adulthood.[208]

953

103

King Louis was returning to Reims, and as he approached the River Aisne he caught sight of a wolf going before him through the fields. Giving free rein to his horse, he set off in pursuit and chased it through out-of-the-way places, eagerly turning his mount in response to all of the wolf's feints and dodges. Nor would he allow it to rest until he had pursued and caught up with the fleeing animal. But as it was being ridden hard over the trackless country, his horse stumbled on a piece of turf and fell. The king was seriously injured in the fall, and he was taken up by his men, who carried him sorrowfully to Reims. He was racked with terrible pains throughout his whole body. After a long period of illness, his internal organs became corrupted due to an excess of humors, and elephantiasis spread painfully throughout his entire body. After suffering for a long time, he died, in the

954

perfunditur. Qua diutius confectus, anno regni sui XVIII,[233] a natu autem XXXVI,[234] diem vitae clausit extremum, sepultusque est in coenobio monachorum sancti Remigii, quod distat fere miliario uno ab urbe, cum multis omnium lamentis.

eighteenth year of his reign and the thirty-sixth of his life.[209] He was buried at the monastery of Saint-Rémi, about a mile from the city of Reims, mourned greatly by everyone.[210]

Note on the Text

Richer's *Historia* survives only in the author's autograph manuscript: Bamberg, Staatsbibliothek MS Hist. 5. The folio that contained Richer's account of Gerbert's speech at the synod of Mouzon has gone missing or perhaps was never inserted into the manuscript. All of Richer's editors have reconstructed this section (chapters 4.102–5) from Gerbert's *Acta* of the synod, which are found in an eleventh-century manuscript from Saint-Mesmin-de-Micy and in the *Ecclesiastical History* of the Magdeburg Centuriators. Frutolf of Michelsberg (d. 1103) and Johannes Trithemius (1462–1516) both made use of a revised version of the *Historia* that once existed at Bamberg and which contained only the first two books. Many of their variant readings, which almost certainly represent revisions that Richer made to the text found in Bamberg MS Hist. 5, are included below. No attempt has been made to document all of the changes Richer made to his autograph manuscript. Only those corrections or deletions thought to be of potential interest to the reader have been included.

Georg Heinrich Pertz produced the first edition of Richer's *Historia* for the *Monumenta Germaniae Historica* in 1839. Georg Waitz revised Pertz's edition for the *MGH* in 1877, and Robert Latouche published a two-volume edition and

translation of the *Historia* with some emendations to Waitz's text in 1930 and 1937. Hartmut Hoffmann produced a comprehensive new edition of the *Historia* for the *MGH* in 2000; his is now the authoritative text. The text printed here is based on Hoffmann's edition, kindly made available by the *MGH,* with some minor changes. While Hoffmann prints Richer's punctuation from Bamberg MS Hist. 5, the text here has been punctuated to accord with modern conventions.

Notes to the Text

ABBREVIATIONS

Frutolf = Frutolf of Michelsberg, *Chronicon,* ed. G. Waitz, *MGH SS* 6. Hanover: Hahn, 1844, pp. 33–223.

Hoffmann = Hartmut Hoffmann, ed., *Richeri Historiarum Libri IIII, MGH SS* 38. Hanover: Hahn, 2000.

L = *Acta concilii Mosomensisi,* Leiden, Bibliotheek der Rijksuniversiteit, Voss. lat. Q 54, ff. 82r–84r.

Latouche = Robert Latouche, ed. and trans., *Richer: Histoire de France (885–995).* Les classiques de l'histoire de France au moyen âge. 2 vols. Paris: H. Champion, 1930 and 1937.

MS = Bamberg, Staatsbibliothek MS Hist. 5.

Pertz = G.H. Pertz, ed., *Richeri historiarum libri IIII.* Hanover: Hahn, 1839, pp. 561–657.

Poinsignon = A.-M. Poinsignon, *Richeri Historiarum quatuor libri—Histoire de Richer en quatres livres.* Reims: P. Regnier, 1855.

Trithemius = Johannes Trithemius, *Annales Hirsaugienses.* Saint-Gall, 1690.

Waitz = Georg Waitz, ed., *Richeri historiarum libri IIII, MGH SRG* 51. Hanover: Hahn, 1877.

Prologue

1   G. *MS*

2   ducendum existimavi *corrected from* ducere volui

3   divae *Pertz*

4   ante te in pontificatu VIII *corrected from* ante te septimus Remorum metropolitanus

5   longe diverso *corrected from* prestantiore : diverso *corrected from* diversissimo

6   orationis *corrected from* ordinationis

7   Sed si ignotae . . . omnia digesserim *added at the bottom of the folio* : digesserim *corrected from* digesta sunt, *which is corrected from* dixerim

Book i

1   -eus *is virtually illegible and perhaps corrected to* Mediterraneum : Mediterraneum interiectum *Pertz* : Mediterraneus interiectus *Latouche*

2   in *corrected from* per

3   autem a Matrona per longum in Garunnam distenditur *corrected from* autem hinc Matrona inde Garunna abluitur

4   efficiunt *added above* habent, *which is not expunged* : efficiunt Frutolf

5   Hiberum, qui Hiberiae regioni nomen indidit usque in oceanum *expunged below* Pireneum

6   Rhodano Ararique *corrected from* provinciae Lugdunensi

7   Pyreneo *corrected from* Hibero

8   Hos . . . christianus *in margin and partially cut off; restored via* Frutolf

9   et cum *Pertz*

10   adprime semper clara victoria *Waitz* : adprime clara semper et illustri victoria *Pertz*

11   abavum *corrected from* avum

12   vix per quadrennium superstite *corrected from* paulo ante amissa

13   provectum *corrected from* commoda

14   in palatio Compendii *Frutolf, Trithemius*

15   eo quod milites mediocri interdum subdi contempnerent *expunged after* habuit.

16   immo et a finibus Galliarum penitus eliminavit *expunged after* compulit

17   quinquennium *correction for* biennium

18   venibat *corrected from* veniebat

19   maritima *expunged after* loca

20   cum exercitu *expunged after* ipse

21   Neustriae *corrected from* Franciae

22   concessisse *corrected from* secessisse

23   caedunt *MS*

24   *rapiuntur MS*

25   aelati *MS corrected from* laetati

26   *erasure after* attrivisse: immo et . . . violenter expugnasse

27   asserebat *corrected from* memorabat

28   aggreditur *corrected from* aggressus est

29   premittit *corrected from* premisit

30   ITERATIO BELLI *expunged in margin*

31   cum regis signo *Pertz*

32   gladio *corrected from* gladiis

33   tirannus *expunged above the line after* regi

34   ait *corrected from* coepit

35   stragem *corrected from* strages

36   Qua conquestio *corrected from* Cuius conquestionis vis

37   regem *Pertz*

38   de privatis multumque *expunged after* Plurimum

39   qui Sequanae Ligerique fluviis interiacent *expunged after* absentia

40   profecti *expunged after* enim

41   tunc *corrected from* adhuc

42   necnon et reliquis *expunged above* aut eorum

43   rei magnitudine permotus *expunged after* comperiens

44   basilica *corrected from* loco qui dicitur

45   diornisii *MS*

46   Cui etiam in primis adolescentiae annis pax atque tranquillitas rei publicae, concordia suorum, commoditas privatorum grata fuere. Id vero in brevi *expunged after* simplicique

47   avarus *corrected from* parcus

48   accommodat *corrected from* accomodavit : Rex ergo principibus stipatus ac multo suorum obsequio inclitus, more regio leges condit ac decreta edicit, Rotbertum quoque *expunged after* accommodat

49   fere per quadriennium *corrected from* plurimum

50   quae est Celticae pars *expunged after* deductus

51   Saxoniam *corrected from* b . . . iam (*possibly* baioariam *Hoffmann*) : *corrected from* Belgicam *Pertz*

52   ubi etiam Heinricum regio genere inclitum ac inde oriundum ducem omnibus praeficit *added at the bottom of the folio*

53   sibi *above* militare, *which is expunged*

54   labem *corrected from* calamitatem

55   Belgicae *over erasure* : Galliarum *Frutolf*

56   urbibus *corrected from* finibus

57   Celticam *over erasure*

58   mediocrem *corrected from* ignobilem

59   indignationem *corrected from* querimoniam

60   eo *corrected from* Rotberto

61   -rumque incommoditatem *in margin* : causarum incommoditatem *Trithemius* : fratrumque incommoditatem *Pertz*

62   mandat *corrected from* spondet

63   Admodum *corrected from* Saevissime

64   pontificis *corrected from* amici

65   adeo *corrected from* admodum

66   condoluere *corrected from* doluere

67   lurida *Trithemius:* lucida *MS*

68   omniumque odio habitus *Trithemius* : omnibus horrori habitus est *Pertz* : omni horrore habitus est *Latouche*

69   caedunt *MS*

70   petitio *Pertz*

71   de rerum dispositionibus fidelissime *corrected from* de amicicia inter se habenda plurimum

72   dolum arbitrans *corrected from* rerum nescius

73   Qua die nihil concordiae, nihil amiciciarum inter eos habitum est *expunged after* cogitur

74 Estimabant *corrected from* Estimaverant : Existimabant *Pertz*

75 enim *omitted by Latouche*

76 A quo etiam *corrected from* ab eo quoque

77 regi Karolo *Pertz*

78 nulla *corrected from* levissima

79 numquam *corrected from* nullo umquam die semet

80 Rotbertus dux *corrected from* principes

81 perciperet *corrected from* perciperent

82 abiectione *Trithemius* : eiectione *Pertz*

83 facit *Pertz*

84 transferre *Pertz*

85 igitur *Waitz* : itaque *Pertz*

86 atque *Pertz*

87 Tandemque *Pertz*

88 et veluti consultantem cum paucis intro dimittunt. Ipsi vero captionem dissimulantes, egrediuntur *expunged after* tenent

89 quidem prius cum paucis *corrected from* cum paucis prius ingreditur

90 sui *corrected from* suos

91 Qui tamen *expunged after* paucis

92 cum paucis *corrected from* duobus tantum

93 Confusique *corrected from* Iratique

94 interiora *corrected from* superiora

95 Tungros *corrected from* Tungris

96 ordinat *corrected from* ordinavit

97 Rotberto duci in regis abiectione favebant *corrected from* cum
Rotberto duce regem abiecerant

98 At rex . . . discesserat *corrected from* At Remorum metropolitani
Herivei consilio usus, Gislebertum qui in Belgica omnibus potior erat, per legatos accersit. Hic enim ab Heinrico persuasus,
cum aliis nonnullis ab rege discesserant. Et accersitus cum multo
honore ante regem admittitur

99 sic *Waitz* : Remensium *Pertz*

100 Heinricum *over an erasure, presumably* Gislebertum

101 tua liberalitate *corrected from* tua liberali ingenio

102 molivolorum *MS*

103 aemersit *MS*

104 at frequentatum et commune *expunged after* singulare

105 Germanorum *corrected from* Belgicorum

106 incautum te *corrected from* sive incauto tibi nescio sive eadem cupienti

107 Germaniam *corrected from* Belgicam

108 Responsio Heinrici *over an erasure*

109 Heinricus *corrected from* Gislebertus

110 his *corrected from* rege

111 expertus *Pertz*

112 Heinricus *over an erasure, presumably* Gislebertus

113 insectabatur *corrected from* impetebatur

114 Quid sibi in animo sit Gisleberto demonstrans, habita apud eum conquestione de quibusdam. Eius quoque consilio militum copias colligit ire volens hostiliter in eos qui nulla penetentia ducti ad sese non redierunt *expunged after* ordinaturus

115 in gratiam resumit *corrected from* multa benivolentia assumit: Enimvero omnibus placita desertoribus fieri parabat. Vixque eos sic revocabat. Necnon et ei sub fidei conservandae acta conditione, sua resitituit vadibus more legali concessis *expunged after* resumit

116 *corrected from* novem

117 duce Gisleberto ordinat. Inde *expunged after* Belgas

118 incendebat *Pertz*

119 dictis *corrected from* collectis

120 signa <cane>re *expunged after* dux

121 gerendum *corrected from* habendum

122 Quo ubi perventum est *expunged after* deducit.

123 frontibus maforto signatis *expunged after* Aquitanis

124 curaverant *Latouche*

125 in augmento *corrected from* quinta

126 cum maximo clamore *expunged after* exercitus

127 collatis *corrected from* infestis

128 Belgae inprovisi prosequuntur *corrected from* Gislebertus cum Belgis inprovisus prosequitur

129 Rotbertus captos *corrected from* quisque ad sua redit. Rotbertus
     vero obsides piratarum

130 An fideliter baptizari spoponderint diligentissime perquirens.
     Comperto vero quia si eis terra mari contigua, quam ipsi quoque
     insectati fuerant sub tributo daretur sese et christianam reli-
     gionem sponte suscepturos et regi Galliarum fideliter militat-
     uros, huic rei non sufficere suum credens consilium, id ordinan-
     dum Wittoni per legatos dirigit Rotomagensium episcopo. Nec
     minus et Heriveo Remorum metropolitano idem pandit ac ab
     eo rationem petit. Hi etenim duo metropolitani et<atis rever-
     entia et vitae merito> in Galliis tunc maxime commendabantur
     expunged after deponit

131 opsidibus *corrected from* hospitibus

132 atque utiliter *MS* : efficacissime *expunged before* atque

133 v.c. *MS* : vir consularis *Pertz*

134 adulto *Frutolf*

135 vel coniugio *above* matrimonio, *which is not expunged*

136 naribus vero iniurias atque contemptum insolenter spirantibus *ex-
     punged after* inquietis

137 in controversiis consensus simul et negatio *expunged after* levi

138 sibique regnum affectabat *expunged after* videbantur

139 municipiis *corrected from* munitionibus

140 largitate *corrected from* dignitate

141 aegit *MS*

142 iulicum *expunged after* partem

143 mox persuasus *crossed out after* et

144 ea socero *del. Pertz* : a (?) socero *Waitz* : a socero *Hoffmann*

145 *two words are expunged after* toleratur; *probably Gis(lebertus) vero*
     Hoffmann

146 Et . . . coniurarent *expunged*

147 tota *corrected from* omni pene

148 Vix etiam spem aliquam sibi relictam, cum a tiranno totum perva-
     sum sit, potestas dominandi, et libertas habendi *expunged after*
     demantur

149 pervasore *corrected from* pervasoribus

150   sui *corrected from* Belgarum magnates

151   equum *MS*

152   *originally* ingredi non valebis; *corrected to* non repetes; repetes *corrected to* irrumpes

153   X *corrected from* VI, *which is corrected from* quinque

154   militiae *corrected from* pugnae

155   Procedit itaque rex *expunged after* unanimes

156   Axonam vero fluvium transmeans, in urbem Suessonicam tendit. Ibi etenim tirannus exercitum collegerat *expunged after* fertur

157   $\overline{VI}$ *over an erasure*

158   v.c. *MS* : virum consularem *Pertz*

159   IIII *corrected from* duobus

160   de militia et famae gloria, priorumque nobilitate et filiorum utilitate *expunged after* quosque

161   ad vim belli *probably added by another hand Hoffmann*

162   prudentia *in margin before* intenderet; *perhaps an alternative for* instinctu *Hoffmann*

163   bello prudentia intenderet *corrected from* in tirannum rueret : bello *perhaps added by the same hand that wrote* ad vim belli *Hoffmann*

164   instinctu episcoporum *Pertz*

165   IIII *corrected from* duobus

166   v.c. *MS* : virum consularem *Pertz*

167   ut corda ad deum elevent eiusque *expunged below* ut dei

168   regni pervasorem *corrected from* tirannum

169   gradive *added by the same hand that wrote* vim belli *Hoffmann*

170   BELL<UM> inter Karol<um> et Rotb<ertum> eiusque fu<...> *expunged in margin* : fuga *Pertz* : furor *Latouche* : fusio *Hoffmann*

171   Irruunt et circumquaque coniurati. A quibus Rotbertus *expunged after* transigit

172   precipitat *MS* ; *corrected from* occubuit : praecipitatus corruit *Pertz*

173   multoque Fulbertus mox *Pertz*

174   intercertans *Pertz*

175   *sic Frutolf* : $\overline{XI}$, *with* CCC *added in the margin and the rest of the number cut away MS*

176   illius *corrected from* sui

177   ecce . . . deducitur *corrected from* Heribertus Hugonem Rotberti filium cum iam pubescentem in prelium deducit

178   rege *below* patre *but not expunged in MS*

179   memorabile *corrected from* insigne

180   ob necem tiranni *corrected from* utpote tiranno interfecto

181   Celtae *corrected from* Galli

182   subito creatum subito *expunged after* regem

183   penitus *Pertz* : pernitiose *Waitz*

184   Gallis *expunged after* Nam

185   sine spoliis in Belgicam retorsit post *corrected from* in Germaniam
     retorsit in Gallias

186   coniuratorum a multitudine *Pertz*

187   *sic Waitz* : ibvenit *MS* : obvenit *Pertz*

188   pyratae *corrected from* Nortmanni

189   Exercitum *corrected from* iter

190   dolose tamen *expunged after* occurrit

191   rem publicam *Pertz*

192   pyratas *corrected from* Nortmannos

193   interiores Burgundiae *corrected from* exteriores Galliarum

194   pyratae *corrected from* Nortmanni

195   Rollonem oculis effossis, suggillant *expunged after* potiti

196   a tergo *expunged after* rex

197   subsecuta atque exagitata est *above* exorta est, *which is not ex-*
     punged

198   Heribert *MS*

199   Karolus liberatur ab Heriberto *Pertz* : Karoli liberatio *Waitz*

200   Heribert *MS*

201   regionem *below* pagum *but not expunged MS*

202   suspectis *added above the line*

203   Sententia papae in Rodulfum petita ab Heriberto reiecta *Pertz* :
     Sententia Romae petita absque effectu *Waitz*

204   Heribert *MS*

205   nonnullos *below* quosque *but not expunged MS*

206   sint *Waitz*

207   bonorum *corrected from* oboedientium

208   neg<ot>ium peracturi *expunged after* properant

209   Heribert *MS*

210   d *corrected from* piae *MS* : divae *Pertz*

211   quibusdam *expunged after* cum

212 ab rege *expunged after* ibique
213 aequitatum *MS*
214 cede *corrected from* prelio
215 Heriberti et Hugonis *Pertz*
216 stabat *Pertz*
217 oppidum *above* castrum, *which is not expunged*
218 Deliberatio contra regem *Waitz* : Heriberti praeparatio contra
     regem *Pertz*
219 excipientes *corrected from* admirantes
220 accersit *corrected from* evocat
221 vos *expunged after* necessitas
222 castri *Pertz* : deditio *Waitz*
223 rationabiliter *expunged after* consciis
224 Ubi postquam *corrected from* cum rex
225 ordinavit *corrected from* ordinaret : ac in predicti tiranni labem, alia
     apud Hugonem disponeret, ac *expunged after* ordinavit
226 petebatur *corrected from* peteret
227 duriter eos cedit *corrected from* durissime urget
228 provinciae *corrected from* regni
229 Turma malorum et prodigia *Pertz*
230 attritione *Waitz*

Book 2

1 divae *Pertz*
2 fautores *corrected from* multi
3 *sic MS*
4 ac Ludovicum accersiendum conclamant *expunged after* cedunt
5 Morinum *corrected from* Bononiam
6 devexi sunt *corrected from* devenerunt : Rex *expunged before* Adel-
    stanus
7 salutantur *Pertz*
8 omnium qui in Galliis potiores sunt *corrected from* omnibus ex
    Galliis faventibus
9 Divae *Pertz*
10 eius *corrected from* Ludovici

11   acsi *expunged before* barbaris

12   per sacramenta *corrected from* iure sacramenti

13   etiam *expunged after* suam

14   iis *corrected from* hiis

15   etiam *expunged after* Cuius

16   et reliqui *corrected from* cum reliquis ; principes *corrected from* principibus

17   revocat *MS*

18   legatum *expunged after* ergo

19   episcopum *corrected from* abbatem

20   sese *corrected from* ei

21   non minus *corrected from* amplius

22   nolint *corrected from* nolunt

23   ei *corrected from* illi

24   cum reliquis Galliarum magnatibus *corrected from* ac reliqui Galliarum magnates

25   navalium *expunged after* multa

26   Ludovicus *corrected from* rex

27   regium *expunged before* equum

28   Heriberto comiti dedit. Ille quoque tandiu armigeravit, donec et ipse iussus Arnulfo comiti redderet. Sic quoque *expunged after* iussus

29   regnandi *corrected from* regnorum

30   quindennis *added above the line*

31   capitque *expunged after* premit

32   sua visurus *expunged after* consentiens

33   invidorum *expunged after* et

34   magnae *below* non minimae *but not expunged*

35   decepto *corrected from* pusillanimo

36   adventus *corrected from* impetus

37   ob principum dissidentiam *expunged after* sevientes

38   gratiam *Pertz*

39   situm *expunged after* Matronam

40   intextis *corrected from* intectis

41   spondet ac iuratus fidem dat *expunged after* proditionem

42   usque *corrected from* ad

43   quo etiam luminis signo per legatos aditum significaverat *corrected*
      from quod etiam luminis signum per legatos mandaverat

44   milites *corrected from* militum cohortem

45   ii *corrected from* hi

46   ad *Pertz*

47   iis *corrected from* his

48   namque *expunged after* rex

49   consentiebant *corrected from* favebant

50   Belgicam *corrected from* Belgicae loca

51   princeps *corrected from* rex

52   propter *corrected from* pro

53   periit atque sessorem inmersit *corrected from* occubuit

54   erepti *corrected from* exempti

55   regiis *corrected from* regis

56   oppugnatione *corrected from* expugnatione

57   malorum *corrected from* mali

58   Ubi *corrected from* Qui

59   tiranni *corrected from* Heribertus et Hugo

60   tiranni *corrected from* Hugo ac Heribertus

61   Lauduni *corrected from* Remorum

62   Interea domni Stephani *expunged after* concedunt

63   provinciarum *corrected from* regnorum

64   vehementer *corrected from* utiliter

65   iis debeatur ruina *corrected from* labe afficiantur labe

66   ingentibus donis *corrected from* humanissime

67   accumulat *corrected from* cumulat

68   celerius *expunged after* tempestivius

69   H. et. H *added above* predictis tirannis

70   obveniens *corrected from* adveniens

71   d... Gallorum *expunged* : de Gallia *Waitz* : duce Gallorum *expunged*
      Latouche

72   ac *corrected from* cum

73   fortuitu *corrected from* nescio

74   vibrabundus *corrected from* fervidus

75   pulvinaribus ac ceteris necessariis stratum *expunged after* gestato-
      rium

76   Desertorisne *corrected from* An desertorisque ne

77 Fervideque *Latouche*

78 iniuriam . . . dissimulans *corrected from* benivolentia . . . simulans

79 iniuria irrogata apud illos *corrected from* iniuria quae ei irrogata a Wilelmo fuerat, cum ab eo surgere a lecto coactus sit, apud illos multam truculentus agitabat indignationem

80 et amici *corrected from* amici quoque

81 pluraque *expunged after* indulturum

82 et loco *expunged after* tempore

83 et quo *expunged after* quando

84 Et ut ille per legatos habendum indicaret, ita ad eius votum penitus susciperetur, illud tantum concederet, ut *expunged after* foret

85 aliquanto *expunged after* sua

86 amico *corrected from* amicis

87 dicere *expunged after* amicicia

88 advectus *corrected from* deductus

89 ac *expunged after* simulantes

90 prestolantem *above* exspectantem, *which has not been expunged*

91 accelerarent *corrected from* valerent

92 procuraturos *corrected from* exsecuturos

93 aliquantisper *corrected from* paulisper

94 strepitu *corrected from* clamore

95 preotissimum *MS*

96 eductis *corrected from* strictis

97 largiens *corrected from* largitus

98 Rodomunt *MS*

99 copiosa *corrected from* multa

100 Thurmodum *corrected from* Turmodum

101 exercitus *expunged before* equitatus

102 densati *corrected from* conglobati

103 *corrected from* $\overline{\text{IIII}}$

104 metropolitanum *corrected from* metropolitano

105 iniuriarum *corrected from* iniurias

106 vim *corrected from* copias

107 sese *expunged after* regem

108 rex *above* Franciae, *which is expunged*

109 excepit *corrected from* habuit

110   regno *expunged after* de

111   illorum *corrected from* sua

112   parent *corrected from* cedunt

113   minuerentur *corrected from* minorarentur

114   Brittanni *corrected from* Brintanni

115   munita *corrected from* minita

116   ut *expunged after* ita

117   parat *corrected from* dat

118   ab *expunged after* duci

119   Quod *corrected from* Id

120   conquerenti *corrected from* conquirenti

121   ingressum negabat *corrected from* ingressus negabatur

122   legationem *corrected from* legatos

123   habuerat *corrected from* habebat

124   resistente et *above the line and possibly erased* : *omitted by Hoffmann*

125   duci non satis creduli *expunged after* vero

126   oblato *corrected from* dato

127   petentes *corrected from* quaerentes

128   Ottonique *corrected from* Ottoni fratri

129   dissentit *corrected from* consentit

130   nec *corrected from* neque

131   Consultumque *corrected from* Deliberatumque

132   discedit *corrected from* discessit

133   Quomodo enim stare potest quem socordia precipitat *expunged after* est

134   ut *corrected from* quae

135   componat *expunged after* militantem

136   Fare *Trithemius*

137   tu *corrected from* te

138   tu *corrected from* te

139   ex *expunged after* et

140   in *expunged after* Et

141   Nec tamen *corrected from* Iamque

142   caedebant *MS*

143   preter suorum conscientiam *expunged after* urbem

144   monstrat *corrected from* mostrat

145   adduxerint *Pertz*

146   omne periculum *corrected from* omni periculo

147   Quod et fertur Bernardi comitis astutia dispositum *expunged after*
       simulantes

148   sese *corrected from* se

149   tempore nocturno *expunged after* videlicet

150   interiora *corrected from* exteriora

151   resisteret *corrected from* resisterat

152   Frederunae *expunged after* reginae

153   in *expunged after* eorum

154   multam *corrected from* atque id la

155   simulans *corrected from* simulat

156   mox sese *expunged after* teriaca

157   donatus *expunged after* successit

158   Belgicae *expunged after* rex

159   Remensem *Pertz*

160   duodecima die *corrected from* decima die : die tercia decima *Trithe-*
       mius

161   excipientibus *above* discutientibus, *which is not expunged*

162   Petetri *MS*

163   Ne *MS*

164   caput *Pertz*

165   contempserat *corrected from* contempsit

166   quae Kl. Aug. habenda indicebatur *expunged after* sinodum

167   universalem *corrected from* generalem

168   Hildinesbeimsis *corrected from* Hildinesbennsis

169   habenda *Pertz*

170   dispondendi *corrected from* ordinandi

171   in sanctam sinodum *expunged after* capitula

172   videntur *above* cognoscimus, *which is not expunged*

173   turbatam *corrected from* turbatum

174   regnorum *above* Galliarum, *which is not expunged*

175   infestetur *corrected from* appetitur

176   multo intuitu, multo caritatis affectu considerandum arbitror ut
       sic *expunged after* confluximus

177   legati *corrected from* vicarii

178 Ludovici regis *Pertz*

179 et usque ad vitae eius suprema ergastulo inclusum esse rogavit
 Pertz : et . . . inclusum servavit *Waitz*

180 extincto *corrected from* capto

181 nobis *underlined and subpuncted* : *omitted by Hoffmann*

182 Rodulfum *corrected from* alium

183 per annum *expunged after* carcerique

184 duos *expunged before* filios

185 coniecit *corrected from* conicit

186 mancipavit *corrected from* mancipat

187 libertatem spopondit *corrected from* reditum spondet

188 acciperet *corrected from* accipiat

189 monendus *corrected from* vocandus

190 tertia huius sinodi die *expunged after* noluerit

191 vim *corrected from* violentiam

192 vobis *corrected from* nobis

193 referamur *corrected from* feramur

194 revocamus *corrected from* ammonemus

195 Artoldus *corrected from* Artaldus

196 nomine *expunged after* porrexit

197 privatur *corrected from* privatus est

198 prolatata *MS*

199 pulso vel abdicato *expunged after* Hugone

200 apud sinodum *expunged after* episcopo

201 fuerant *expunged after* evocati

202 Post haec *corrected from* Atque hiis gestis

203 post haec *expunged after* et

204 His expletis *corrected from* Interea

205 ab *expunged after* confectus

206 Interea *corrected from* Quibus gestis

207 exercitu . . . collecto *corrected from* exercitus . . . colligitur

208 Hugoni datur r *expunged*

209 caedunt *MS*

210 conferrt (*sic*) *corrected from* conferre

211 adortus *corrected from* adorsus

212 iter truculentus reflectit *corrected from* truculentus refertur

213 ig<ne> *expunged after* DLX

214 in ipsa hieme *expunged after* ut

215 acceleret *over expunged* mittat *followed by expunged* licet ipse exercitum collectum remiserit et usque post ver non reversurum : et usque post ver non reversurum *corrected from* et non usque post hiemem reversurum

216 Ottone *corrected from* rege

217 Refert *corrected from* Contulit

218 quidem *expunged after* magnum

219 pilleatis *corrected from* obvolutis

220 eliguntur *expunged after* iurati

221 rex *corrected from* dux

222 Iulio mense *corrected from* August. tempore

223 insignis *corrected from* insigniter

224 presul *corrected from* princeps

225 rex *expunged after* ergo

226 bene ac *expunged after* veniente

227 XXX *evidently corrected from* XX

228 Latronculos *MS*

229 cum Gerberga *expunged after* indignans

230 omnia *expunged after* uxori

231 educatur *corrected from* educatus est

232 merore *corrected from* luctu

233 XVIII *corrected from* XVII

234 XXXVI *corrected from* XXII *MS* : anno vite sue, ut Richerus monachus ait, tricesimo septimo, regni autem octavo decimo *Trithemius*

Notes to the Translation

ABBREVIATIONS

Acta concilii Mosomensis = Ernst-Dieter Hehl, ed., *Die Konzilien Deutschlands und Reichsitaliens 916–1001,* vol. 2, *MGH Concilia* 6.2. Hanover: Hahn, 2007, pp. 495–507.

Acta concilii Remensis = Ernst-Dieter Hehl, ed., *Die Konzilien Deutschlands und Reichsitaliens 916–1001,* vol. 2, *MGH Concilia* 6.2. Hanover: Hahn, 2007, pp. 380–450.

Barth = Rüdiger E. Barth, *Der Herzog in Lotharingien im 10. Jahrhundert.* Sigmaringen: Thorbecke, 1990.

Bubnov = N. Bubnov, ed., *Gerberti Opera Mathemtica.* Berlin: R. Friedländer, 1899.

Flodoard, *Annales* = Philippe Lauer, ed., *Les Annales de Flodoard,* Collection de textes pour servir à l'étude et à l'enseignement de l'histoire. Paris: Alphonse Picard, 1905.

Flodoard, *HRE* = Martina Stratmann, ed., *Flodoardus Remensis: Historia Remensis Ecclesiae, MGH SS* 36. Hanover: Hahn, 1998.

Gerbert, *ep.* = Pierre Riché and J. P. Callu, eds., *Gerbert d'Aurillac: Correspondance,* Les classiques de l'histoire de France au moyen âge. 2 vols. Paris: Les Belles Lettres, 1993.

Hoffmann, "Die *Historien*" = Hartmut Hoffmann, "Die *Historien* Richers von Saint-Remi." *Deutsches Archiv für Erforschung des Mittelalters* 54 (1998): 445–532.

Hoffmann, *Historiae* = Hartmut Hoffmann, ed., *Richer von Saint-Remi: Historiae, MGH SS* 38. Hanover: Hahn, 2000.

JK = Philipp Jaffé, ed., *Regesta pontificum Romanorum ab condita ecclesia ad annum post Christum natum MCXCVIII,* 2nd ed. by F. Kaltenbrunner, P. Ewald, and S. Loewenfeld. 2 vols. Graz: Akademische Druck, 1956 [Leipzig, 1885–1888].

Latouche = Robert Latouche, ed. and trans., *Richer: Histoire de France (885–995).* Les classiques de l'histoire de France au moyen âge. 2 vols. Paris: H. Champion, 1930 and 1937.

Lauer, *Louis IV* = Philippe Lauer, *Le règne de Louis IV d'Outre-Mer.* Geneva: Slatkine, 1977 [Paris: É. Bouillon, 1900].

Lauer, *Robert I*ᵉʳ *et Raoul de Bourgogne* = Philippe Lauer, *Robert I*ᵉʳ *et Raoul de Bourgogne, rois de France (923–936).* Geneva: Slatkine, 1976 [Paris: H. Champion, 1910].

Lot, *Hugues Capet* = Ferdinand Lot, *Études sur le règne de Hugues Capet et la fin du X*ᵉ *siècle.* Geneva: Slatkine, 1975 [Paris: É. Bouillon, 1903].

Lot, *Les derniers Carolingiens* = Ferdinand Lot, *Les derniers Carolingiens, Lothaire, Louis V, Charles de Lorraine (954–991).* Geneva: Slatkine, 1975 [Paris: É. Bouillon, 1891].

MGH = *Monumenta Germaniae Historica.* Hanover, etc. 1826ff.

PL = Jacques-Paul Migne, ed., *Patrologiae cursus completus, series latina.* 221 vols. Paris: 1841–1864.

SRG = *Scriptores rerum germanicarum in usum scholarum separatim editi*

SS = *Scriptores* (in folio)

PROLOGUE

1   Gerbert of Aurillac, archbishop of Reims (991–998) and later Pope Sylvester II (999–1003).

2   Hincmar, archbishop of Reims (845–882).

3   Gerbert was actually the ninth archbishop after Hincmar. The or-

der of succession after Hincmar was as follows: Fulk (882–900), Hervey (900–922), Seulf (922–925), Hugh (925–931, 941–946), Artald (931–940, 946–961), Odelric (962–969), Adalbero (969–989), Arnulf (989–991), and then Gerbert (991–998).

4   The *Annals of Saint-Bertin* (*Annales Bertiniani*). Hincmar wrote the final section, covering the years 861–882.

5   Flodoard of Reims (d. 966) wrote both a *History of the Church of Rheims* and an *Annals* covering the years 919–966. The latter work, to which Richer is referring here, is Richer's most important source.

Book i

1   Orosius, *Hist.* 1.1–2.

2   The Riphaean Mountains were a mythical range supposedly located in the far north. Jerusalem was thought to be the center of the earth, based on Ezek. 5:5. Lake Maeotis is the modern-day Sea of Azov.

3   Isidore of Seville, *Etymologiae* 14.4.25. Isidore derives the word "Gaul" from the Greek *gala* (milk).

4   Caesar, *Gal.* 1.1.

5   Isidore, *Etymologiae* 14.4.4.

6   Jerome, *Contra Vigilantium* ch. 1.

7   Sulpicius Severus, *Dialogi* 1.8.5.

8   Richer's Latin is ambiguous. He may be speaking of a single victory here, namely Clovis's defeat of King Alaric II of the Visigoths at the Battle of Vouillé in 507.

9   King Charles III ("the Simple") of West Francia (r. 893–923, d. 929).

10   Richer is confused. Charles the Simple's father was King Louis II ("the Stammerer") (877–879); his paternal grandfather was Charles the Bald (r. 843–877, imp. 875–877). Carloman (879–884) was the second son of Louis the Stammerer and his first wife, Ansgard. He briefly shared the kingdom of West Francia with his older brother, Louis III (879–882). Thus Carloman was Charles the Simple's half-brother, not his father.

11   Louis the Stammerer died on April 10, 879. Charles the Simple was born on September 17 of the same year, five months after his father died. His mother, Adelaide, Louis's second wife, lived until at least 901.

12   I.e., Normandy.

13   This appears to be a reference to the treaty of Saint-Clair-sur-Epte (911), by which Charles the Simple granted the lands that would make up the core of the future duchy of Normandy to Rollo and his followers. If so, Richer's chronology is highly confused.

14   King Odo (888–898). He was crowned in February 888, making Charles eight years old at the time.

15   According to the *Annals of Saint-Vaast*, Odo's election took place at Compiègne. See B. De Simson, ed., *Annales Vedastini, MGH SSRG* 12 (Hanover: Hahn, 1909), p. 64.

16   Robert the Strong (d. 866).

17   Robert the Strong's father was not Witichin but a certain Rutpert (or Robert) who held comital power around Worms and the upper Rhine.

18   A passage that Richer later expunged in the manuscript explains that Odo was unable to keep the peace "because the *milites* occasionally scorned to be subject to a person of middling status."

19   By ounces and drachmas Richer may be referring to solidi and denarii.

20   Twelve denarii made up a solidus.

21   The Battle of Montpensier (892).

22   Cf. Livy 4.12.6.

23   Archbishops Ratbod of Trier, Hatto of Mainz, and Hermann of Cologne.

24   Richer telescopes the five years between the coronation of Charles (893) and the death of Odo (898), making it appear as though Odo died soon after Charles was crowned.

25   Robert I, duke of Neustria and later king (922–923).

26   King Henry I ("the Fowler") of Germany (919–936). Richer's assessment of Charles the Simple's dominion over Saxony is inaccurate, the result either of bias against the non-Carolingian Henry or of reliance on Flodoard, who refers to Henry as *prin-*

ceps (not *rex*) up until the year 923. Henry did not rule as duke of Saxony under the overlordship of Charles; he was elected king by the German magnates at Fritzlar in May of 919.

27 At this point Richer begins using the *Annals* of Flodoard as his primary source; he continues to do so until 3.21.

28 Flodoard, *Annales s.a.* 920, p. 2.

29 Archbishop Fulk of Reims (883–900).

30 Count Baldwin II of Flanders (879–918).

31 These were vassals of the archbishop of Reims.

32 Flodoard, *HRE* 4.10, pp. 402–3.

33 Cf. Hegesippus, *Bellum Iudaicum* 1.45.9.

34 Flodoard, *HRE* 4.10, p. 403.

35 Archbishop Hervey of Reims (900–922). He was ordained bishop on July 6, 900.

36 Flodoard, *HRE* 4.11, pp. 403–4.

37 Flodoard's *History of the Church of Rheims (Historia Remensis Ecclesiae).*

38 Flodoard, *Annales s.a.* 920, pp. 2–3.

39 Flodoard, *Annales s.a.* 920, p. 3 says that Charles was "encamped against" Henry.

40 Flodoard, *Annales s.a.* 920, p. 3.

41 Flodoard, *Annales s.a.* 920, p. 3.

42 The bishop of Soissons in 920 was not Riculf but Abbo (ca. 909–937). See Hoffmann, *Historiae,* p. 59 n. 2.

43 Flodoard, *HRE* 4.15, p. 408.

44 Flodoard, *Annales s.a.* 920, pp. 3–4.

45 Richer originally wrote (and later crossed out) that Charles negotiated with Gislebert of Lotharingia (for whom, see chs. 34–35 and n. 36 below) rather than Henry I. Likewise, it was originally Gislebert, not Henry, who heard Hervey's speech at 1.23 and responded to it at 1.24.

46 Cf. Sallust, *Iug.* 31.1.

47 Sallust, *Epistula ad Caesarem* 2.1.1.

48 Sallust, *Epistula ad Caesarem* 2.1.1–2.

49 Sallust, *Epistula ad Caesarem* 2.1.4.

50 Sallust, *Epistula ad Caesarem* 2.2.1.

51 Richer of Prüm, bishop of Liège (920/921–945).

52 Pope John X (914–928).

53 Flodoard, *Annales s.a.* 922, p. 7.

54 Probably Trosly-Loire.

55 Flodoard, *HRE* 4.16, p. 409.

56 Flodoard, *Annales s.a.* 921, p. 5.

57 Count Ricuin of Verdun (d. 923).

58 Flodoard, *Annales s.a.* 921, p. 5.

59 Possibly the viscount of Brioude. See Hoffmann, *Historiae,* p. 66 n. 3.

60 Sallust, *Cat.* 59.5 and 58.11.

61 Cf. Sallust, *Cat.* 59.1. It is not clear where the battle that Richer describes here took place, or if it took place at all. Flodoard, *Annales s.a.* 921, p. 6, says only that "Count Robert besieged the Northmen, who had taken control of the Loire river, for five months." Richer may be harking back to the Battle of Chartres (911), in which Duke Robert and Richard the Justiciar, the duke of Burgundy, inflicted a major defeat on a Viking army led by Rollo.

62 Cf. Livy 5.44.6.

63 Richer evidently invented this synod based on Flodoard's mention of the efforts that Archbishop Hervey took to convert the Normans after the Battle of Chartres in 911 (*HRE* 4.14).

64 Flodoard, *HRE* 4.14, p. 407. Flodoard reports that Hervey's treatise contained twenty-three, rather than twenty-four, chapters.

65 Reginar Longneck (d. 915) may have been Count of Hainaut, but this is uncertain. He was lay abbot of the important monasteries of Echternach, Stavelot-Malmedy, Saint-Servatius, and Saint-Maximin of Trier, and he held lands in northern Lotharingia along the Scheldt and the middle and lower Meuse. See Barth, pp. 15–38.

66 Gislebert of Lotharingia (ca. 880–939) inherited the possessions of his father, Reginar, and was recognized as duke in Lotharingia by Henry I of Germany in 928/929. See Barth, pp. 39–82.

67 Gislebert's father, Reginar, was a grandson of the Carolingian emperor Lothar I (d. 855).

68   Gerberga (ca. 913–968/969) was married to Gislebert from 928/929–939 and to Louis IV from 939–954.

69   Richer draws heavily here on the description of Julian the Apostate in the *Historia Tripartita* (7.2.16), a compilation of the fourth–fifth century AD Greek histories of Socrates Scholasticus, Sozomen, and Theodoret translated into Latin by Cassiodorus.

70   Cf. Sallust, *Cat.* 5.4.

71   The dispute between Charles and Gislebert that Richer describes at 1.36–38 took place ca. 920–922, several years before Gislebert married Henry's daughter Gerberga. If Gislebert did indeed flee to Henry's court, he was not taking refuge with his father-in-law.

72   The identity of *Litta* is uncertain. It has been variously identified with the town of Lith (or Lithoijen) in the southern Netherlands or Leten, west of Maastricht.

73   Richer, following Flodoard, employs *Sarmatae* to refer to the Slavs (he uses the term *Sclavi* once, at 2.18). The use of the term "Sarmatians" (strictly speaking, ethnic Iranian pastoralists who migrated to the western Eurasian steppe in late antiquity) by Latin authors to refer to the inhabitants of Eastern Europe derives from Pliny (*Nat.* 4.80) and later authors like Orosius.

74   Sallust, *Cat.* 5.6.

75   The text of this chapter has been crossed out in the manuscript, but it is of sufficient length and potential interest to the reader that I have chosen to include it here.

76   June 29/30, 922.

77   Flodoard, *Annales s.a.* 922, p. 10.

78   Archbishop Seulf of Reims (922–925).

79   Flodoard, *HRE* 4.18, pp. 409–10.

80   Sallust, *Cat.* 58.7; Hegesippus, *Bellum Iudaicum* 5.4.1.

81   Flodoard, *Annales s.a.* 923, p. 13.

82   The Battle of Soissons: June 15, 923.

83   Sallust, *Cat.* 60.2.

84   Flodoard does not in fact provide casualty figures for the Battle of Soissons, either in his *Annals* or in his *History of the Church of Rheims*.

85 Hugh the Great (d. 956), future duke of the Franks.

86 Count Heribert II of Vermandois (d. 943).

87 Flodoard, *Annales s.a.* 923, p. 13, states unequivocally that Hugh and Heribert were victorious.

88 This directly contradicts Flodoard, *Annales s.a.* 923, p. 13, who says that after the battle Hugh and Heribert took Charles's camp and seized spoils.

89 That is, it was strategically dangerous to seize spoils from the battlefield with Robert's army still lurking nearby.

90 Flodoard, *Annales s.a.* 923, p. 13.

91 Flodoard, *Annales s.a.* 922, p. 11.

92 Flodoard, *Annales s.a.* 923, p. 14.

93 Richard the Justiciar, duke of Burgundy (d. 921).

94 King Radulf of West Francia (923–936).

95 According to Flodoard, *Annales s.a.* 923, p. 15, Charles was first imprisoned at Château-Thierry and only later transferred to Péronne.

96 Flodoard, *Annales s.a.* 923, pp. 14–15.

97 The manuscript reads *Germani,* but this makes little sense and is most likely a mistake for *Galli* or *Belgae.*

98 Duke William II ("the Younger") of Aquitaine (d. 926).

99 Flodoard, *Annales s.a.* 924, pp. 19–20.

100 Flodoard, *Annales s.a.* 924, p. 23.

101 Count Manasses II of Langres and Dijon (d. after 927), Warnerius, count of Troyes and viscount of Sens (d. 924), Bishop Gauzlin of Langres (924–931), and Bishop Ansegis of Troyes (914–960/970). The Battle of Chalmont took place on December 6, 924.

102 *Gallia citerior* ("Hither Gaul") is Richer's rendering of Flodoard's *Burgundia.*

103 Flodoard, *Annales s.a.* 925, pp. 26–31.

104 According to Flodoard, *Annales s.a.* 925, pp. 31–32, Heribert of Vermandois and Arnulf of Flanders attacked Eu, while the king remained in the county of Beauvais.

105 Richer originally included the following phrase here, which he later crossed out: *Rollonem oculis effossis, suggillant* (they strangled Rollo after gouging out his eyes).

106   Flodoard, *Annales s.a.* 925, pp. 31–32.

107   The battle was fought at Faucembergues.

108   Hildegaud II, Count of Ponthieu (d. 926).

109   Flodoard, *Annales s.a.* 926, p. 33.

110   Flodoard, *Annales s.a.* 926, p. 34. The eclipse occurred on April 1, 926.

111   According to Flodoard, *Annales, s.a.* 927, p. 37, Heribert wanted the county of Laon for his son Odo, but King Radulf granted it to Roger, son of the recently deceased count of the same name.

112   Flodoard, *Annales s.a.* 927, p. 37.

113   William Longsword, duke of Normandy (927–942).

114   Richer originally described the death of Rollo at 1.50, but later expunged it. See n. 105 above.

115   Flodoard, *Annales s.a.* 927, pp. 39–40.

116   The cropped margins of this folio of the manuscript make it impossible to determine the title of this chapter with certainty.

117   According to Flodoard, *Annales s.a.* 928, pp. 41–42, it was Wido, marquis of Tuscany, who imprisoned Pope John X.

118   Flodoard, *Annales s.a.* 928, pp. 40–43.

119   Archbishop Hugh of Reims (925–931, 940–946).

120   Flodoard, *Annales s.a.* 925, pp. 32–33. Hugh was not yet five years old when he received the appointment.

121   Richer makes it appear as though Heribert's request for the see of Reims followed on the heels of his reconciliation with Radulf and his subsequent reimprisonment of Charles the Simple. In point of fact, Richer has gone back three years in time, from 928 to 925 to pick up the story of Hugh's appointment to the see of Reims.

122   Odelric, bishop of Aix-en-Provence (ca. 928–947). Bishop Abbo of Soissons administered the see of Reims from 925 to 928.

123   That is, a prebend of the canons of the cathedral of Reims. Flodoard, *HRE* 4.22, p. 414, reports that Odelric received only a single clerical prebend.

124   Flodoard, *HRE* 4.22, p. 414.

125   Flodoard, *Annales s.a.* 929, p. 44. Charles died on either September 6 or October 7, 929.

126   According to Adémar of Chabannes (*Chronicon* 3.20) the battle was fought at a place called *Ad Destricios,* perhaps to be identified with Estresse, near Beaulieu-sur-Dordogne. See Lauer, *Robert Ier et Raoul de Bourgogne,* p. 59 n. 2.

127   Flodoard, *Annales s.a.* 930, p. 45.

128   Richer seems to have invented this detail to explain the origin of the dispute between Hugh and Heribert. Flodoard does not say that the see of Reims was a point of contention between them.

129   Flodoard, *Annales s.a.* 930, p. 45.

130   Flodoard, *Annales s.a.* 931, p. 49.

131   Again, the cropped margins of the manuscript here make it impossible to read the complete chapter title.

132   Flodoard, *Annales s.a.* 931, pp. 49–51.

133   Cf. Hegesippus, *Bellum Iudaicum* 1.35.1.

134   Artald, archbishop of Reims (931–940, 946–961).

135   Flodoard, *Annales s.a.* 931, p. 51.

136   Bovo, bishop of Châlons-sur-Marne (ca. 913/917–947).

137   Adele, a daughter of King Robert.

138   Flodoard, *Annales s.a.* 931, p. 51.

139   Bishop Ayrard of Noyon (923/924–932).

140   Walbert, abbot of Corbie, and later bishop of Noyon (932–936/937).

141   Flodoard, *Annales s.a.* 932, pp. 52–53.

142   Count Raymond III Pons of Toulouse (d. 944/961).

143   Count Ermengaud of Rouergue (d. 936/940).

144   Richer borrowed this account of Lupus Aznar and his horse from Flodoard, *Annales s.a.* 932, p. 53. Lupus is otherwise unknown (see Hoffmann, *Historiae,* p. 95 n. 5). At the time, Sancho Garcés bore the title of Count of Gascony and exercised dominion over Gascony as a whole.

145   Flodoard, *Annales s.a.* 932, p. 53.

146   Flodoard, *Annales s.a.* 934, p. 59.

147   Flodoard, *Annales s.a.* 935, p. 62.

148   That is, the church of the monastery of Saint-Columba.

149   Flodoard, *Annales s.a.* 936, p. 63.

150   The plural *regna* refers to the various principalities that consti-

tuted *Gallia,* the area that historians today call West Francia. These included ethnically distinct territories such as Aquitaine, Brittany, Gothia (Septimania), and Gascony. In his account of the coronation of Hugh Capet in 987 (*Hist.* 4.12), Richer reports that Hugh was made king over "the Gauls, the Bretons, the Normans, the Aquitainians, the Goths, the Spanish, and the Gascons."

Book 2

1   King Louis IV "d'Outremer" (b. 920/921, r. 936–954).

2   Louis's mother, Eadgifu, was the daughter of King Edward the Elder of Wessex (899–924) and the half-sister of King Aethelstan (924–939). She had taken refuge in England with Louis after her husband, King Charles, was deposed and imprisoned.

3   Richer originally named the town of the envoys' departure as Boulogne *(Bononia).* He later changed this to Thérouanne *(Morinum),* a town that does not border the sea. He may have been prompted to make this change by a passage in Caesar, *Gal.* 4.21.3, where the author states that the shortest crossing over the English Channel was in the territory of the Morini.

4   Flodoard, *Annales s.a.* 936, p. 63.

5   Apparently some of the magnates, particularly those who had been loyal supporters of Robert, feared that Louis would seek revenge against them.

6   Cf. Sallust, *Iug.* 22.2.

7   As the expunged *acsi* before *barbaris* makes clear, Richer is not offering his opinion about Hugh and the Franks, but instead representing Aethelstan's distrust of them.

8   Flodoard, *Annales s.a.* 936, p. 63.

9   Oda, bishop of Ramsbury (923/927–941/942) and later Archbishop of Canterbury (941/942–958).

10   A passage in the manuscript that Richer later crossed out states that Louis asked Hugh to hand his arms over to Heribert of Vermandois, who then turned them over to Arnulf of Flanders.

11   Louis was crowned on June 19, 936.

12 Flodoard, *Annales s.a.* 936, pp. 63–64.

13 Hugh the Black, duke of Burgundy (936–952). Hugh had seized Langres after the death of his brother, King Radulf.

14 Bishop Heiric of Langres (ca. 934–943/948).

15 Flodoard, *Annales s.a.* 936, p. 64.

16 Flodoard, *Annales s.a.* 937, p. 65.

17 Flodoard, *Annales s.a.* 937, p. 65.

18 Although the second part of 2.7 has its own marginal title and would normally be considered an independent chapter, Richer's first editor, Georg Heinrich Pertz, included all of this material as a single chapter, and this convention has been followed by subsequent editors.

19 Flodoard, *Annales s.a.* 937, pp. 65–66.

20 The identity of the town that Richer calls *Guiso* and Flodoard *Guisum* is uncertain. Lauer, *Louis IV*, p. 31 n. 1, suggests Guines. Wissant is another possibility.

21 Count Arnulf I of Flanders (918–965).

22 Flodoard, *Annales s.a.* 938, pp. 68–70.

23 Flodoard, *Annales s.a.* 938, p. 70.

24 Flodoard, *Annales s.a.* 938, p. 70.

25 Count Erluin of Montreuil (d. 945).

26 Flodoard, *Annales s.a.* 939, p. 72.

27 Flodoard, *Annales s.a.* 939, p. 72.

28 Flodoard, *Annales s.a.* 939, p. 74.

29 Flodoard, *Annales s.a.* 939, p. 72, reports that the Lotharingian magnates who came to King Louis were Gislebert of Lotharingia, Count Otto of Verdun, Count Issac of Cambrai, and Count Thierry of Holland.

30 The coastal regions mentioned here are the territories of Arnulf of Flanders, whom Aethelstan (in Richer's account) evidently suspected of some disloyalty to the king.

31 Flodoard, *Annales s.a.* 939, pp. 72–73.

32 Otto I, king of Germany (936–973) and Holy Roman Emperor (961–973).

33 Count Thierry II of Holland (d. 988).

34 Count Isaac of Cambrai (d. ca. 946).

35   Flodoard, *Annales s.a.* 939, p. 73.

36   King Henry I of Germany (919–936).

37   In fact, Charles was thirty-nine years old when Henry was elected king in May of 919.

38   Flodoard, *Annales s.a.* 939, p. 72.

39   The Battle of Andernach. Otto himself was not actually present at the battle.

40   Flodoard, *Annales s.a.* 939, pp. 73–74. A year before Louis married Gerberga, Hugh the Great had married another of Otto's sisters, Hadwig, making the king and the duke of the Franks brothers-in-law.

41   That is, Duke William of Normandy. "Pirates" is Richer's preferred term for the Normans.

42   Flodoard, *Annales s.a.* 940, p. 75.

43   Heribert of Vermandois had captured Chausot, which belonged to the see of Reims, two years earlier. See 2.8 above.

44   Flodoard, *Annales s.a.* 940, pp. 75–76.

45   The convent of Avenay and the monastery of Saint-Basle de Verzy were both within the diocese of Reims.

46   Flodoard, *Annales s.a.* 940, pp. 76–77.

47   Hugh had been chosen Archbishop of Reims at the behest of King Radulf in 925, and then deposed in favor of Artald in 931. In the intervening nine years he had been staying with Bishop Wido of Auxerre, who had ordained him as a deacon.

48   Laon's position at the top of a hill made the city extremely difficult for invading forces to capture.

49   Flodoard, *Annales s.a.* 940, p. 77.

50   Richer appears to have misunderstood Flodoard, who says that the king had been in Burgundy for six or seven weeks when he returned to Reims. Since the king had left for Burgundy before Hugh and Heribert attacked Reims, the siege itself had not been going on for that long. See Lauer, *Le règne de Louis IV,* p. 57.

51   Bishop Wido I of Soissons (937–ca. 970).

52   Flodoard, *Annales s.a.* 940, pp. 77–78.

53   The synod of Soissons took place on March 27–28, 941.

54   Arnold, the count, or castellan, of Douai.

55 Flodoard, *Annales s.a.* 941, pp. 80–81.

56 Flodoard, *Annales s.a.* 941, reports that Louis's two companions were Archbishop Artald of Reims and Count Roger of Laon.

57 Flodoard, *Annales s.a.* 941, pp. 82–83.

58 Pope Stephen VIII (939–942).

59 The pallium was a band of white woolen cloth traditionally bestowed upon archbishops by the pope.

60 Flodoard, *Annales s.a.* 942, pp. 83–84.

61 Count Roger of Laon.

62 William III "Towhead," count of Poitou and Auvergne, and duke of Aquitaine (934–963).

63 Alan II Barbetorte, count of Nantes and duke of Brittany (d. 952).

64 Flodoard, *Annales s.a.* 942, pp. 84–85.

65 Flodoard, *Annales s.a.* 942, pp. 85–86.

66 Flodoard, *Annales s.a.* 943, p. 86.

67 Duke Richard I of Normandy (942–996).

68 According to William of Jumièges (*Gesta Normannorum ducum* 3.2), her name was Sprota.

69 Flodoard, *Annales s.a.* 943, pp. 86–87.

70 Possibly Sihtric Sihtricsson, brother of King Olaf Sihtricsson, who briefly ruled over the Viking kingdom of York (943–944; 950–952).

71 Flodoard, *Annales s.a.* 943, p. 88.

72 The monastery of Saint-Basle-de-Verzy.

73 Although Richer gives the impression that the king received Artald at Compiègne, in a letter that Artald later sent to the Synod of Ingelheim (948) he stated that after leaving the monastery of Saint-Basle he went to find the king at Laon. See Flodoard, *HRE* 4.35, p. 432.

74 Flodoard, *Annales s.a.* 943, p. 87.

75 For his account of the symptoms preceding Heribert's death Richer borrows heavily from a medical manuscript he found at Chartres (Chartres, Bibliothèque municipale, MS 62), which he almost certainly read during his journey there in 991 (see 4.50 below). See MacKinney, p. 366 and n. 49.

76 The monastery of Saint-Quentin in Vermandois.

77 The sons of Heribert II of Vermandois were Odo, count of Amiens (d. 946), Robert, count of Troyes and Meaux (d. after 966), Heribert III ("the Old"), count of Omois (d. 980/984), Adalbert, count of Vermandois (d. 987/988), and Hugh, archbishop of Reims (d. 962).

78 Flodoard, *Annales, s.a.* 943, pp. 87–89. According to Flodoard, the king first received Archbishop Hugh, before any of his brothers, after they had agreed that the abbeys of Avenay and Saint-Basle would be restored to Artald, who would also be provided with another bishopric.

79 Although Richer does not say so specifically, Flodoard, *Annales, s.a.* 943, p. 89, confirms that Erluin killed William's murderer before cutting off his hands.

80 Flodoard, *Annales s.a.* 943, p. 89.

81 That is, he became her godfather. The girl's name was probably Mathilda. See Lauer, *Louis IV,* p. 107 n. 4, and Hoffmann, *Historiae,* ch. 39 p. 126 n. 1.

82 Flodoard, *Annales,* s.a. 943, pp. 89–90. Flodoard says that Louis granted Hugh the duchy of Francia (*ducatus Franciae*) and that he put all of Burgundy under his dominion as well. The latter grant came at the expense of Duke Hugh the Black of Burgundy.

83 Raymond III Pons, count of Toulouse.

84 Flodoard, *Annales s.a.* 944, pp. 90–91.

85 Amiens had been held by Heribert II of Vermandois since at least 932; at some point it passed under the control of his eldest son, Odo. In 944, members of King Louis's household conspired with Derold, bishop of Amiens (for whom see 2.59 below), whose men handed the city over to them. Richer passes over the betrayal of Amiens in silence. See Flodoard, *Annales s.a.* 944, p. 91 and Lauer, *Louis IV,* p. 111.

86 Included in Erluin's possessions (*sua*) may have been the members of his family, whom Arnulf had shipped to England after his capture of Montreuil in 939. See Lauer, *Louis IV,* p. 113.

87 Flodoard, *Annales s.a.* 944, p. 91.

88 Count Judicael Berengar of Rennes (d. ca. 970).

89   Alan Barbetorte.

90   Flodoard, *Annales s.a.* 944, p. 94, whom Richer follows almost ver-
        batim in this chapter, reports that it was Dol, rather than
        Nantes, that was captured by the Normans.

91   Flodoard, *Annales s.a.* 944, pp. 93–94.

92   Probably the rest of the cities of Normandy, but the phrase *cum
        reliquis* is vague.

93   Flodoard, *Annales s.a.* 944, p. 95.

94   Count Bernard of Senlis (d. after 945).

95   Theobald le Tricheur ("the Trickster"), Count of Blois, Chartres,
        Tours, and Châteaudun (d. ca. 975).

96   Flodoard, *Annales s.a.* 945, p. 96.

97   I.e., not Bernard of Senlis, mentioned at 2.43 above. Various other
        candidates have been proposed, including Count Bernard of
        Rethel, Count Bernard of Beauvais, and Count Bernard of Por-
        cien. See Hoffmann, *Historiae,* ch. 44 p. 130 n. 2.

98   The nephew of the aforementioned Bernard, according to Flodo-
        ard, *Annales* s.a. 945.

99   Flodoard, *Annales s.a.* 945, pp. 96–97.

100   Count Reginald of Roucy.

101   According to Flodoard, *Annales* s.a. 945, p. 97, the meeting took
        place around the feast of Saint John, i.e. June 24th, and the duke
        (and probably the king) negotiated through intermediaries, not
        in person.

102   Flodoard, *Annales s.a.* 945, p. 97.

103   Archbishop Theotilo of Tours (ca. 932–945).

104   Theotilo's death probably occurred on April 29, 945, before the
        beginning of the siege, which, according to Richer's informa-
        tion, concluded on May 21. See Hoffmann, *Historiae,* ch. 46 p. 131
        n. 1, and Lauer, *Louis IV,* pp. 129–130 n. 4. Flodoard, *Annales s.a.*
        945, p. 97, whom Richer follows closely in this chapter, says only
        that Archbishop Theotilo was stricken with illness *(aegritudine
        corporis . . . deprimitur)* during his journey. In accordance with his
        usual procedure, Richer invents a specific disease as the cause of
        death and gives a detailed account of the symptoms.

105   Flodoard, *Annales s.a.* 945, pp. 97–98.

106   This Harald, who may have been the son of the Turmod killed at 2.35, was evidently an independent Norman chief who had taken advantage of the power vacuum following the death of William Longsword to assert control over Bayeux. See Lauer, *Louis IV,* pp. 287–302.

107   Flodoard, *Annales s.a.* 945, pp. 97–98.

108   Charles (945–ca. 953). The elder of the two sons of Louis and Gerberga was Lothar, who succeeded to the throne upon the death of his father in 954.

109   Wido was the son of Count Fulk the Red of Anjou, one of Hugh's vassals.

110   Theobald le Tricheur.

111   Flodoard, *Annales s.a.* 945, p. 99.

112   King Edmund of England (939–946).

113   As the son of Edmund's half-sister Eadgifu, Louis was the English king's nephew, not his cousin. Richer may have assumed that Edmund was King Aethelstan's son, rather than his brother.

114   Flodoard, *Annales s.a.* 946, p. 101.

115   Flodoard, *Annales s.a.* 945, p. 99.

116   Sallust, *Jug.* 10.1

117   Sallust, *Cat.* 44.5.

118   Latouche, *Richer,* Vol. I, pp. 210–11 n. 2 points out that Richer's assertion that Louis went to Compiègne after being released by Hugh was probably just an educated guess.

119   Flodoard, *Annales s.a.* 946, p. 101.

120   Sallust, *Iug.* 14.23–24.

121   King Conrad "the Peaceful" of Burgundy and Provence (937–993). Richer calls Conrad king of the *Genauni,* a name he probably derived from Horace, *Carm.* 4.14.10, in order to differentiate Conrad's kingdom of imperial Burgundy, which lay east of the Rhône-Saône river basin, from the duchy of Burgundy to the west.

122   Cf. Hegesippus, *Bellum Iudaicum* 5.3.1.

123   Flodoard, *Annales s.a.* 946, p. 102.

124   Flodoard, *Annales, s.a.* 946, p. 102, reports that Hugh met with his brother-in-law Arnulf of Flanders, Count Udo of Wetterau, who

was married to one of his aunts, and Duke Herman of Swabia, Udo's brother.

125   Flodoard, *Annales s.a.* 946, pp. 102–3, says that Hugh and his men left the city on the third day of the siege. Trithemius, in summarizing this chapter, reports that it was on the eighth day of the siege.

126   Flodoard, *Annales, s.a.* 946, pp. 102–3.

127   Archbishop Frederick of Mainz (937–954).

128   Archbishop Ruotbert of Trier (931–956).

129   Flodoard, *Annales, s.a.* 946, p. 103.

130   At this point in the manuscript (fol. 23ʳ) there is a line that Richer crossed out, which states that the ruse employed by the young men was devised by a certain Count Bernard: *Quod et fertur Bernardi comitis astutia dispositum.* Which Bernard is meant is not clear. See Lauer, *Louis IV,* p. 272.

131   I.e., Normandy.

132   Flodoard, *Annales, s.a.* 946, p. 103.

133   Bishop Derold of Amiens (929–946).

134   Flodoard, *Annales, s.a.* 946, p. 103.

135   Richer originally identified the queen as Frederuna (d. 916/917), the first wife of Charles the Simple, but he later crossed out the name. Hoffmann, *Historiae,* ch. 59 p. 140 n. 4, notes that the queen in question may have been Charles's second wife, Eadgifu.

136   Since it is difficult to imagine how poison could be hidden between these two fingers, it makes sense to accept the conjecture of Guadet, p. 217 n. 1, that Richer meant the ring finger *(annularis)* rather than the index finger *(salutaris).*

137   Bishop Gibuin of Châlons-sur-Marne (947–ca. 998), son of Count Hugh of Dijon.

138   Flodoard, *Annales s.a.* 947, p. 104.

139   Flodoard, *Annales s.a.* 947, p. 104.

140   Flodoard, *Annales s.a.* 947, p. 104, states on the contrary that it was the duke's men who persuaded him to undertake the siege of Reims.

141   Flodoard, *Annales s.a.* 947, p. 104.

142 Flodoard, *Annales s.a.* 947, p. 105, states that the meeting between Louis and Otto took place at the beginning of August.

143 Flodoard, *Annales s.a.* 947, p. 105.

144 Bishop Theobald of Amiens (947–975).

145 Flodoard, *Annales s.a.* 947, pp. 104–5. Flodoard says that Hugh was encamped between the strongholds of Douzy, which was located just north of the Chiers, and Mouzon, which was several kilometers south of the river. This distinction is important: by occupying a position south of the river, Hugh's presence prevented any attempt by Louis and Otto to attack Mouzon. See Lauer, *Louis IV*, p. 161.

146 Although Richer states that the parties agreed to postpone further discussion to "another synod," the meeting beside the Chiers between Louis and Otto did not itself constitute a synod. Flodoard, *Annales s.a.* 947, p. 105, makes this point more clearly: *Et quia synodus tunc convocata non fuerat, altercatio determinari non potuit.*

147 Flodoard, *Annales s.a.* 947, p. 105, says only that the synod would be held in the middle of November (*circa medium mensis Novembris*).

148 Flodoard, *Annales s.a.* 947, p. 105.

149 See *MGH Concilia* 6.1, pp. 128–31.

150 Bruno, brother of King Otto I, later archbishop of Cologne and duke of Lotharingia (953–965). At the time he was abbot of Lorsch.

151 Einold, abbot of Gorze (933–959), and Odilo, abbot of Stavelot (938–954).

152 January 13, 948. See *MGH Concilia* 6.1, pp. 132–34.

153 Pope Agapitus II (946–955).

154 The nineteenth chapter of the Council of Carthage of 419 declared that the case of a bishop who was accused of a crime would be brought before the primate of his province. See C. Munier, ed., *Concilia Africae* 345–525, *CCSL* Vol. 149, p. 140.

155 Flodoard, *Annales s.a.* 948, pp. 107–9.

156 Marinus was the bishop of Bomarzo, not Ostia.

157 Flodoard, *Annales s.a.* 948, p. 109.

158 See *MGH Concilia* 6.1, pp. 135–63.

159 The synod of Ingelheim convened on June 7, 948, not on August 1, the date decided upon at the end of the synod of Mouzon.

160 Flodoard, *Annales s.a.* 948, pp. 109–11. *Lioptacus Ribunensis* and *Liefdach Ripunensis* are the same person: Liafdag, bishop of Ribe.

161 Flodoard, *Annales s.a.* 948, p. 111.

162 Flodoard, *Annales s.a.* 948, pp. 111–12.

163 Artald's speech to the synod of Ingelheim, the so-called *libellus Artoldi,* is reproduced in Flodoard, *HRE* 4.35, pp. 428–34. See also MGH *Concilia* 6.1 pp. 149–57.

164 Flodoard, *Annales s.a.* 948, p. 112, says only that Artald delivered his account of the strife between himself and Hugh in accordance with the instructions he had received from Pope Agapitus; he does not say that the pope sent a letter ordering Artald to be restored to the see of Reims.

165 Flodoard, *Annales s.a.* 948, pp. 112–13, says that the letter was translated into German for the benefit of the kings. Having married a sister of Otto, Louis may have been conversant in her native tongue. See Lauer, *Louis IV,* pp. 182–83 n. 1.

166 According to Flodoard, *Annales s.a.* 948, p. 113, this was the same letter that Hugh had sent to the synod of Mouzon (see 2.67 above).

167 Flodoard, *Annales s.a.* 948, pp. 112–13.

168 Flodoard, *Annales s.a.* 948, pp. 113–14.

169 Popes Innocent I (402–417), Alexander I (ca. 106–115), Symmachus (498–514), Sixtus III (432–440), Celestine I (422–432), Zosimus (417–418), Leo I (440–461), and Boniface II (530–532). These canons are taken in part from the Pseudo-Isidorian Decretals. Those of Innocent, Zosimus, Boniface, Celestine, and Leo are found in the *Collectio Dionysiana.* See Hoffmann, *Historiae,* ch. 80 p. 157 n. 2; Lauer, *Louis IV,* pp. 184–85; and, *Gesta synodalia* ch. 13, *MGH Concilia* 6.1, pp. 162–63.

170 Flodoard, *Annales s.a.* 948, pp. 114–15.

171 Flodoard, *Annales s.a.* 948, p. 115, says that the synod dealt with incestuous marriages (*incestis coniugiis*) and churches usurped by laymen, but says nothing about priestly marriages. Similarly,

the *Acta* of the synod (*Gesta synodalia* ch. 12, *MGH Concilia* 6.1, p. 162) contain a prohibition against marriages by close relations, but say nothing about marriages by priests.

172 Flodoard, *Annales s.a.* 948, p. 115.

173 Duke Conrad the Red of Lotharingia (d. 955). He assumed control of the Duchy of Lotharingia after the death of Count Otto of Verdun in 944 and married Otto's daughter Liudgard in 947. He was deposed from office in 953 after joining a conspiracy against King Otto led by the king's son, Liudolf, duke of Swabia, and killed at the Battle of Lechfeld in 955.

174 Richer's chronology is confused. According to Flodoard, *Annales s.a.* 948, pp. 115–16, four weeks after the synod of Ingelheim (i.e., in July 948) the troops that Louis was promised by Otto arrived under the command of Conrad the Red. There followed campaigns against Mouzon, Montaigu, and Laon, after which a meeting of bishops was held in the church of Saint-Vincent of Laon to excommunicate Theobald le Tricheur. The council that Richer describes here actually took place in October 948 at Trier, not at Laon (see MGH *Concilia* 6.1, pp. 164–70), and according to Flodoard, *Annales, s.a.* 948, p. 118, the only bishops present were Artald of Reims, Wido of Soissons, Rodulf of Laon, Wicfrid of Thérouanne, Ruotbert of Trier, and the papal legate Marinus.

175 Hugh fled Reims in September 946 (see 2.55 above). He was deposed from office at the synod of Mouzon on January 13, 948 (2.67).

176 See 2.64 above.

177 Theobald le Tricheur.

178 Heribert the Old, count of Omois.

179 Flodoard, *Annales s.a.* 948, pp. 118–21.

180 Bishop Rorico of Laon (949–976).

181 Flodoard, *Annales s.a.* 949, p. 121.

182 Cf. Livy 43.18.

183 Flodoard, *Annales s.a.* 948, pp. 115–16.

184 Flodoard, *Annales s.a.* 948, p. 116. The siege of Laon described here is not found in Flodoard, who says only that the bishops met

in the church of Saint-Vincent at Laon to excommunicate Theobald.

185 Flodoard, *Annales, s.a.* 948, p. 117, says only that about forty people were killed in and around the church of the village of Cormicy. The same number is found in Flodoard's *HRE* 4.36, p. 437, although in one manuscript the number of those killed is estimated at about four hundred.

186 Flodoard, *Annales s.a.* 948, p. 117.

187 Flodoard, *Annales s.a.* 949, p. 122.

188 Flodoard, *Annales s.a.* 949, p. 122.

189 Flodoard, *Annales s.a.* 949, pp. 122–23.

190 Flodoard, *Annales s.a.* 949, pp. 124–25. According to Flodoard it was Arnulf of Flanders who burned the outskirts of Senlis.

191 Flodoard, *Annales s.a.* 949, p. 125.

192 Flodoard, *Annales s.a.* 949, p. 125.

193 Flodoard, *Annales s.a.* 949, p. 125.

194 Flodoard, *Annales s.a.* 950, p. 126. Flodoard says that it was Duke Conrad, along with "certain bishops and counts," who went to speak to Hugh.

195 Rom. 13:1: "Let every soul be subject to higher powers. For there is no power but from God: and those that are ordained of God."

196 Adalbero of Metz and Fulbert of Cambrai.

197 Flodoard, *Annales s.a.* 950, p. 127.

198 Charles-Constantine, count of Vienne (d. 962) was the son of Louis the Blind, king of Provence (d. 928) and the grandson of Boso, king of Burgundy (d. 887). His paternal great-grandfather, Bivin, was a count under Louis the Pious. Richer seems to be assuming that Boso was an illegitimate son of Bivin, or perhaps that Bivin himself was illegitimate. This rumor of illegitimacy in the family line might have originated to explain why Charles-Constantine did not inherit the kingdom of Provence from his father, Louis the Blind. (It went to King Rudolf II of Upper Burgundy instead.)

199 Count Letald of Mâcon (d. 961).

200 Flodoard, *Annales s.a.* 951, pp. 129–30.

201 Flodoard, *Annales s.a.* 951, pp. 129–30.

202 Count Anglebert of Brienne; Gozbert was his brother. See Lauer, *Louis IV,* p. 218.

203 Brienne-le-Château.

204 Flodoard, *Annales s.a.* 951, p. 131.

205 Count Heribert the Old.

206 Flodoard, *Annales s.a.* 951, p. 132.

207 The future Charles of Lotharingia.

208 Flodoard, *Annales s.a.* 953, p. 136.

209 Louis IV died on September 10, 954. In *Hist.* 2.4, Richer says that Louis was fifteen years old when he was crowned king in 936. This would make him thirty-three, not thirty-six at the time of his death.

210 Flodoard, *Annales s.a.* 954, p. 138.

Bibliography

EDITIONS

Hoffmann, Hartmut. *Richeri historiarum libri IIII, Monumenta Germaniae Historica SS* 38. Hanover: Hahn, 2000.

Pertz, G. H. *Richeri historiarum libri IIII,* in *Monumenta Germaniae Historica SS* 3, pp. 561–657. Hanover: Hahn, 1839.

Waitz, Georg. *Richeri historiarum libri IIII, Monumenta Germaniae Historica SRG* 51. Hanover: Hahn, 1877.

TRANSLATIONS

Guadet, Jerome. *Richer, Histoire de son temps.* 2 vols. Paris: Jules Renouard, 1845–1846.

Latouche, Robert. *Richer: Histoire de France (885–995).* Les classiques de l'histoire de France au moyen âge. 2 vols. Paris: H. Champion, 1930 and 1937.

Poinsignon, A.-M. *Richeri Historiarum quatuor libri — Histoire de Richer en quatres livres.* Reims: P. Regnier, 1855.

Von der Osten-Sacken, Karl. *Richers vier Bücher Geschichte.* Berlin: Besser, 1854.

SELECTED STUDIES

Giese, Wolfgang. *"Genus" und "Virtus": Studien zum Geschichtswerk des Richer von St. Remi.* Augsburg: W. Blasaditsch, 1969.

Glenn, Jason. *Politics and History in the Tenth Century: The Work and World of Richer of Reims.* Cambridge: Cambridge University Press, 2004.

Hoffmann, Hartmut. "Die *Historien* Richers von Saint-Remi." *Deutsches Archiv für Erforschung des Mittelalters* 54 (1998): 445–532.

Kortüm, Hans-Henning. *Richer von Saint-Remi: Studien zu einem Geschichtsschreiber des 10. Jahrhunderts.* Stuttgart: Franz Steiner, 1985.

Lauer, Philippe. *Le règne de Louis IV d'Outre-Mer.* Geneva: Slatkine, 1977 [Paris: É. Bouillon, 1900].

———. *Robert Ier et Raoul de Bourgogne, rois de France (923–936).* Geneva: Slatkine, 1976 [Paris: H. Champion, 1910].

Lot, Ferdinand. *Les derniers Carolingiens, Lothaire, Louis V, Charles de Lorraine (954–991).* Geneva: Slatkine, 1975 [Paris: É. Bouillon, 1891].

———. *Études sur le règne de Hugues Capet et la fin du Xe siècle.* Geneva: Slatkine, 1975 [Paris: É. Bouillon, 1903].

MacKinney, L. C. "Tenth-Century Medicine as Seen in the *Historia* of Richer of Rheims." *Bulletin of the Institute of the History of Medicine* 2 (1934): 347–75.

Riché, Pierre. *Gerbert d'Aurillac, le pape de l'an mil.* Paris: Fayard, 1987.